PROPERTY OF
B O C E S
SARATOGA   WARREN CO.
Henning Rd., Saratoga S____gs

Each pupil is responsible for the return
of every Text Book charged against him.
He will be required to pay for books that
are lost and for damage to books assigned.
If a book is not in good condition when it
is loaned to the pupil that fact must be
noted on the book when it is assigned.

Date of Purchase . . . .

Book No. . . . .

Course . . . .

Cos. . . . .

Name of Student (In Ink)	Condition	Date Issue

6.

Food Service Careers

Revised

Food Service Careers
Revised

Ethelwyn G. Cornelius

Former Director of Home Economics, Ithaca, N. Y., Public Schools, and Instructor of Home Economics Education, New York State College of Human Ecology.

Edited by Marion L. Cronan

Former Director of Homemaking and School Lunchrooms, Public Schools, Brookline, Massachusetts.

CHAS. A. BENNETT CO., INC.

Peoria, Illinois 61614

Library of Congress Catalog No. 77-81072
Printed in the United States of America

ISBN 87002-206-7

V-H 5 4 3
83 82

Table of Contents

Preface

Food Service Careers is a beginning text which explores careers in food service. I hope it will help you to make wise choices in planning your future.

The book concentrates on the skills and attitudes needed for successful employment in the food service industry. It gives you basic and current information on many kinds of food service operations. It provides detailed information on the training requirements, responsibilities, and duties of various food service jobs.

As part of your study, you will have practice in developing food service skills through both on-the-job and class laboratory experiences. This should not only be fun for you, but it should also increase your value as an employee in the work world.

Words to Know, at the beginning of each chapter, lists some of the key words and phrases which are used in the food service industry. Be sure you understand these words—they can be of great help to you if you decide on food service as a career.

Let's Think It Over and *Let's Investigate,* which appear at the end of each chapter, can help you to review the material you have covered. They also give you an opportunity to apply the information to job situations in your locality.

Student Resources at the end of the book lists books, other publications, and magazines. These can be helpful in increasing your knowledge in specific areas of the food service industry. Your teacher can also direct you to new resources as they become available. The trade magazines provide ways to acquire new ideas and to continue learning about food service. Some of these may be available in your training center.

The illustrations in the text can help you to become familiar with food service equipment and work methods.

As you study food preparation and service, ask yourself if you have the interests and abilities to work in this field.

Acknowledgments

The author makes grateful acknowledgment to the manufacturing companies, government departments, state and city home economics departments, equipment companies, advertising agencies, the National Restaurant Association, and the many restaurant operators who have contributed materials and ideas for this book.

She wishes to express special appreciation for resources, teaching ideas, and pictures to Mrs. Jean Snyder, teacher of Food Service at Board of Cooperative Educational Services (BOCES), Ithaca, New York; Marion Cronan, former Director of Homemaking and School Lunchrooms, Public Schools, Brookline, Massachusetts; the editors; and to Don Daverman for his cartoons.

Chapter **1**

The Food Service Industry and You

Most likely you are familiar with one or more sections of the food service industry. As a student, you probably eat away from home quite often. You may eat lunch in the school lunchroom or at a nearby hamburger stand. Perhaps after school you drop by a drive-in, a snack shop, or other eating place. You generally meet your friends, talk about the day at school, make plans for later in the evening, and, while doing all this, have a soda or a snack. Any place where you eat "away from home" is a part of the food service industry.

When did people begin to "eat out"? How did this great industry have its beginnings? The first coffee house was opened in 1554 in Constantinople. During the sixteenth and seventeenth centuries, inns and taverns were estab-

lished along main, well-traveled routes. Why? People needed food, rest, and lodging as they traveled the dangerous and difficult roads. In those early days, inns were located approximately a day's journey apart, in or near towns. Gradually, more and more eating places were established to meet the basic needs of travelers.

Today, the industry includes many different types of food service establishments. Some provide only food while others also offer lodging. Many also have recreational facilities such as swimming pools and exercise rooms.

Food service is one of the nation's fastest growing industries. Recent surveys, sponsored by the U. S. Department of Agriculture (USDA) Economic Research Service and the

H. J. Heinz Co.

Nearly 4 million people find interesting jobs in the food service industry.

food service industry, show that "the food service industry may have more total outlets and workers than any other single kind of business."

Nearly 4 million men and women find interesting and important work in the food service industry. The U. S. Department of Labor reports that about 2.5 million or over 60 percent of these are women, engaged in jobs such as waitresses, cooks, cashiers, hostesses, dietitians, and managers.

If you are considering food service as a career, learn all you can about the industry and how it operates. In this chapter, we will give some facts about the food service industry as big business.

Students often enjoy meeting friends after school at their favorite snack shop.

H. J. Heinz Co.

WORDS TO KNOW

Food service industry
In-plant feeding
Subsidize
Customer
Labor market
Food service unit
Table or counter service
Self-service
Buffet table
Cafeteria
Snack counter
Vending machine
Automat
Restaurant unit
Limited menu
Quick-service units
Catering units
Food preparation and assembly units
Central kitchens
Commissaries
Pre-portion
Assemble
Off the premises
Contract feeding company
Institutional feeding units

GROWTH OF THE INDUSTRY

The food service industry is now the fourth largest in size, based on total sales, of all industries in the nation.

Certain changes in American life have created a great demand for food services and caused rapid growth in the industry. These changes include greater national prosperity, higher family income, longer life span, more

13

The attractive service of food encourages the selection of nutritious foods and increases the sale of menu items.

women workers, and more emphasis on leisure activities.

Food service is now available in about 500,000 establishments in this country. Millions of dollars a year are spent by food service operators to provide meals which meet the public demand. The total annual food and drink sales is estimated at $59 to $64 billion. Here are some other facts in which you may be interested.

The ten states with the largest number of commercial restaurants are California, New York, Pennsylvania, Illinois, Texas, Ohio, New Jersey, Massachusetts, Michigan, and Florida.

Today, about one out of every three meals is eaten away from home. By 1985, people may divide their food spending evenly between eating at home and eating away from home.

IMPORTANCE OF FOOD SERVICE

How does the food service industry affect American life? What makes it so important? *Fast Food*, a magazine for people in the restaurant business, made a study recently of the growth of the industry. It said, "The food service industry now emerges as a potent force in the national economic scene. This strong food service industry is providing and will continue to provide jobs for workers, services for the consumer, and opportunities for investors."

Satisfies People's Needs

The food service industry satisfies a growing public need. Eating places are planned and located to take care of many interests and occupations. How is this done? Let us discuss school lunchrooms as an example. Schools must serve simple, nutritious meals quickly because of short meal periods. Food prices are

Today, one out of every three meals is eaten out.

low because students generally have a limited amount of money to spend. Colleges serve nutritious meals two or three times a day for students. The cost is also kept as low as possible.

Large industrial plants, located away from business centers and eating places, must provide food service or *in-plant feeding* for their employees. In-plant feeding has grown greatly in recent years. Some companies subsidize the food operation. To *subsidize* means that the company pays part or all of the cost of meals for its employees. (The government also subsidizes school lunches.) Some industrial plants and businesses often set up a series of vending machines which offer hot and cold food. These meet the needs of employees not only for coffee breaks but also for meals. Large businesses may also provide special dining facilities for their executives.

Hospitals must provide tray service for their patients. Many institutions also have cafeteria, counter, and snack bar service for guests and staff members.

Railroad, bus, and airline terminals have established restaurants, cocktail lounges, and counter service twenty four hours a day to meet the needs of travelers.

People traveling by car can easily find drive-in restaurants for quick meals or motel and hotel restaurants for leisurely dining.

Influences Social Life

The food service industry influences the social life of a community. It has become a custom for friends and families to eat out together. Supper clubs, recreational clubs, night clubs, and special restaurants add to the social

Tray meals may be prepared in centrally located kitchens or catering restaurants for service on airlines, trains, or at special events.

Restaurants, clubs, and community groups often serve food buffet style in order to provide faster customer service.

15

Wedding receptions are often held in restaurants. For this luncheon reception, the head table has been arranged next to the wedding cake.

life of a community by providing food, music, atmosphere, and entertainment. Civic groups use restaurants and hotels for luncheon or dinner meetings and sometimes for parties. Social activities such as teas and wedding receptions are commonly held in restaurants.

Affects Business Life

The increasing demand for food service away from home has affected the business life

The food service industry is an important market for businesses such as food processors, equipment manufacturers, and interior designers.

of the nation. The following facts, compiled by the National Restaurant Association, give some indication of the effect the food service industry has on business. The food service industry uses almost twenty percent of all the food produced in the United States. Over $25 billion in food and beverages is purchased yearly by the nation's food service establishments. The amount is growing every year. More than $1 billion in food service equipment is purchased annually. In addition, food service is a major market for such industries as furniture and other furnishings, floor coverings, maintenance materials, cleaning supplies, heating and air conditioning, and construction.

This means that businesses such as farms, food processors, transportation companies, equipment manufacturers, paper and linen suppliers, and others share in the growth of food service.

Affects Labor Market

The labor market is also vitally affected by the food service industry. Because of the need for personal service in most eating establishments, many kinds of jobs are provided for a large number of workers. The following figures from the National Restaurant Association show the number of people employed in food service in 1960 and 1970, with a prediction for 1980. This will give you some idea of the importance of the food service industry to the labor market.

National Employment in Food Service Industry

    1960 total..........................2,500,000
    1970 total..........................3,500,000
    1980 total estimate...........over 4,000,000

About 250,000 new workers are needed each year in the food service industry. Will you be one of them?

As you can see by the figures above, the food service industry has grown remarkably since 1960. If this growth rate continues, the industry will require *each year* for the next ten years:

- 75,000 workers in newly created jobs
- 175,000 workers as replacements in existing jobs
- $\overline{250,000}$ total new workers each year

Thus you can see from the above figures that jobs in the food service industry will be available for years to come.

Where will these jobs be? Different kinds of food service units have developed to meet

If you are interested in a food service career, you can get first-hand information from someone successfully employed in the field such as a dietitian.

the needs of people who use them. Let us review the types of units in which you might work if you decide on a food service career.

FOOD SERVICE UNITS

A *food service unit* provides hot or cold, ready-to-eat food for customers. Some units both prepare and serve the food. Others act as central kitchens—they prepare the food but transport it to another location for serving. Others only serve food that has been prepared elsewhere, either in a central kitchen or by a food manufacturer.

Before we discuss the different types of food service units, let us review the basic methods of serving food to customers.

Table or Counter Service

Food is served to the customer by a waiter or waitress. This may be either at tables, booths, or sit-down counters.

Self-Service

Self-service units generally have a display of ready-to-eat items, ranging from a few snacks to dozens of elaborately prepared foods. Customers serve themselves from a buffet table, a cafeteria line, a snack counter, or vending machines. Self-service units may have a fixed price for a meal or they may charge by the items selected.

In a *cafeteria* or at a buffet or *snack counter*, customers collect their food on plates, which are often placed on a tray. They then take the food to a table. Sometimes waitress service is provided to carry trays to tables. Limited table service may be available such as waitresses who serve beverages.

Automated self-service makes use of *vending machines*. Some of the machines contain cold foods such as sandwiches, salads, and beverages. Others offer hot foods such as soups and main dishes. The customer places coins in a slot in the machine and pushes the right button. The food comes out of an opening. Some vending installations sell frozen foods and provide small electronic ovens. The customer buys the frozen item from the machine and places it in the electronic oven to heat for a few minutes. Restaurant experts predict great growth in this area of fast food service. An *automat* is another form of self-service. It has a display of food, with each item behind a small glass door. The customer puts the correct amount of coins in a slot, and the door opens, allowing food to be removed.

Typical self-service units include cafeterias, buffets, and vending stations in office buildings and in bus, railroad, and airline terminals.

Occasionally, the two types of service are combined. A restaurant may feature table service with a salad bar. Customers select their own combinations of greens and dressings at the salad bar. However, they are served the rest of the meal while seated at tables.

Any of these serving methods may be used by most of the food service units discussed on pages 20–23.

Restaurant Units

A restaurant or commercial feeding establishment serves food to the general public. It usually offers a menu and has table and/or counter service.

Dudley-Anderson-Yutzy

Restaurants may specialize in certain types of ethnic foods. This restaurant features Polynesian food, and carries out the Polynesian theme in the beverage servers.

Some table service restaurants have a salad bar featuring an assortment of salads and dressings.

Sheraton Inn

Vending machines provide both hot and cold foods for fast self-service.

Canteen Corp.

Table service restaurants may have a special brunch menu, such as this, served buffet style.

Institutions/VFM

Some restaurants cook food in full view of the customers.

Fast service restaurants can prepare short orders quickly by the use of well-organized food units such as this.

Jimbo Restaurant, Cape Coral, Fla.

Table-service restaurants generally have a menu which offers a wide number of choices. They may have after-theatre supper service and perhaps private dining rooms for parties and banquets. If the restaurant is part of a hotel or motel, room service is generally available. This provides guests with table or tray service in the privacy of their rooms. Table-service restaurants vary widely in design and atmosphere. Some have special decorative themes such as the Gay 90's, Early American, or Old English, with elaborate menu items. Others may specialize in ethnic foods such as Chinese, German, Greek, or Mexican. Some are primarily supper clubs and night clubs. There are also restaurants in large department stores, on sea-going ships, and on trains.

Quick-service restaurant units provide simple table and/or counter service to save time for the customers. They may have waitress service or they may be self-service. These units usually offer a limited menu choice and often provide take-out service. Typical quick-service units include cafeterias, tea rooms, coffee shops, diners, snack bars, drive-ins, fountain-grill service, and vending machines.

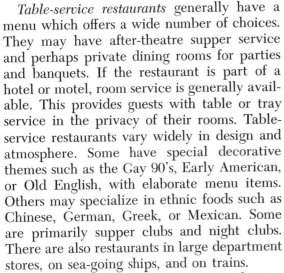

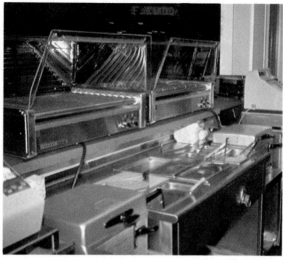

The arrangement of this counter service unit provides simple but fast service to customers.

This drive-in also has table service.

Some restaurants provide an extra portable hot unit for fast lunch service to busy business people.

Snack bars serve a variety of sandwiches, beverages, and short orders, but usually do not have table service.

Atlanta, Ga., Public Schools

Commissary workers load pans of food into delivery carts.

Catering Units

Catering units usually serve food at a location specified by the customer such as a private home, a club, or a hall. Generally the food is ordered for special occasions such as weddings, club parties, or business entertaining. The service is a convenience for the customers. They may choose from a wide menu selection and may also select the type of service they would like such as buffet or table service. The food is generally prepared by the caterers in their own kitchens. It is transported in special insulated containers, which help to keep the food at the right serving temperature. Oftentimes, table linen, silver, and dishes, as well as labor, are supplied by the catering unit. These units may be operated by restaurants as a part of their service, or by individual caterers.

Food Preparation and Assembly Units

Food preparation and assembly units are large kitchens, called *central kitchens* or *commissaries*. Foods such as salads, sandwiches, desserts, beverages, and/or complete meals are prepared in quantities. These foods are *preportioned* or divided into individual servings and then assembled or packaged. They are eaten *off the premises,* meaning at some other location. Some units deliver the food as well as prepare it. The food prepared in these central kitchens may be delivered to schools, airplanes, ships, businesses, and vending machines.

One special type of food preparation and assembly unit is the *food vending* or *contract feeding company*. A large organization may operate several divisions to serve different purposes such as:

- Make sandwiches, salads, desserts, and complete meals for automatic vending machines.
- Provide food, workers, and management for industrial cafeterias, office buildings, military bases, hospitals, schools, and universities.
- Provide complete frozen meals for freighters, tankers, airlines, and trains.
- Provide frozen full meals, platter meals, or bulk foods of ten to twenty servings. These are shipped to distribution spots and delivered to restaurants, drive-ins, and automats for service to customers.

The commissaries of vending companies may be located near residential areas, away from business areas. This makes it convenient to hire homemakers to work full or part-time.

Typical preparation and assembly units include food vending commissaries, automat restaurant commissaries, carry-out food shops, airline flight kitchens, and kitchens for public school systems.

Institutional Feeding Units

These units provide food service in institutions such as hospitals, public schools, or colleges. Institutional feeding units are operated by governmental agencies or by private or charitable organizations. Sometimes a commercial company is hired by the institution to provide food service. Institutional units feed large groups of people daily. Emphasis is on providing nourishment, rather than on making a profit. Menu choice is usually limited. Both table service and cafeteria service are common. In hospitals, tray and mobile cart service is provided for patients.

Typical institutional feeding units include public and parochial schools, hospitals, prisons, Salvation Army units, nursing homes, colleges and universities, and Red Cross units.

In-Plant Feeding Units

In-plant feeding has grown rapidly in recent years. Many business offices, manufacturing plants, banks, and others are situated in areas where restaurants are not available for workers. Therefore facilities are provided within the plants or office buildings to serve meals to employees.

The service may be limited to beverages and vending machines for short coffee breaks. Some plants provide twenty-four hour service, including snacks and meals, for shifts working around the clock.

The service in in-plant feeding may be cafeteria, vending, snack bar, or table service. Sometimes elaborate facilities are provided for service to executive or board members.

Employers have long recognized that food service to employees helps morale. Some companies are so convinced that good food builds health and thereby reduces absenteeism that they subsidize meals to employees.

Florida Dept. of Citrus

Elementary schools often provide informal cafeteria service for children.

Canteen Corp.

Vending units are used for meals in institutions.

Food items sold in cafeterias and snack bars and from vending machines need to be displayed attractively.

Florida Dept. of Citrus

23

Let's Think It Over

The food service industry has grown rapidly in size and importance, especially since the 1940's. There have been many changes which have influenced the development of this industry.

1. How have the following changes affected this business?

    Population growth.
    Increased travel.
    Job commuting or work away from home.
    More women working.
    Higher standards of living.
    Developments in technology.

2. How does the food service industry rank with other industries in size and number of people employed?
3. List the businesses that are affected by the food service industry. How are they affected?

Let's Investigate

1. Make an appointment to talk with a school lunchroom or restaurant manager. Find out the following:

- Was there an increase or decrease in the number of meals and/or people served this past year? What percentage?
- Number of employees. How many employees left this past year and had to be replaced? (This is called *employee turnover*.)
- Kinds of food service jobs available in your area.

2. Classify and describe the kinds of food service units in your community. Make a chart, using the following headings:

    Types of units.
    Name and location.
    Description.
    How are customers' needs met?

3. Think about the growth and importance of the food service industry. Are you aware of what it has done for your community? Are there any large food service units that have contributed to the economic growth of your locality? It would be interesting for you to talk with friends or neighbors who are in the food service business. See how they feel about this growing, expanding industry.

Chapter **2**

Opportunities

and Training

You are probably thinking seriously about the kind of job you want to have when you graduate. Since you will probably spend a good part of your life working, you will want to take time to select a career that you enjoy and find rewarding. Government surveys show that a man will spend forty or fifty years of his life on a job, six to eight hours every working day. A woman, even if married, may spend as many as 25 years of her life working at a job. You can make the most of your future right now by exploring job areas.

OPPORTUNITIES IN FOOD SERVICE

Think about food service as a career. Investigate the advantages and opportunities it offers. Consider your interests. Do you enjoy working with food? Do you like to work with

Now is the time to think seriously about the type of work you will do when you graduate.

people? Now is the time to try to determine if this field of work suits you.

When you invest in your future by training, you want some assurance that, once you are ready to work, there will be a job for you. As far as can be predicted, jobs will be available in food service in the future. Today, one out of six persons employed in industry is in some phase of the restaurant business. With the expected growth mentioned in Chapter One, job opportunities with chances for career promotions seem certain.

WIDE JOB CHOICE AND FLEXIBLE HOURS

Many types of food service jobs are available. For example, if you like to help the sick or aged, there are jobs in hospitals and nursing homes. If you enjoy being around young people, there are jobs in school lunchrooms and dining halls. If you like meeting many different people, there are jobs in motels, hotels, and institutions.

If you want to work part-time or short hours, jobs are often available in broken shifts. For instance, you may work three or four hours at a time in institutions and 24-hour restaurants, or in specialty food stands with limited service.

Many resorts and recreation areas offer short-term food service jobs during after-school hours or summer vacations. After-school and weekend jobs are also available in restaurants, snack bars, and drive-ins where business is heaviest during the late afternoon and evening hours.

On-the-Job Experience

On-the-job experience is one of the best ways to learn about food service. It is also possible for you to earn money during your training period. For instance, school food service co-op programs may provide an opportunity to earn on a job while you learn other basic skills in school. You might do kitchen work, or serve in a restaurant or a drive-in for a few hours a day and weekends. When you go on to full-time work, most employers provide the additional training necessary for specific jobs.

A Business of Your Own

Eventually, would you like to be the boss? There are many opportunities for an ambitious person to develop his own business in food service. Of course, you need money to invest and a willingness to work hard. You need to have an interest in people, a flair for food, and the ability to organize. As much experience as possible in food service work will help.

Today, there are national franchise operations which help finance a person who wants a business of his own. Other national food service chains have local, company-owned outlets which provide an opportunity for those who may have management ability.

People have started their own food service businesses in many ways. Some with a special talent for cooking may start in their own kitchen and sell their special food to friends and neighbors. This may result in a small neighborhood business.

The National Restaurant Association tells us that about twenty percent of all the restaurants in the nation are family businesses operated by father, mother, and children. Often families start a business in a small way, perhaps a restaurant featuring food specialties that may become popular. As the business grows they can expand, hire extra help, or even start other restaurants.

What other possibilities are there? If you own a car, you might deliver orders for a local pizza or chicken parlor. You might prepare and sell homemade pies, jellies, jams, pickles, or a specialty food. Perhaps you might be able to create a new idea. Generally, people who start a business of their own and succeed do so because they are creative, imaginative, and work hard to get their ideas across to others.

Franchise Food Business

When a company has established a successful food operation, they may allow others to use their name, methods, and building design. In return, they receive a fee for this privilege. This type of business is known as a *franchise*. Specific legal documents are required, setting forth the rights of both the franchisor (the one who originated the system) and the franchisee (the one who will operate the system.) Naturally, the franchisor wants his name and standards upheld and may specify that certain items be bought from him.

Ithaca Country Club

A part-time job as a waitress offers excellent training and experience in food service.

In recent years franchising has grown rapidly, especially in the area of fast foods. There are opportunities in this field for persons with business knowledge and experience in food service. Often a franchisor will train prospective franchisees in all phases of the business. Investment capital, or money to buy the franchise and set up business, is required.

Look carefully into the contract and the possible volume of business in the area before accepting a franchise. As in any business, a poor decision may result in failure; a wise decision could bring great rewards.

There are many opportunities in food service to go into business for yourself.

H. J. Heinz Co.

Food service workers learn to arrange food creatively so it is more appealing to customers.

In addition to school laboratory work, food service students attend classroom sessions.

Hospitals offer many types of food service jobs for those who like to help people.

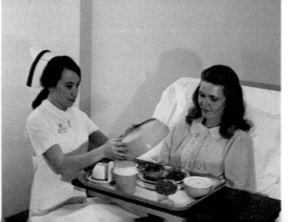

Company-Owned Food Service Operations

National food companies develop and operate chains of restaurants which are known as *company-owned units*. Food executives claim that company-owned operations are five to six times more profitable than franchised ones, probably because trained personnel are in charge, with constant supervision.

It is possible to develop a business of your own in these outlets. A manager is selected and trained by the parent company to operate each outlet. If you qualify for a manager's position, you usually have considerable freedom in operating the business. You do not have the heavy financial risks such as owning the building. Your income is derived from the profits of the business. Some companies may also guarantee a specified income for a period of time to a manager who is starting a new business. Other companies may pay the manager a fixed salary plus a bonus based on the profits. You may develop your own income through your ability to build up the business, and thus increase the profits.

You are not, of course, entirely on your own in a company business. Remember, the company is your partner. It provides a usually distinctive style of building, management training, supervision, and national advertising. You usually agree to pay a certain percentage of the gross income or building rent to the parent company. You must buy and sell specified foods and supplies. You must follow a specific method of operation in relation to menu, food preparation, and service personnel. High standards are promoted by company supervisors, who regularly check on food preparation, customer service, and building maintenance.

The major food companies generally offer benefits, which may include hospitalization, surgical, major medical, and disability benefits, group life insurance, and vacations.

Remember, if you plan to work for a company-owned operation, study the contract carefully before you sign it.

Family Meal Aides

If you prefer a more personalized type of work, you may enjoy serving as a *family meal aide* or *family dinner specialist* in private homes. Many individuals and families need a competent worker to prepare and serve food in the home because:

- Both husband and wife may have full-time jobs.
- Elderly family members are unable to prepare meals.
- The homemaker may be ill or convalescent.
- The homemaker may need help in entertaining guests.

The job of a family meal aide may be short-term, part-time, or full-time, depending on the needs and circumstances.

JOB SPECIALIZATION

The food service industry needs workers who are interested in specializing in one area. There are four major areas in most food service units: *management, production, sales and service,* and *sanitation. Specialization* means learning to do one type of work well to the point of becoming an expert. This can lead to better jobs and better pay.

Food service jobs are available in . . .

Caddy Corp.

Sanitation.

H. J. Heinz Co.

Management.

Food production.

H. J. Heinz Co.

Sales and service.

Holiday Inn

Let us look at some of the job titles generally used to indicate responsibilities in each of the four areas.

Management Area

Manager
Assistant manager
Executive chef
Supervisor
Dietitian
Owner

Production Area

Chef
Assistant chef
Pantry worker
Baker
Cook
Assistant cook
Kitchen helper
Assistant baker

Sales and Service Area

Hostess
Head waiter
Food checker
Food runner
Waiter/waitress
Carhop
Counter worker
Cashier
Dining room helper
Busboy/girl

Sanitation Area

Dishwasher
Porter
Busboy/girl
Stock clerk
Kitchen helper

The number of people employed in each area depends on the type and size of the operation. In a large operation, specialization is generally required. However, in small operations duties may be combined. For instance, a large restaurant kitchen may have a chef, assistant chef, cook, assistant cook, baker, salad maker, and kitchen helper. On the other hand, a small operation such as a coffee shop or a snack bar may have only one or two persons who do all of the food preparation.

If you have limited training and experience, you can start in a job that requires little skill. As you learn new skills, you can move on to a better job in the same or another area. Of course, in-school or on-the-job training will help you to advance.

Have you considered the kind of food service job you might want? Have you thought about the kind of education and training you will need? Let us examine food service training.

As part of the management team, the dietitian is responsible for planning nutritious, flavorful meals. To do this, she must keep up with the latest developments in her field.

H. J. Heinz Co.

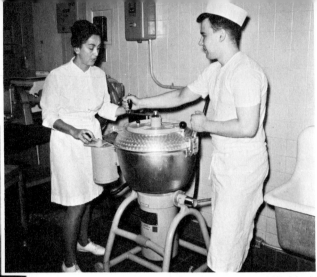

In a large restaurant, a helper may be responsible for one job such as cutting vegetables. Here a student learns how to use the vertical cutter to shred vegetables.

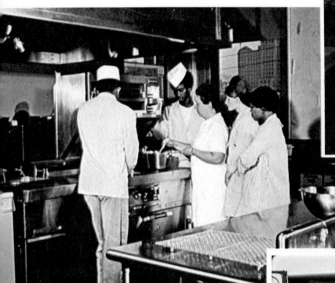

Most food service units offer on-the-job training for new employees.

A student begins his career in food service by working as a deliveryman for the school breakfast program.

Student obtains training and experience in vegetable preparation in food service classes.

TRAINING REQUIREMENTS

Every job in food service is important. What kind of training prepares you for these jobs? The following charts show the job levels in each area of food service. Information is also given as to training needed.

Beginning Jobs

Beginning jobs usually require some basic training in food service.

Food Service Area	Beginning-Level Jobs
Production	Cook's helper
	Kitchen helper
	Pantry girl/man
	Salad girl/man
	Sandwich maker
	Hot food packer
	Baker's helper
	Formula room worker
	Caterer's helper
	Food assembler and packer
Sales and service	Family meal aide
	Dining room helper
	Waiter/waitress
	Busboy/girl
	Counter employee
	Carhop
	Fountain worker
Sanitation	Dishwasher
	Ware washer
	Storekeeper
	Cart, equipment cleaner
	Porter

Beginning jobs require at least one year of vocational food service courses. Two or more years are preferred. Food service courses are also offered in the adult education and other community programs for out-of-school youths and adults. In many large food service units, on-the-job training is available.

Intermediate Jobs

Intermediate jobs require a higher level of work skills, knowledge, and experience.

Food Service Area	Intermediate-Level Jobs
Production	Kitchen supervisor
	Roast or meat chef
	Pastry supervisor
	Pantry cook
	Baker
	Butcher
	Vegetable cook
	Food supervisor
Sales and service	Host, hostess
	Head waiter
	Head waitress
Sanitation	Sanitation supervisor

Intermediate jobs require two to four years of training in any of the following: vocational-technical high schools; manpower training courses sponsored by the federal government in local communities; technical and community colleges; and hotel and restaurant schools.

Students learn basic food

production techniques . . .

BOCES, Ithaca, N. Y.

How to serve food attractively.

Brookline, Mass., Public Schools

How to follow a recipe.

Brookline, Mass., Public Schools

How to serve food in correct portions.

How to use specialized equipment.

How to use equipment properly.

Taylor Freezer

Erie Co. BOCES #1

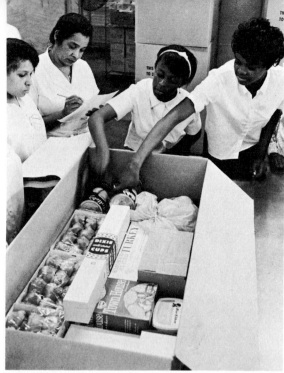

Dudley-Anderson-Yutzy

How to pack lunches for delivery to schools.

How to wash dishes and trays properly.

Brookline, Mass., Public Schools

It is also possible for you to work up to an intermediate job by doing a good job at a beginning level.

Management Jobs

Management jobs require a high professional level of skill, knowledge, and experience.

Food Service Area	Management-Level Jobs
Production	Caterer
	Chef or chief cook
	Dietitian
	Executive chef
	Food production manager
	Manager
	Supervisor
Sales and service	Caterer
	Dietitian
	Executive chef
	Food service supervisor
	Manager
	Bookkeeper
	Caterer
	Sales supervisor
	Special function manager
Sanitation	Sanitation engineer

Management jobs are usually open to graduates of colleges, universities, and hotel schools. However, some are available to graduates of two-year technical schools or colleges.

It is also possible to work up through the ranks into management-level jobs.

35

Beginning jobs in food service . . .

H. J. Heinz Co.

Cashier.

Cayuga Inn, Ithaca, N. Y.

Waitress.

BOCES, Ithaca, N. Y.

Dining room helper.

Storeroom worker.

Sarasota, Fla., Public Schools

Dishroom worker.

Brookline, Mass., Public Schools

36

Education and on-the-job experience can lead to management jobs . . .

Food service consultant.

Manager.

Chief dietitian.

Executive chef.

Photos this page courtesy H. J. Heinz Co.

HOW WILL YOU
FIT INTO FOOD SERVICE?

It may not be easy to find a job immediately that you feel is just right for you, one in which you can be a success. Your first task in job-seeking will be to sell yourself. What can you offer? Size yourself up and match your qualifications with the requirements listed by food service employers. Take an honest inventory of yourself, but *do not underrate* your ability as you answer the following questions.

What Is Your Background?

Education	Employers Prefer	Because You Need To
Can you read and follow directions accurately?	A high school graduate, although it is not necessary in some beginning food jobs.	Understand menus, recipes. Carry out written directions.
Can you write clearly?	Legible handwriting.	Write food orders, requests for supplies.
Can you use simple arithmetic?	Accurate use of arithmetic.	Figure and measure food quantities. Figure food sales checks.
Are you able to use correct English in writing and talking?	Pleasing voice. Good grammar.	Communicate with workers and employers intelligently. Talk to customers.
Have you had any training in food service?	Some training and courses in food service.	Know basic skills.
Have you had any jobs in food service?	Some actual experience in a food service job.	Produce good results.

What Is Your Physical Condition?

Health	Employers Prefer	Because You Need To
Is your health good?	A physical examination; general good health.	Be free from diseases when handling food.
Do you have good posture?	Good posture.	Work efficiently.
Is your weight average?	Average weight.	Present a good appearance and work efficiently.

Are your feet and legs in good condition?	▷ Freedom from enlarged veins.	▷ Be on your feet during many work hours.
Are your clothes clean, well-pressed, comfortable?	▷ Neat, clean, attractive appearance. Clean uniform or clothes appropriate to job.	▷ Look clean and attractive when handling food and serving it to customers.
Is your skin healthy, clean, and attractive?	▷ Clear skin, well-cared-for hands.	▷ Present a clean, healthy appearance.
Is your hair arrangement right for the job?	▷ Clean, well-arranged hair.	▷ Feel comfortable and have confidence in yourself.

What Are Your Personal Qualities?

Personal Traits	Employers Prefer	Because You Need To
Are you dependable?	▷ Employees who are on time and work with little absenteeism. Employees who do not wait to be told what to do.	▷ Contribute to the efficient operation of the business.
Are you capable of doing the work?	▷ Employees who know how to perform necessary tasks and get work done on time.	▷ Finish tasks in allotted time and do your share of the work.
Are you willing to accept directions?	▷ Employees who obey rules and regulations.	▷ Help maintain standards and quality.
Do you make an effort to learn and improve?	▷ Employees who accept criticism and are willing to learn.	▷ Take criticism and supervision.
Are you courteous and friendly?	▷ Employees who are friendly, tactful, and who move quietly.	▷ Act in the best interest of the customers and the employer, as well as yourself.
Are you honest?	▷ Employees who do not cheat.	▷ Protect your employer's interests and your own reputation.
Are you loyal?	▷ Employees who have pride and interest in the business and in themselves.	▷ Promote the business and your own status.

Food Service Careers

How will you fit into food service?

Sheridan Vocational Center, Broward County, Fla.

Are you friendly and courteous?

Brookline, Mass., Public Schools

Do you make an effort to learn and to improve your work?

BOCES, Ithaca, N. Y.

Can you work on your feet for many hours and still be efficient and good-natured?

Can you follow instructions accurately?

Brookline, Mass., Public Schools

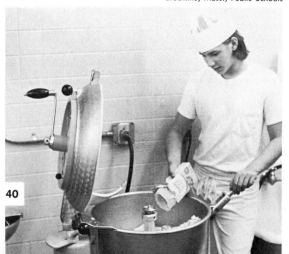

Can others depend on you to get your job done?

Caddy Corp.

40

Do you have the qualifications that employers desire? Why is it that some individuals have trouble obtaining and keeping a job, while others seem to succeed easily?

Young people looking for their first job may find pretty rough going. They wonder why they failed. Employers report that the mistakes made by most young people in *getting* and *holding* jobs are found in the following areas:

- Appearance.
- Attitude and behavior.
- Ignorance of labor market and unrealistic wage demands.
- Misrepresentation of age, education, and experience.
- Insufficient training.
- Failure to notify employer of absence.
- Unsuitability for job.
- Accompanied by friend or relative when applying for job.
- Lack of reliability and responsibility.
- Inability to get along with others.

The way you manage yourself and the techniques you use in getting and holding a job are important keys to success.

Investigate Your Personality

The ability to get along with all kinds of people is a great asset on a job. Employers say their biggest problem is the employee who clashes with others or causes friction. Learn to work well with others and to maintain a good relationship with your employer. It is important to understand that everyone may have some faults. However, tact and consideration for the other person will help you as well as him.

BOCES, Ithaca, N.Y.

Success in food service depends on your willingness to work and to learn.

On page 42 is a list of personal traits valuable in food service work. The questions give you clues for judging your own personality. Answer each question in the proper column—Excellent, Good, Average, or Poor. Rate yourself three times during the year to see if you can have a better score by the end of the year.

Your Chances for Success

As you learn about the food service industry, the job opportunities, and where you may fit in, keep in mind your chances for success. Consider both the advantages and disadvantages of the many areas of food service. Would you be willing to put up with the disadvantages? Do the advantages appeal to you?

How Do You Rate?

Friendliness

Do you like to work with other people?

Do you like to listen to others?

Do you feel like helping other workers?

Is it easy to ask help from the people you work with?

Are you shy or self-conscious?

Do you say very little to your co-workers?

Are you pleasant but quiet when you are working?

Can you smile and be enthusiastic about your work?

Can you show people that you like them?

Do you have many friends at school or where you work?

Do you make an effort to compliment others?

Dependability

Do you tell the truth on the job, at home, and at school?

Are you always on time for a job?

Do you get all assigned work done on schedule?

Do you look for more to do when your work is done?

Do you notify the employer or teacher when you are late or unable to be on a job?

Do you see work that needs to be done without being told?

Thoughtfulness

Can you be calm when under pressure?

Can you keep from gossiping and blaming other people?

Do you try to understand the other person and his job?

Do you use good manners when talking and working with others?

Do you show appreciation to the boss and co-workers when they help you?

Do you avoid rude behavior such as interrupting conversations?

Advantages in Food Service

What?	*Why?*
Work is steady.	Many types of food services are available in all communities.
There is constant demand for new employees.	Food service industry is growing.
You can secure work readily in any location.	Food service jobs are similar throughout the country.
Wages are reasonably good.	Pay range varies depending on job level. Tips may help to increase your basic wage.
Working conditions usually are pleasant.	Many food service units are modern and attractive. You are with people your own age and meet many others.
Fringe benefits are increasing.	Meals and uniforms are often furnished; other benefits may be paid vacations, bonuses, pension plans, hospital and group insurance, profit sharing.
Shorter work weeks are increasing.	Working hours vary from 40–48 a week.
Many part time jobs are available.	Short hours, broken shifts, early and late shifts can be arranged to fit needs of worker.
Opportunities for self-improvement and promotion exist.	On-the-job training and advancement through experience are offered.
Possibilities for starting your own business may occur.	Businesses such as franchises offer opportunities to experienced persons.

Disadvantages in Food Service

What?	*Why?*
Hard physical labor is required such as carrying heavy trays, pots, and pans.	Food must be produced in quantity and within specific time periods. It must usually be carried to the customer.
Work is often done under pressure.	Peak serving periods and increased food production demand a faster pace.
Working conditions may be uncomfortable.	Hard floors, hot kitchens, and limited space may cause fatigue.
Working hours may not be convenient.	Food must be served evenings, weekends, holidays, and Sundays.
Dealing with the public is not always pleasant.	Customers may be unreasonable, irritating, and demanding.

Let's Think It Over

1. When you work, you come in contact with all kinds of people. Part of your job depends on how well you get along with your employer, supervisor, and co-workers.

   - Why do employers always check the personal traits of employees? How do employers find out this information?
   - Identify and discuss the personal traits which are essential in order to succeed on a job.
   - List and discuss the kinds of behavior which would indicate to an employer that you possess the following personal traits:
       Dependability.
       Loyalty.
       Honesty.
       Tact.
       Responsibility.
   - What should you do when you make a mistake on the job? What should you not do?

2. The food service industry employs a large number of people in many jobs at all levels.

   - Discuss the differences in training for beginning, intermediate, and management jobs.
   - What are some of the beginning jobs in food service? How do responsibilities differ in these jobs?
   - Explain the meaning of *employee turnover*, *work experience*, and *on-the-job training*.

3. The food service industry offers possibilities for advancement to employees who are interested and willing to work.

   - How would you advance from a beginning to an intermediate job?
   - List the most important characteristics employers look for in a worker.
   - In order to succeed in food service, what should you consider when choosing a job?
   - Describe the advantages and disadvantages of food service work. How do you think you might overcome the disadvantages?
   - What physical and personal qualities are needed to get ahead in a food service job?

Let's Investigate

1. Make an appointment to interview a restaurant manager. What are his requirements for new employees regarding education, experience, and ability? Discuss these in class.

2. Observe the actions of food service employees whenever you eat out. How might these actions lead to advancement or to loss of a job? How do you think a loss of job might have been prevented in any specific case? Report on or role-play some of these situations in class.

3. Investigate and discuss the opportunities that are available in the food service industry in your locality. What are the opportunities for specialization? Make a chart showing the job choices for the class bulletin board.

Chapter **3**

Operation of Food
Service Units

As a food service customer, have you ever wondered why a hamburger costs $.45 at a hamburger stand, $.75 in one restaurant, and $1.50 or more in another? What determines the amount of your check?

Have you ever wondered how restaurants manage to serve perhaps a hundred meals an hour while each customer waits no more than a few minutes to be served? How are restaurants operated to make this possible?

To answer these questions, let us look behind the scenes of an average restaurant. We will start by examining the economics—the dollar-and-cents operation—of the food service business.

ECONOMICS OF FOOD SERVICE

The *economics* of food service means the management of expenses and income. Careful, progressive management is essential to success. Management must control:

- Food and supplies—the cost of food, china, glassware, paper, and linen, and other supplies.

<table>
<tr><th colspan="2">WORDS TO KNOW</th></tr>
<tr><td>Turnover</td><td>Teamwork</td></tr>
<tr><td>Profit</td><td>Front of the house</td></tr>
<tr><td>Gross receipts</td><td>Back of the house</td></tr>
<tr><td>Net receipts</td><td>Lines of authority</td></tr>
<tr><td>Economics</td><td>Overhead</td></tr>
</table>

H. J. Heinz Co.

Why does the price of a hamburger and French fries differ from restaurant to restaurant?

Some restaurants have high overhead, food, and labor costs and therefore charge higher prices for the food they serve.

Corning Glass Works

- Labor—the wages of employees including all fringe benefits.
- Overhead—the cost of rent, utilities, maintenance of equipment, and repairs.
- Turnover—the number of customers served during the day.

The expenses involved in food service— food, supplies, labor, and overhead—must be balanced against the income. Income depends on volume of business.

Restaurant owners must make a profit to stay in business. Therefore the prices of items on their menus are based on the costs of food, labor, and overhead. Restaurants with elaborate decor and formal waiter service have high overhead and labor costs. As a result, the customers must be charged higher prices for the food. Some food service units such as those in institutions do not operate for profit. Therefore their menu prices are lower than those found in commercial restaurants.

Let us examine the food service operation in Art Turner's restaurant. How do the economics of food service work for him?

Art Turner operates a restaurant in the business section of a small city. His meal prices and operating costs may change in times of inflation or depression. However, the percentages used to determine profit and loss remain approximately the same. His restaurant offers only table service for 75 customers at one time. The menu prices are average—about $7.00 for a meal of meat, vegetables, salad, beverage, and dessert. Each day at closing time Art Turner counts the money he has taken in. Today, it adds up to $700. This amount is his *gross receipts*. However, he cannot keep all this money as his profit. Why not?

46

Food costs average 35 to 40 percent of a restaurant's gross receipts.

About 30–35 percent of a restaurant's income is used to pay employee wages.

First, Art Turner must pay for the food. In food service units, food costs average 35 to 40 percent of the gross receipts. Today his food costs are $252 or 36 percent out of his $700.

Second, he must pay his labor costs, which amount to $231 for the day, including his own salary. Thus he must take out 33 percent of $700 to pay the cost of labor. This includes wages and fringe benefits for cooks, dishwashers, kitchen helpers, waitresses, and anyone else who is employed in the restaurant. Labor costs in food service average 30 to 35 percent of gross receipts.

Third, he must pay his overhead costs, which amount to $175 today. This means he must take out 25 percent of $700 to pay the cost of overhead. This includes rent, electricity, gas, telephone, repairs, maintenance of equipment, and supplies. Overhead costs in food service average 20 to 30 percent of gross receipts.

Between 20 and 30 percent of a restaurant's income is used for overhead such as utilities and maintenance of equipment.

The $42 left are the *net receipts* for the day's business, which usually amount to 3 to 5 percent of his gross receipts. Because Art owns this business, he does not share with a partner or stockholder. Therefore the net receipts are also his *profit*.

The profit that Art Turner makes each day depends on the turnover of customers. The costs in daily operations are generally the same from day to day. However, the turnover usually varies. It is necessary to have a large volume of customers to make a profit.

Like Art Turner, food service owners base their operation on the economic principle which may be summarized as follows: If the cost of food, labor, and overhead is high and the customer turnover is low, higher menu prices are necessary to make a profit. If the cost of food, labor, and overhead is low, and the customer turnover is high, a profit can be made even with low menu prices.

Art Turner makes a small profit with 100 customers a day. If he served only 75 customers, he would have to charge more for his meals. He might even be forced out of business. The average cost of an American restaurant is $1,500 per seat. Since Art Turner can seat 75 people at a time, he has about $112,500 invested in his business. He cannot afford to lose customers.

If Art Turner can serve 150–200 customers a day, he will increase his gross receipts with little or no increase in the cost of operation. He could either have a larger profit or lower his menu prices.

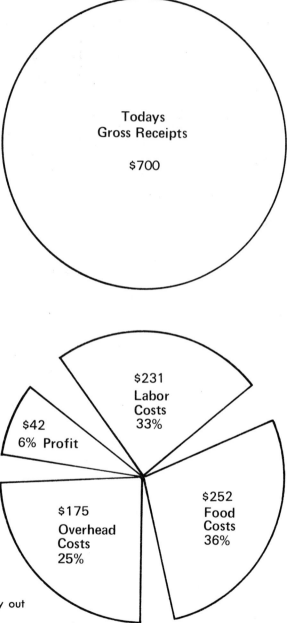

These are the average costs which a restaurant must pay out of the day's gross receipts.

Restaurant owners use different methods to increase their customer turnover. They may advertise their restaurant, emphasizing food specialties or stressing quick service or leisurely dining. They may have daily specials. Some develop a high reputation for a certain recipe or food item. Others may offer specials during slow periods such as early morning or mid-afternoon to bring in more customers.

A good location is important in attracting customers. A restaurant in a shopping center would probably be used by shoppers and store employees. A restaurant located in a business area could expect to serve businessmen and office workers during coffee breaks and lunch hours. If it were in a high-crime area, it would get little if any business during evening hours.

Cape Coral Country Club, Fla.

A restaurant's profits often depend on the ability of the chef. For example, this chef has become well known for his unusual sauces.

What other areas must management control? The success of any business depends upon efficient management of all operations. To do this, management must have a well-organized plan or system of operation.

ORGANIZATION OF UNITS

Have you ever thought about the number of activities that must take place in a food service operation? The food must be purchased, stored, prepared, and then served and sold to the public. Usually this is all done on the premises. A food service unit is very much like a factory, where the product is manufactured, warehoused, and sold in one place. However, in the food service business the product is often consumed on the premises.

Operations are organized into two main areas—the back of the house and the front of the house.

Back of the House

The back of the house is the area where food is delivered, stored, and prepared. It includes storerooms, kitchen, pantry, and dishwashing area. The back of the house contributes to success by purchasing and preparing high-quality foods with minimum labor costs. Therefore careful planning is needed to insure an efficient arrangement of floor space and labor-saving equipment. Storage areas for dry, refrigerated, and frozen foods are placed near the back door where the raw food supplies are received. The kitchen is placed so that there is easy access to the pantry area and the storerooms. The dishwashing area is convenient to the dining room.

The dining area is the salesroom of the house. Attractive, appealing displays and service of food are essential.

A well-planned storeroom is essential in the back-of-the-house area. Note that all like foods are placed together with the cans arranged so that the labels are easy to read.

Front of the House

In restaurant units, the front of the house is the salesroom of the business. It is the area where food is served, sold, and consumed. It includes the reception area, dining rooms, coat rooms, and rest rooms. It is most important·to have attractive, clean, and comfortable dining rooms. Customers want to feel relaxed while eating. Heat, noise, and confusion should be eliminated.

Many restaurants promote specialties in food and service. Some invest in unusual decorations to create an atmosphere which will attract customers to their dining room. Clever merchandising of food and decor can spell success.

Rooms in the front of the house should be organized so that there is an easy flow of customer and service traffic.

In assembly units, the front-of-the-house operations are handled by means of vending machines, automats, or carry-out service.

In institutional feeding units, the front-of-the-house operations vary. For instance, cart and tray service is generally used in hospitals. Cafeteria or counter service is generally used in universities and schools.

50

Lines of Authority

Every type of food service unit must have a well-defined plan for operating. This plan establishes the lines of authority among the staff and sets up the duties and responsibilities for each employee. The plan depends on the type of food service unit. There are *three key factors*:

- *The menu.* This specifies the kind of food that is to be served. The menu is important. It indicates what foods must be bought and prepared. It determines what equipment is needed to store, cook, serve, and sell this food. It also determines the work load of the employees.
- *Type and quality of service.* This can vary from simple counter service to elaborate table service. The food, equipment, personnel, and overhead will vary with each type of service. Can you give an example of this from your observations?
- *Size of operation.* This determines the number of customers served and the number of meals that must be prepared each day. It influences personnel needs, food purchasing, storage, and equipment. Customer turnover must be considered here. Why?

The lines of authority are set up to meet the needs of each operation. Remember, when a person has responsibility he must also have authority. Why is this necessary? What are these lines of authority? Who is responsible to whom?

The chart on page 58 shows the lines of authority in an average restaurant such as that of Art Turner.

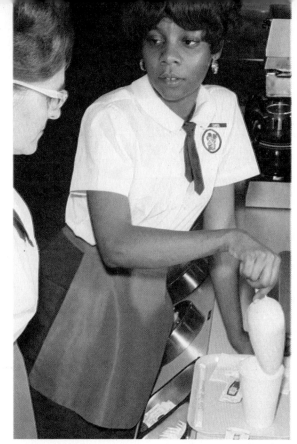

H. J. Heinz Co.

Back-of-the-house and front-of-the-house activities are often combined such as in this counter service unit. Counter workers are also responsible for simple food preparation such as fountain specialties.

The type of food a restaurant decides to serve determines the equipment it will need, the food that must be bought, and the work load of the employees. Some foods such as pizza require specialized equipment.

H. J. Heinz Co.

51

Food Service Careers

Some restaurants offer elaborate table service. Here a student learns the art of serving foods flambé or flaming.

Cooperation among food service workers is essential. Every worker is responsible for proper food storage. Here trays of cold food have been placed on a cart and rolled into the refrigerator.

Here is an assortment of appetizing desserts prepared in a small coffee shop from soft-serve ice cream.

52

In this organization, a waitress is directly responsible to the hostess. A kitchen helper is responsible to the cook. The hostess and cook are responsible to the manager. In a well-planned system, each person knows exactly where he is in the line of authority. Can you see how necessary this is? Wouldn't it be confusing to work in a kitchen and not know whose instructions you were to follow?

Responsibilities of Each Position

A good operating plan sets up duties and responsibilities for teams of food service workers. Each worker can be said to be part of a team—each person does his special job, but each depends on the work of others. Cooperation is necessary for teamwork.

For example, the job of the dishwasher is an important part of the back-of-the-house team. The major responsibility of the dishwasher in Art Turner's restaurant is to keep an adequate supply of clean, sanitary dishes, glassware, and silver ready for the kitchen and the dining room. If he is slow getting started, or if he stops to visit with a friend, what happens? The chef runs out of dinner plates, the salad girl needs more salad plates, and the waitresses want silver. The customers have to wait for service and become dissatisfied. The whole line of operation slows down, fewer customers are served, and Art Turner worries about his profit. All of the workers depend on the dishwasher to do his job right.

The manager depends on his dishwasher to keep him informed about food left on the used dishes. Why? Because this helps to indicate which menu items are popular and whether the food preparation is satisfactory.

Do you begin to see that cooperation is necessary for smooth operation? Can you give an example of good and poor teamwork in food service that you may have experienced or observed?

Why Is Organization Important?

Let us think again about the basic economics of restaurant operation. To establish a restaurant represents a large outlay of money. The cost of building or buying a restaurant may range from $100,000 to $250,000. Remember, the owner or manager must make a reasonable profit to stay in business. If he cannot realize at least a five to ten percent profit, it would be better to invest his money in some other way.

Some restaurant owners do fail. Why does this happen? There may be many reasons such as poor location, inefficient organization, inaccurate records, or inability to control costs. However, if the manager can set up a good system of operation and maintain it with the help of his employees, he has a greater chance for success.

HOW CAN YOU HELP KEEP EXPENSES DOWN?

Each employee can cooperate in many ways. Following established procedures is one. For example, if you give a friend a big scoop or double portion of food, the business is losing money. It is important to handle, store, and serve food exactly as directed to maintain the standards set by management and to avoid waste.

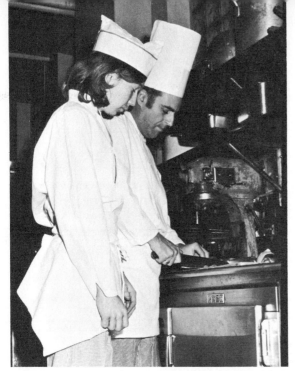

Brookline, Mass., Public Schools

Standards set by management must be maintained. Here a trainee learns the right way to pre-prepare food for the grill.

Brookline, Mass., Public Schools

One of these workers has a few spare minutes, so he uses the time to help a co-worker with his job.

By handling dishes and glassware carefully, you can help avoid costly breakage.

BOCES, Ithaca, N. Y.

Do you know that the cost of dishes, linen, and silverware may run into thousands of dollars? A cup and saucer may cost $2.50, a dinner plate $2.00, a knife $1.00. You can help reduce costs by handling dishes and glasses carefully so they do not break. Be sure silverware is not dropped into the garbage. Avoid spills that stain the linens badly.

What other ways can you help? Turn water taps off tightly. Turn off lights, gas, and power when they are not in use. Perhaps you could do something extra such as help another employee if you have a few spare minutes. Make your time produce more. Save steps by carrying several items in one trip. Learn to use both hands when you work.

You probably will not be involved directly in the management of the food operation at first. However, your cooperation and your efficient work habits can help the business to be successful. Try not to let your employer or the customers down. You can get satisfaction from your job by being an efficient part of a successful team. You may also benefit by being promoted. If you help to keep the business a success, it will make your job more secure.

Let's Think It Over

Building or buying a restaurant means a large outlay of money to the owner. He must operate the business efficiently so that he can make a profit.

- Define the general economic principle that is involved in restaurant operation.
- What parts of a food service operation must management control to be successful? Define each one.
- Define the following terms as they relate to a food service.

Economics	Gross receipts
Profit	Net receipts
Capital investment	Turnover

- If a restaurant owner took in $650 gross receipts for one day, how much of this would he have to pay out for . . .
  Food costs at 35 percent?
  Labor costs at 34 percent?
  Overhead costs at 25 percent?
  What would his day's profit be?

- What do the terms "front of the house" and "back of the house" mean?
- List and explain the three key factors that influence the operating plans of food service units.
- What is the importance of teamwork in food service?
- List several ways an employee can help prevent waste.
- Name several ways of becoming an efficient, productive employee.

Let's Investigate

1. Interview your school lunchroom manager or a restaurant owner about his system of operation. Draw a diagram of this operation showing the lines of authority.
2. Interview two managers—one from a commercial restaurant and one from an institutional food service unit such as a hospital or school. Compare the volume of business and the costs of food, labor, and overhead. How do the variety and quality of food and service compare? Is any part of the institutional food service subsidized? Why? Discuss your findings in class.

Chapter **4**

How Do Food Service

Teams Function?

In the previous chapter, we discussed the success of a food service operation. Success usually depends on the combined skills of all the employees, from the manager to the kitchen helper. Think of the employees in each department as a team, ready to cooperate with each other and with members of other teams.

What are the responsibilities of each team? How does each operate and cooperate with others? What part does each play in a successful food service operation? Let us examine the responsibilities of each team.

WORDS TO KNOW

Management	Inventory
Receiving	Side stand
Storing	Purchasing agent
Issuing	Central store
Requisition	Work station
Commissary	Pre-preparation
Service station	Pantry

WORK STATION

Each team generally operates at a work station. This is an area which contains the equipment, work space, and storage space needed to carry on the team's activities.

MANAGEMENT TEAM

The management team is responsible for the overall operation. This includes managing money; hiring, training, and supervising workers; and purchasing food. This team is also responsible for the quality of the food and service. This is the top level of authority.

It would be ideal if each worker had only one boss. However, in reality there may be several bosses to whom workers are responsible. The illustrations on pages 58 and 59 show how management teams might operate in small and large food service operations.

In a small operation such as a diner or coffee shop, a husband and wife might be both owner and manager. Together they would plan the overall operation. Both might be responsible for the cashiering, bookkeeping, and menu planning. However, the husband might oversee the food purchasing and preparation while the wife concentrates on the service or the front-of-the-house operation. Note the chain of command in the illustration on page 58. The cook and hostess report directly to the owner or manager. If you were a counter worker, who would be your boss? Who would be your boss if you were the dishwasher?

In larger operations, there may be several people on the management team, each with a specific job. In the illustration on page 59, the owner or manager plans and controls the overall operation. The cashier and bookkeeper, also members of the management team, take care of the financial accounting. The front-of-the-house operation is supervised by the hostess while the back-of-the-house operation is supervised by the chef. Both are responsible to the manager. If you were a waitress, who would be your boss? Who would be your boss if you were a salad maker? Why?

RECEIVING, STORING, AND ISSUING TEAM

The functions of receiving, storing, and issuing usually occur in one department located in the back of the house. Generally, the department is adjacent to the delivery area, with convenient access to the kitchen. This operation is important to all other activities because food must be kept in prime condition—not spoiled or wasted. It must be available when needed to meet the preparation and service schedules.

Receiving means checking in all purchases as they are delivered. The receiver must make sure that the quantity delivered is the same as the amount ordered. The products must be examined to determine if they meet standards of quality. Accuracy in judging grades, quality, and weights can save money for the employer.

Storing means putting the supplies away in the storeroom, refrigerator, freezer, or cupboards. This must be done promptly so that perishable foods will not spoil. A plan of storage has generally been established so that foods and supplies may be located easily.

Issuing means supplying each department with the items they call for or *requisition*. The storeroom worker assembles and delivers the least perishable foods first, then the most perishable. Can you tell why? He keeps a record of all food and supplies coming in and going out. This is known as the *inventory*. In this way he can tell quickly what is on hand. By checking his inventory, he knows what item is low and needs to be ordered.

FRONT OF THE HOUSE   OWNER—MANAGER—CASHIER   BACK OF THE HOUSE
(HUSBAND)

HOSTESS
(WIFE)

COOK

COUNTER WORKER   WAITRESS   HELPER   DISHWASHER

Lines of authority in a small restaurant.

FRONT OF THE HOUSE   MANAGER   BACK OF THE HOUSE

CASHIER—
BOOKKEEPER

HEAD CHEF

HOSTESS

RECEIVING
CLERK

COOK

BAKER

WAITRESS   DINING ROOM
HELPER   DISHWASHER   KITCHEN
HELPER   SALAD
WORKER   DESSERT
WORKER

Lines of authority in a large restaurant.

Food Service Careers

RECEIVING CLERK

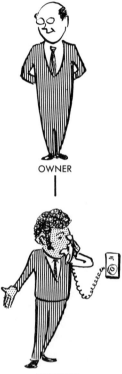

OWNER

STOREROOM WORKERS

In a large food service unit, the receiving clerk is in charge of the storeroom and reports to management.

MANAGER

Some owners prefer to hire a manager to run the restaurant for them.

Storeroom and food service workers are required to check and arrange equipment and supplies, restocking them as needed.

BOCES, Ithaca, N. Y.

Owners and/or managers in small operations may receive, store, and issue food supplies direct to workers. Since they do not need extra help in this area, it becomes part of the management team responsibility.

In larger food service units, the team may have from two to four workers. The receiving clerk is in charge and reports to the management. Other storeroom workers take care of receiving and issuing and keep the inventory. They are responsible to the receiving clerk.

Many large institutional food service units such as those in schools, colleges, and state hospitals maintain a central store or *commissary*. Do not confuse this type of commissary with a central kitchen, which is also called a commissary, discussed in Chapter One. A *purchasing agent* buys food in large quantities in order to provide a ready supply of food for each unit. Buying in quantity also reduces the cost. Each unit in the institution orders its supplies from the commissary as needed. The purchasing agent in charge of the commissary is a management person.

The *receiving, storing, issuing station* is sometimes called *stores*. Equipment includes worktables, carts, scales, dollies, shelves, and movable pallets. Men are usually employed in this area because of the heavy lifting involved. In large storage areas, mechanical fork lifts are used to move stock.

What do you have to be able to do at this station?

- Requisition, receive, store, and issue food, equipment, and supplies in accordance with a definite policy.
- Know and use the proper equipment to store and transfer items.

- Keep necessary records.
- Clean and maintain the area and the equipment.

Here are some typical jobs that you may have as a beginner in this area:

- Count, check, or weigh produce as it is received.
- Store cases on pallets as directed.
- Open cartons and place items on shelves.
- Refrigerate fresh produce.
- Receive requisitions from work areas.
- Weigh and portion supplies as requisitioned.
- Deliver to stations at specified times.
- Clean shelves, floor, and equipment.

FOOD PREPARATION TEAM

The work of the food preparation team is vital to the success of the food service unit. The team must be efficiently organized and expertly scheduled, especially in large establishments where many workers are involved. Cooperation is essential so that the work of each contributes to the whole operation.

This team is responsible for the preparation of every item on the menu. Food must be well-prepared, appetizing, and attractively served in pre-determined portions.

The size of the food service operation generally determines the number of workers. In a small restaurant, the manager may be in charge of both dining room and kitchen. One cook and an assistant take care of all the kitchen work and may also assist in the dining room. In a much larger operation, the head chef is usually in charge of the kitchen workers.

The work of the food preparation team is divided into three steps:

- *Pre-preparation (preliminary preparation)*—preparing raw food for cooking such as chopping meat and washing and cutting vegetables. Kitchen helpers and assistant cooks are generally responsible for this work.
- *Cooking*—combining and preparing foods by various methods according to standard recipes. Chefs and cooks are responsible for the cooking.
- *Finishing*—putting prepared food into serving containers. Kitchen and dining room workers are responsible for this work.

These three steps—pre-preparation, cooking, and finishing—are carried on at specific work stations. These are the pre-preparation, hot food or range, cold food, and bake stations. A food service unit may need all of the stations or combinations of several, depending on its type and size. It is important to understand the organization of these work stations since you may soon be a worker on one of the teams.

Pre-Preparation Work Station

An example of a pre-preparation work station is vegetable pre-preparation, where fresh vegetables are washed and prepared for cooking. The station is located near a sink and within easy access of any equipment needed.

In a small unit such as a coffee shop, the members of the food preparation team may report direct to the manager.

MANAGER

COOK

ASSISTANT COOK

HELPER   DISHWASHER

HEAD CHEF

COOK

BAKER

DISHWASHER

KITCHEN HELPER

SALAD WORKER

DESSERT WORKER

In a large restaurant, the head chef is responsible for the activities of the food preparation team.

Vegetables and fruits needed for salads and sandwiches may also be pre-prepared here and stored in the cold food station.

Who works at this station?

A head vegetable person.
Kitchen helpers (number depends on size of operation).

What equipment is used at this station?

Sinks.
Potato peelers.
Vegetable choppers.
Vegetable slicers.
Vertical cutters.
Colanders or strainers.
Platform scales.
Chopping boards.
Bowls, pans, trays.
French knives.
Paring knives.
Shears.
Table scales.

What do you have to be able to do at this station?

- Know the safe and proper use and care of hand and machine equipment.
- Select the right equipment for each job.
- Know the correct methods for pre-preparation of fresh fruits and vegetables.
- Plan own work for each task assigned.
- Become skillful in quantity preparation of foods prepared here.

As a beginner at the vegetable pre-preparation center, you may be asked to:
- Wash and scrape fresh vegetables such as carrots.

Sheridan Vocational Center, Fla.

A cook's helper learns to trim beef tenderloin properly, an important pre-preparation job.

- Wash salad greens.
- Slice, chop, or cube vegetables.
- Operate an electric chopper, slicer, or vertical cutter.
- Clean machines, sinks, worktables, and small equipment.

Hot Food or Range Work Station

The work performed here includes cooking meats, poultry, fish, seafood, soups, gravies, sauces, and vegetables.

The organization of the hot food station varies with the size and type of food service operation. For example, there may be a division of work. Short order cooking may be done on charcoal broilers or grills. Long-cooking foods such as fried chicken may be prepared on one range or in a fry kettle. Vegetables may be prepared on another range or in a steamer. A chef or a head cook may be in charge at each section. The food prepared here may go to a steam table or be transferred to a wagon or a cart equipped with thermostatic heat controls.

Who works at this station?

Executive chef.
Chef.
Head cook.
Counter worker.
Second and third cooks.
Short-order cook.
Vegetable cook.
Cook's helper.
Kitchen helper.

What equipment is used at this station?

Deep fat fryers.
Gas and electric ranges and oven.
Charcoal broilers.
Grills.
Steam-jacketed kettles.
Trunnion kettles.
Steamers.
Electric mixers.
Pots and pans.
Stirring and measuring utensils.
Portion tools.
Knives.

Sheridan Vocational Center, Fla.

A kitchen helper adds chopped tomatoes to the soup pot.

A cook's helper removes a roast from the oven.

BOCES, Ithaca, N. Y.

What do you have to be able to do at this station?

- Know the safe and proper use and care of the equipment, tools, and work area.
- Select the proper equipment and tools for the job assignment.
- Follow written directions and recipes accurately.
- Be skillful in the proper preparation methods for assigned tasks.
- Organize own work methods efficiently.

What do you do? Here are some of the tasks performed by beginning workers at the hot food station:

- Assemble ingredients and tools.
- Measure and weigh foods.
- Bread foods.
- Arrange raw portions of meats and poultry in pans for roasting.
- Slice and portion roast meats.
- Add sauces to meats, poultry, and fish.
- Reconstitute dehydrated or freeze-dried products.
- Store the cooked and left-over foods.
- Portion cooked foods.
- Clean work area, equipment, tools, and utensils.

Cold Food Work Station

This station is arranged for the preparation of salads, appetizers, cold sandwiches, and cold meat and seafood items. In some food units, this may be called the *pantry* or *service station*. Fountain items and breakfasts may also be handled at this station. Hot and cold beverages may be prepared and picked up here.

In some food establishments, this work is organized into two separate but related areas. This helps waiters and waitresses to pick up orders rapidly, thereby giving faster dining room service. Salads, sandwiches, cold meats, seafoods, and appetizers are prepared at the *cold food station*.

Prepared foods such as salads and cold meats are given finishing touches at the *cold food pick-up, pantry, or service bar*. Hot and cold beverages are also prepared in this area.

The wide variety and the last minute assembling and garnishing of these foods require a good deal of hand labor. The foods need to be fresh, chilled properly, and served attractively. Many salads, cold plates, seafood cocktails, and sandwiches are often assembled "on order." This means they are not prepared until the customer orders them, which requires well-organized, fast food production.

The station where cold foods are prepared and assembled should be well arranged. Sufficient work space located near the refrigerator and sink is required. The area also has a cold table, which is a refrigerated space or one filled with chopped ice. Equipment, tools, and utensils need to be placed within easy reach and place of first use so that the work can move fast and efficiently. *Place of first use* means that if a scoop is needed, it is located where a worker may reach it easily as he begins his task. This is a general rule for management efficiency.

The work is organized to provide a smooth sequence in work flow such as that found in an assembly line. Workers should use both hands, making every movement count. These efficient methods of work are usually learned on-the-job or in special training classes.

Sheridan Vocational Center, Fla.

Workers peel shrimp for appetizers at the cold food station.

Brookline, Mass., Public Schools

A student learns to slice ham for sandwiches at the cold meat station. Notice that he guides the meat with his right hand and keeps his left hand away from the sharp cutting blade.

A well-organized salad preparation center with efficient workers speeds the last-minute assembling of salads.

Canteen Corp.

6

An assortment of baked desserts is prepared at the bake work station.

Dudley—Anderson—Yutzy

Who works at this station?

- The head salad and/or sandwich worker.
- The assistant pantry worker.
- The kitchen helpers.

What equipment is used at this station?

- Sinks.
- Refrigerators.
- Cold table or counter.
- Shelving and storage.
- Portion scoops, serving tools.
- Slicers.
- Mixers.
- Measures.
- Scales.
- Hot plates.
- Dishes, plates.
- Containers.
- Cutting boards.
- Knives—French, grapefruit, paring.
- Cheese and egg slicers.
- Forks.
- Spatulas.
- Beverage urns and equipment.

What do you have to be able to do at this station?

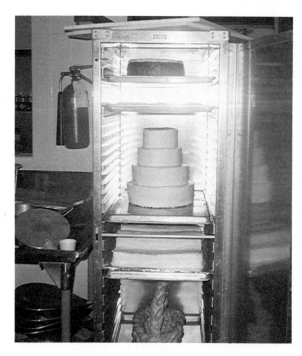

A mobile storage cabinet may be used at the bake station to hold finished products which need no refrigeration. This cabinet holds three cakes and a basket made of yeast dough.

Sheridan Vocational Center, Fla.

- Know the safe and proper use and care of all the equipment and tools.
- Select the right equipment for each job.
- Know the correct methods for the preparation of cold foods.
- Organize own work methods in assembly line fashion and in correct sequence.
- Follow written directions and recipes accurately.
- Assemble and portion menu items properly.
- Develop skill in working quickly under pressure.

Some of the tasks a beginner may be asked to do at the cold food station are:

- Make sandwich fillings and sandwiches.
- Assemble salads, cold plates, and first-course cocktails.
- Clean refrigerator, cold table, and utensils.

Bake Work Station

The bake station or bake shop is equipped for the preparation of pastries, cakes, breads, quick breads, and desserts. Here, a great amount of knowledge and skill is required.

Equipment and supplies must be organized to save time and to make efficient work methods possible. For example, large containers of flour, sugar, and other staples are placed on dollies or casters under or near work areas. Small containers of food supplies such as baking powder and spices are labeled and placed within easy reach. The necessary equipment is located in or near the area. This would include proof cabinets with controlled temperatures in which yeast breads rise, balance scales,

pan racks, and storage cabinets for breads, pastries, and desserts.

Who works at this station?

- Pastry chef or head baker.
- Second baker.
- Baker's helper.
- Pastry helper.

What equipment is used at this station?

- Deck or convection ovens.
- Proof cabinets.
- Storage racks.
- Dry storage bins.
- Pans.
- Bowls.
- Dough dividers.
- Mixer with beater and dough hook.
- Trunnion steam cooker.
- Oven scrapers.
- Pastry cloths.
- Pastry bags.
- Stockinettes.
- Scales.
- Measuring equipment.

What do you have to be able to do at this station?

- Know the safe and correct use and care of equipment, tools, and work areas.
- Select or assemble proper equipment, tools, and utensils for assigned work.
- Measure accurately with scales and measures.
- Follow written recipes and production charts accurately.
- Be skillful in pre-preparation and portioning of desserts, pastries, and breads.
- Organize own work methods efficiently.

If you are a beginner in the bake shop area, you may be asked to:

- Grease or line pans.
- Weigh ingredients.
- Scale batter into pans.
- Scoop muffin batter.
- Shape or cut dough.
- Remove baked food from pans.
- Portion, cut, and wrap products.
- Clean baker's bench and utensils.
- Clean racks and ovens.

SANITATION TEAM

This group is responsible for the cleanliness, sanitation, care, and maintenance of the physical plant. This includes the kitchen and its equipment as well as all parts connected with the food service unit. The number of workers on the sanitation team depends on the size of the operation, the hours of food service, and the kind of equipment.

Generally, the sanitation team includes the dishwasher, the helpers, and the porters. The dishwasher is usually in charge of the dishwashing room. The illustration on page 71 shows the sanitation team in a small operation. Notice that, even though the dishwasher is in charge of the room, all of the team members are directly responsible to the manager. The illustration on page 73 shows the sanitation team in a large food service unit. Here, the assistants, helpers, and porters are responsible to the head dishwasher. The head dishwasher may be responsible to the head chef, the assistant manager, or the manager, depending on the size of the operation.

Although the work of this team is hard and often tiring, it is most important. High standards of sanitation must be met in order to safeguard the health and well-being of the customers and the employees.

Why are cleanliness and sanitation so important in food service work? Harmful germs and bacteria, which are present in foods and on all surfaces, will grow and multiply if food is not handled in a sanitary manner. Serious illnesses have been traced to restaurants that were careless with sanitation. Such illnesses have resulted in costly law suits against the restaurants. You will find out more about the importance of sanitation in Chapter Thirteen.

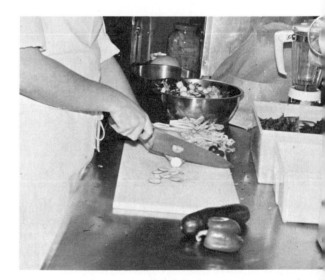

Every food service worker should understand the importance of sanitation. This student keeps the work area clean and well organized while working with the French knife.

BOCES, Ithaca, N. Y.

OWNER AND/OR MANAGER

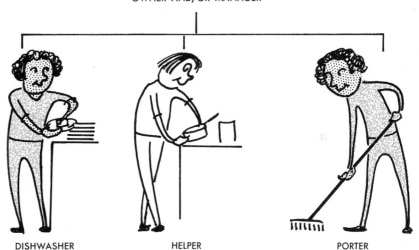

In a small unit, the owner or manager is generally in charge of the sanitation team.

DISHWASHER HELPER PORTER

The work of the sanitation team is generally divided into three major operations:

Care of the physical plant. This includes cleaning, repairing, and maintaining the building and grounds, both inside and outside. If the food service unit is located in a building that has other activities such as a hospital, some of this work may be done by the building maintenance workers. However, kitchen porters and cleaners usually remove the trash. In addition, they clean floors, walls, hoods, and some equipment.

Maintenance of equipment and utensils. This includes cleaning and sanitizing pots, pans, and utensils used in receiving, storing, preparing, and serving food. This operation, generally located near the hot food station, is handled by the pot and pan washers.

Dishwashing or warewashing. This includes washing and sanitizing the china, plastic, glass, and silver used in serving the food. This operation is usually located in a separate area near the dining room door. It may be called the *dishwashing station or dishroom.* Dish machines are used in most operations, but some smaller units may wash dishes by hand. Dish machine operators and dishwashers work in this area.

What equipment and supplies are used by this team?

- Dishwashing equipment:
    Prerinse machine.
    Dish machine.
    Silver burnisher.
    Glass washer.
    Ware washing sink.
    Pot sink.

- Refuse disposal equipment:
    Cans.
    Grinders.
    Garbage and trash cans.

- Cleaning supplies, and equipment:
    Detergents.
    Insect repellents.
    Wax.
    Mops.
    Brushes.
    Sponges.
    Pails.

Floor scrubbers.
Waxers.
Brooms.
Hose.

What do you have to be able to do at this station?

- Select, use, and clean equipment as required.
- Know the correct amount of various cleaning agents needed for each job.
- Be thorough in cleaning, polishing, and sterilizing.
- Organize work area and equipment for efficiency.
- Properly handle and store sanitized utensils.

Beginning jobs in the sanitation area may include:

- Operating a dish machine or hand dishwashing.
- Sterilizing or burnishing flatware.
- Trucking dishes to and from dishroom.
- Sweeping, mopping, polishing, and general cleaning.
- Removing waste and disposing of trash.
- Maintaining grounds.

SALES AND SERVICE TEAM

This team may involve any number of employees, depending on the type and size of the operation. The sales and service team . . .

- *Receives the customers.* The hostess, headwaiter, or waitress is responsible for greeting and seating guests comfortably and for presenting the menu.

HEAD DISHWASHER

ASSISTANT DISHWASHER

PORTER OR HELPER

POT AND PAN WASHER

The dishwashing station is arranged efficiently for disposing refuse and washing and sanitizing china, glassware, and silver.

In a large restaurant, the head dishwasher is responsible for the sanitation team.

OWNER AND/OR MANAGER

WAITRESS   CASHIER

In a small unit, the sales and service team may consist only of waiters or waitresses.

- *Sells and serves the food.* Waitresses or waiters are responsible for making menu suggestions and helping to sell food specialties. It is also up to them to serve the food promptly, neatly, and attractively.
- *Controls the sales.* The cashier, waitress and/or counter workers receive the money for the sales, make accurate

change, and keep records of the sales. Some operations use food checkers to check on size of portions and the number of menu items served.

Although management may have spent a great deal of money on advertising and decor, much of the success of the operation depends on the sales and service team. This team has direct contact with the customer and has the opportunity to sell the merchandise. Service must be courteous, speedy, and geared to the needs of the customers. If service is slow or sloppy, customers will not return. Can you see why a smiling, gracious, efficient worker is so important?

The sales and service team includes the maître d'hotel, hostess, headwaiter, waiters, waitresses, counter workers, busboys, and dining room helpers. The team may be small, consisting of only one or two waitresses, as shown in the illustration on this page. Compare this with the illustration on page 75, which shows the sales and service team in a large operation.

The work of this team is performed in the dining area and may involve several work stations such as cashier, hostess, and side stand. As a beginning worker, you will probably be concerned first with the side stand.

A waiter or waitress is usually assigned to a group of tables or counter stools. This is the *station.* The supplies needed for service are located near the station or between the station and the kitchen. This supply table is known as the *side stand, service unit,* or *service station.* A tray stand is also provided at each station. What equipment and supplies are used by this team?

MANAGER

ASSISTANT MANAGER

HOSTESS OR MAÎTRE D'HÔTEL

CASHIER—BOOKKEEPER

WAITRESS

WAITER

COUNTER WORKER

BUSBOY/GIRL

DINING ROOM HELPER

The sales and service team in a large restaurant may include the hostess or maître d'hôtel, waiters, waitresses, counter workers, busboys/girls, and dining room helpers.

Courteous, efficient service by this counter worker encourages customers to return.

In a carry-out unit such as this, the counter worker also serves as the cashier.

Cold food served in a cafeteria is properly stored in refrigerated compartments under the counter, ready for immediate use.

In a cafeteria, the sales team is responsible for accurate portion control. Notice how the filling for each roll is carefully measured.

Much of the success of a restaurant depends on the sales and service team. Guests appreciate courteous, prompt service.

The supplies kept at the side stand may be:

- China.
- Glasses.
- Silverware.
- Linen.
- Paper supplies.
- Trays.
- Rolling tray units.
- Condiments.
- Ice.
- Water.
- Butter.
- Hot coffee in glass pot or thermos jug.
- Individual service items.
- Carts or containers for soiled dishes.
- Clean side towels.
- Roll warmers.

What do you have to be able to do at this station?

- Organize and assemble all foods and utensils.
- Know proper handling and service rules.
- Know menu offerings.
- Work efficiently and courteously.
- Be accurate.

Beginning jobs may include:

- Replenishing tray stands with food and dishes.
- Removing soiled dishes.
- Cleaning and setting tables.
- Serving food and beverages.
- Receiving money and making change.

Can you begin to see how each job in food service relates to the whole operation? Remember, you are part of a team. By working together with your fellow employees and by following the planned procedures, you will find your work easier and more satisfying.

Nutritious food, attractively served, is the result of cooperation between management, food production, sanitation, and sales and service teams.

Sheridan Vocational Center, Fla.

"The steak was *that* thick and the best I've ever eaten!" Happy customer compliments chef and waitress on the excellent meal he has just had.

CHRIE

Let's Think It Over

1. A successful food service operation requires the combined efforts of all employees in a well-planned system.

  - List the types of workers and the general responsibilities of each of the following teams.
    Management.
    Receiving, storing, issuing.
    Food preparation.
    Sanitation.
    Sales and service.

2. All food preparation and service must be well organized and scheduled to meet the demands of the menu.

  - Discuss the three main steps in food preparation which are generally followed by food service units.
  - Where is the pre-preparation work station usually located? What food is prepared at this station?
  - Describe the hot food work station. Discuss the activities of this station.
  - Would there be a difference in the organization of the cold food work station in a large food service unit as compared with a small one? Why?

  - Who works at the bake work station? What foods are prepared in this area?
  - Describe the three major responsibilities of the sanitation team.
  - Why is the work of the sales and service team so important to the success of a food service business?
  - What work stations are used in the operation of the sales and service team?
  - Describe the supplies needed at the side stand.
  - Discuss beginning jobs at each station for which you might qualify.

Let's Investigate

1. Interview your school lunch manager or a restaurant manager concerning their system of operation. Draw a diagram, similar to the ones in this chapter, showing the lines of authority.
2. Ask a manager of a restaurant what qualifications are needed for employment as a counter worker, waiter, or any beginning job. Discuss these in class. Which jobs could you fill now?
3. Invite an administrator from a restaurant organization to discuss the functions and importance of management in food service.

Chapter **5**

Jobs in

Food Preparation

When people eat out, they want appetizing, well-prepared, and safe-to-eat food. Good food, properly served, is the responsibility of the food preparation team.

You will no doubt have opportunities in class and on the job to study and practice the work done by the food preparation team. These activities include use of commercial equipment, quantity food preparation and service, food storage, and sanitation. As you develop your skills and knowledge, you may begin to sense an increasing satisfaction with food service work. This may mean that you are on the road to a successful career in food service.

Have you ever read of men and women who started in simple food preparation work and later became famous as chefs, teachers,

television performers, or authors in the culinary field? For instance, Maurice Moore-Betty of New York cooking school fame became interested in food when he was a young boy, cooking on camp-outs and fishing trips. Eugene Scanlon, director of food and beverage at the Waldorf-Astoria Hotel in New York City, learned to love cooking when he experimented with recipes in his mother's kitchen. How do such people become successful?

A top professional chef spends years in training and apprenticeship. He works his way up through the stations in the back of the house. He proves that he is capable and creative and that he has business sense and leadership qualities. The result is success, prestige, and the right to wear the master chef's cap.

As a beginner in food service, you should become familiar with the chef's cap, which you may someday wear. In French, this cap is called *la toque blanche*. It is worn by cooks and chefs for sanitary reasons. However, the toque blanche also has an important meaning —its height usually indicates the rank of the chef. Master chefs, for instance, wear the highest hat, which is 12 inches high. Famous chefs may even have their hats custom made.

The toque blanche has an interesting tradition. Some say it is one of the first symbols of high rank to be given to a profession by the kings of early times. The kings decreed that their own royal headdresses, which were tall, ribbed with gold, and made of elegant fabric, be copied for their loyal personal chefs. However, the copies were made of plain fabric, and pleats were used instead of gold ribs. Starch turned the plain fabric into a tall, stiff hat.

The chef, wearing a toque blanche, discusses food orders with one of his helpers.

CHRIE

This honor was given to loyal chefs for several reasons. It recognized their skills in the kitchen. It also expressed gratitude for their loyalty—the chefs were responsible for protecting the kings from poisons that enemies might want to slip into royal food. Chefs generally were well paid, which increased their prestige and discouraged bribery.

Down through the years, the styles and colors of the caps changed with the fashions of the day. However, the chef's cap has always been a symbol of status and distinction. Today, it means that the chef has reached the peak of excellence in the food he serves. It is considered the mark of achievement and perfect performance. It is a respected symbol in the food service industry. If your goal is to wear a chef's cap someday, you will need to begin now by learning the basics of good food preparation.

In Chapter Four, we discussed back-of-the-house areas. They may vary from small, back-of-the-counter kitchens to large kitchens with a number of departments. Because of this, a great number of jobs are available in this area. In this chapter, we will discuss the requirements, benefits, and general duties of food preparation jobs at beginning levels.

WORDS TO KNOW	
Toque blanche	Trayline worker
Kitchen helper	Caterer's helper
Salad worker	Cook's helper
Formula room worker	Beverage maker
Pantry worker	Food checker
Dessert worker	Baker's helper
Food assembler	Sandwich maker

JOB REQUIREMENTS

Employers, when hiring, usually look for specific skills and abilities. They will ask you questions about your education, experience, health, and abilities. This is to determine whether you will meet their special requirements and fit into the job. There are also some general, minimum requirements that all employers in food service look for in employees. These are:

- The ability to speak, read, and write English.
- A high school diploma, although this is not always required.
- An age range of 18–55 years, male or female.
- A standard physical examination.
- Neatness, and cleanliness. Good health with no physical handicaps.

HOURS, WAGES, AND BENEFITS

Full-time food service employees generally work eight hours a day and five days a week. However, the hours and days off may be irregular, depending on the type of operation.

Food service employers generally pay wages equal to those accepted in the local community. As a rule, beginning workers are paid the minimum wage. You can find out about the minimum wage in your area by asking employers or your local state employment office.

Fringe benefits in the food service industry vary. They may include uniforms, laundering of uniforms, one or two meals daily, paid vacations and/or holidays, and group insurance.

If you are a beginner, you can increase your salary by gaining experience and proving you

81

are a good worker. The opportunity for getting ahead is good if your work is satisfactory and you are ambitious. The line of advancement in food preparation work follows a pattern: kitchen helper to cook or baker's helper; cook's helper or assistant to cook; baker's helper to baker; caterer's helper to caterer; pantry worker to pantry supervisor.

In a hospital kitchen, you also have a chance to advance as your work improves and you gain experience. Usually, you advance from a trayline worker to a food checker, and then to a diet aide.

BEGINNING FOOD PREPARATION JOBS

The titles, duties, and responsibilities of beginning jobs may vary with the size and type of food service unit. For example, a pantry worker in a small operation may prepare sandwich fillings, make sandwiches, and prepare

Experience in food preparation can bring advancement to the rank of chef.

Canteen Corp.

salads each day. In a larger operation, a pantry worker may spend the whole day washing and preparing lettuce and other greens for salads. A kitchen helper may have a variety of duties in a small kitchen. However, in a large operation, he may have only one job such as assisting the cook.

Although food preparation jobs throughout the industry may have different titles, the workers generally do similar work. For this reason, the jobs discussed in this chapter are combined into job clusters.

Job Clusters	*Other Titles*
Kitchen helpers.	Cook's helpers, baker's helpers.
Pantry workers.	Salad workers, sandwich makers, dessert workers, beverage makers.
Caterer's helpers.	A variety of titles.
Food assemblers.	Food packers. Assembly line workers.
Family meal aides.	Family dinner service specialists.
Trayline workers.	Loaders, passers, food checkers.
Formula room workers.	No other title.

The intention of this chapter is to help you become acquainted with the duties and the basic skills needed in each type of job cluster. The training you receive through work and in-school laboratory experience can make your job easier and your advancement faster wherever you are employed. Now let us look more

closely at the beginning level food preparation jobs.

Kitchen Helper

If you like to cook, working as a kitchen helper can be satisfying. You will have a chance to observe and to learn from the chefs, cooks, bakers, and other special workers.

With the food service industry growing rapidly, many kitchen helper jobs are usually available. You can find them in the kitchens of restaurants, drive-ins, school lunchrooms, industrial cafeterias, hospitals, nursing homes, motels, hotels, vending companies, airlines, trains, and ships. Although the duties vary according to the needs of the food service unit, the *kitchen helper* generally does the following:

- Cleans and washes small equipment and pots and pans used in cooking.
- Cleans and maintains kitchen work areas, sinks, large equipment, refrigerators, storage areas, floors.
- Cleans and prepares vegetables and fruits for storage or cooking.
- Stores staple supplies in storeroom.
- Brings staples to work areas when needed.

The *cook's helper* generally does the following:

- Cleans all vegetables for storage and cooking.
- Grinds meat for storage.
- Makes meatballs to specific size.
- Breads meats for frying.
- Browns stew meats.
- Strains soup stock.

Dudley–Anderson–Yutzy

After preparing the meatballs, the cook's helper stores them in the walk-in refrigerator.

- Slices meats and cheeses.
- Stores staple supplies in storeroom.
- Stores meat, poultry, and fish in refrigerator or freezer.
- Stores eggs, milk, butter, and cheese in refrigerator.
- Cleans and washes small and large equipment and utensils used in cooking.
- Cleans and maintains cook's work area.

Let us take a look at a typical day's routine for a cook's helper who works eight hours, from 8:00 a.m. to 5:00 p.m., in a table service restaurant.

8:00–9:00 a.m.—Arrives at station in a clean uniform. Washes hands, covers hair. Checks with supervisor and/or chief cook and gets work schedule. Assembles all supplies needed.

9:00–10:00 a.m.—Prepares vegetables, soups, and some meat mixes for noon meal, following recipes and work schedule. Cleans work area and utensils after each duty.

10:00–10:15 a.m.—Rest or coffee break.

10:15–12 Noon—Follows work schedule, helping with vegetable preparation and short orders. Completes jobs according to schedule.

12:00–12:30 p.m.—Lunch period.

12:30–3:00 p.m.—Washes pots and pans. Cleans work area and large equipment. Follows work schedule in helping to prepare vegetables, soups, and meats for dinner and/or next day. Stores foods.

3:00–3:15 p.m.—Rest or coffee break.

3:15–5:00 p.m.—Continues as before coffee break.

The *baker's helper* does many of the simple, routine jobs for the baker. He generally takes care of the following:

- Assembles, measures, and weighs ingredients needed by baker or pastry cook.
- Prepares fruits for pies and pastries.
- Prepares fillings for cookies, cream puffs, and éclairs.
- Prepares mixes and toppings for coffee cakes, cakes, and biscuits.
- Prepares sauces for puddings.

A student, learning to frost a cake in the bake shop, improvises a cake stand when she finds no rotating stand is available.

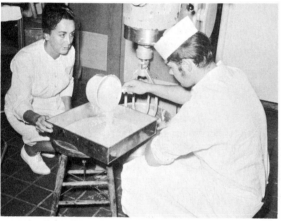

A baker's helper learns to dip batter into an appropriate pan.

- Shapes rolls and cookies for baking.
- Cleans and maintains pastry center, baker's table, and dessert storage area.
- Cleans and cares for small and large equipment used in the baking center.
- Stores baked items.
- Cuts cakes and pies as directed for serving.
- Portions cookies and puddings as directed.

Pantry Worker

The pantry worker is generally responsible for preparing simple foods such as salads. As a pantry worker, you may work in one special area of the kitchen or in a pantry room near the kitchen. This job requires special care because the food materials are expensive and easily spoiled. If you are a pantry worker, you are responsible for handling food in a safe, sanitary way without waste. Pantry work can be pleasant and interesting. It is sometimes combined with waiting on customers.

Larger restaurants, cafeterias, and vending companies are most likely to have special pantry workers for each major step of preparation. This is known as assembly work.

A pantry worker generally does all or part of the following jobs:

- Uses hand and electric equipment.
  Dices celery with French knife.
  Makes melon balls with cutter.

The baker demonstrates cake decorating methods to students.

Slices eggs with hand egg slicer.
Operates electric food mixer and chopper.
Extracts juices with electric extractor.
Slices cold meat and cheeses on electric slicer.

- Prepares and makes salads, relishes, and cocktails.
    Fruit and vegetable combinations, and potato salads.
    Chef's green salads and variations.
    Molded salads.
    Seafood salads.
    Seafood cocktails and canapes.

- Makes salad dressings and sauces.
    Mayonnaise variations.
    French, Italian, and Roquefort dressings.
    Tartar sauce, cocktail sauce, and whipped cream.

- Prepares for buffet service.
    Makes cold meat sandwiches.
    Arranges cold meat plates and salad plates.
    Arranges assorted relish dishes.
    Prepares and arranges deviled eggs.
    Carves cold chicken, turkey, and other meats.

- Utilizes leftovers.
    Makes chicken, ham, seafood, mixed fruit, and vegetable salads.
    Prepares creamed foods on toast points.

- Makes refrigerated desserts.
    Prepares whips, melbas, mousses, gelatins, fruit shortcakes, and sauces for puddings.

United Fresh Fruit and Vegetable Assoc., Esquire Diner

Attractive service helps sell food.

Food service workers learn to prepare, arrange, and serve attractive meals.

United Fresh Fruit and Vegetable Assoc., Stouffer

85

Food Service Careers

Sheridan Vocational Center, Fla.

Students, as pantry workers, learn to prepare attractive, appetizing canapés.

Salads, prepared in the pantry area, give students an opportunity to be creative.

Edison Community College, Ft. Myers, Fla.

Brookline, Mass., Public Schools

A pantry worker learns to portion desserts as directed.

- Handles pantry service.
  Cuts and serves pies and cakes.
  Prepares dinner salads.
  Prepares and serves combination cold plates.
  Prepares and serves cold sandwiches.
  Prepares and serves à la carte salad bowls.

- Cleans equipment and utensils.

- Cleans work center, refrigerator, and sink.

- Stores and cares for pantry foods.

Caterer's Helper

Work as a caterer's helper may be full time, part time, or seasonal. It is interesting work with a variety of responsibilities. The duties fall into much the same pattern as kitchen helpers or pantry helpers and often include the jobs done by both. Sometimes the caterer's helper must provide waiter or waitress service. Some understanding of the catering business will help you to see your responsibility as a caterer's helper or assistant. See Chapter Nine for information on catering.

Food Assembler

A food assembler's work is likely to differ from that of the workers who prepare food on the premises of a restaurant. Food assemblers may work in carry-out food service units or in commissaries. For carry-out service, they assemble the menu items and/or meals and package them on order, as the customer waits. In commissaries, the food assembler generally prepares, assembles, and packages menu items and/or meals in large numbers. The assembler may be part of a team working at a movable belt or may work alone or with one or two others.

Packaged foods are stored in refrigerators, cold rooms, or freezers for delivery to vending installations, restaurants, schools, or other food service units.

Here is a typical day's routine for a food assembler who works eight hours a day, 12 noon to 8:30 p.m., in the commissary kitchen of a vending company.

11:45 a.m.—Arrives at work and changes into uniform. Freshens up, washes hands, covers hair. Checks with supervisor and receives work production schedule. Goes to work station.

Ft. Meyers Tech. School, Fla.

Operating a potato peeler machine may be one of the responsibilities of a food service worker.

A food assembler in a carry-out packages chicken dinners. Food, paper cartons, and supplies are conveniently arranged for fast assembling.

Kentucky Fried Chicken

12:00 Noon–3:00 p.m.—Makes sandwiches, using fillings prepared the day before. Packages sandwiches in individual or bulk servings according to schedule. Stores packages in cooler in designated area, where route man picks them up. (Sandwich makers can prepare 10–12 sandwiches a minute using automatic equipment and appropriate methods.) Cleans utensils and work area when sandwiches are completed.

3:00–3:10 p.m.—Rest period or coffee break.

3:10–6:00 p.m.—Prepares desserts and salads according to production schedule. Packages and stores salads and desserts in cooler for route man to pick up. Cleans utensils and work area after each preparation.

6:00–6:30 p.m.—Dinner period.

6:30–8:30 p.m.—Pre-prepares puddings, sandwich fillings, and salad ingredients for the next day. Cleans utensils, work area, and refrigerator.

Family Meal Aide

Some families may desire help in preparing and serving food in their homes. Perhaps both husband and wife work or have unusually heavy responsibilities. The homemaker may want a worker who will prepare and serve family meals every day, or she may just need help for special parties. The family meal aide is responsible for planning, preparing, and serving attractive, nutritious meals that meet the needs of a family.

This work, like catering, provides an opportunity to develop a business of your own, or it may provide a steady job with one family with whom you enjoy working.

As a family meal aide, your duties would vary with the needs of each employer. You may perform some or all of the following tasks:

- Plan a variety of meals.
- Select and purchase foods.
- Prepare and serve family meals and/or special occasion meals.
- Use, store, and care for kitchen equipment and supplies.
- Store food and food products.
- Use left-over foods as specified.
- Clean and wash dishes, glassware, silver, and cooking utensils.
- Clean and care for kitchen work area.

As you can see, your work would be similar to the work you might do in your own home. However, you will need to follow the policies and instructions of the specific family with whom you work.

You can see from the duties described that the work generally involves shopping, assembling food and supplies, preparing and serving food, and cleaning up.

Hospital Specialties

Do you have an interest in helping the sick and convalescent? If so, you may find working in a hospital or nursing home rewarding. The food preparation jobs previously described are available in the kitchens of hospitals and nursing homes. However, specialty jobs such as tray-line and formula room work meet the special needs of these institutions. Following are the duties performed by workers in these specialty jobs.

Tray-line Worker

Hospitals and larger nursing homes prepare patients' food trays on an assembly line. Special equipment provides speed and accuracy in filling the trays. Equipment in an assembly line operation includes conveyor tray belts, individual hot food carriers, and hot and cold food tables. Supplies such as sugar, cream, salt, and pepper are usually packaged individually for sanitary handling.

A tray-line worker is part of the team on the tray assembly line. Titles depend on the worker's responsibility such as Position No. 1, 2, 3, or 4, server, loader, passer, or food checker. Position No. 4 is often that of the food checker.

When preparing meal trays for patients, the duties of the tray-line workers vary according to the position in the assembly line. Workers are assigned to handle specific food items or jobs. As trays move to their positions, they read the individual diet menus accurately and assemble the food items on the trays in the correct position.

The food checker is usually a worker with more experience than the others on the line. She checks each menu item on the tray at the end of the line to be sure it matches the diet order. Patients often have special diets ordered by their doctors. Therefore the trays must be properly prepared and checked before they are sent to the patients. After the trays are checked, they are transferred to portable carts and taken to the patients.

Tray-line workers usually work in one of two over-lapping shifts:

1st shift: 6:30 a.m. to 2:30 p.m.; includes breakfast and lunch service.

2nd shift: 11:00 a.m. to 7:00 p.m.; includes lunch and dinner service.

Following are the tray-line worker's duties before meal service:

- Brings menu orders from office.
- Checks heated dishes needed for hot food items.
- Gets equipment ready.
- Operates heat devices as instructed.
- Assembles utensils, silverware, paper supplies, and accessories needed for meal service in proper place.
- Arranges cold foods, condiments, beverages, dishes, and silver in proper place.
- Makes coffee and other beverages at noon and evening meal.

Following are the duties of the different positions during meal service:

Server: Serves all hot items onto heated container.

Line Position #1: Reads diet order. Prepares tray and tray cover. Assembles napkin, salt (or substitute), pepper, silver, and hot food containers on each tray in correct position.

Line Position #2: Reads diet order. Prepares and assembles on each tray, in correct position, bread, butter, fruits, salad, and cold sandwich.

Line Position #3: Reads diet order. Prepares and assembles on each tray, in correct position, juice, cream, jelly, cereal, dessert, and beverage.

Line Position #4 or Food Checker: Checks all menu items on tray for accuracy.

Photos on this page courtesy of Caddy Corp.

The hospital assembly line is organized for fast, efficient loading of patients' trays. Workers wear white gloves to emphasize sanitation in food handling.

Worker uses tongs to place portion of chicken on plate.

Trayline workers . . .

Worker arranges food supplies at her station.

Worker passes plate to vegetable server.

Bread and butter are placed on appropriate plates, ready to be loaded on trays.

Plate with entrée and vegetables is placed on patient's tray.

90

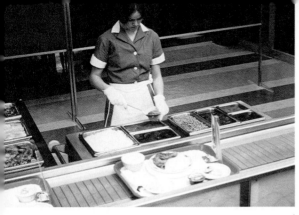

Some vegetables such as stewed tomatoes are served in individual containers.

Food checker compares loaded tray with patient's prescribed diet to be sure there are no mistakes.

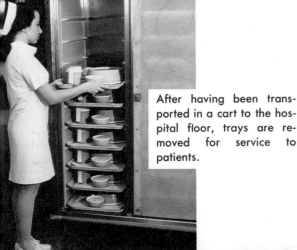

After having been transported in a cart to the hospital floor, trays are removed for service to patients.

Loader: May help checker, but usually loads trays on carts, delivers to floor designated.

Passer: Stationed on each floor of the hospital in the food service room or area. Prepares toast during breakfast service or any food needing to be prepared immediately before serving. Places on trays. Serves trays to patients on her floor.

These are the tray-line worker's duties after meal service:

- Turns off steam table, conveyor belt, and other equipment.
- Puts food items away properly.
- Empties waste containers.
- Cleans equipment and work area.
- Prepares tray and delivers special nourishments, as directed, to patients at 10:00 a.m., 2:00 p.m., and 4:00 p.m. (Special nourishments are eggnogs, fruit juices, and other special items prescribed by doctors.)

As we discussed above, the duties of tray-line workers differ from those of kitchen helpers. Naturally, their day's routine is also different. Here is a typical day's schedule for a tray-line worker on the early shift (6:30 a.m. to 2:30 p.m.) in line position #1.

6:15 a.m.—Arrives at work, puts on clean uniform. Eats breakfast; washes hands. Puts on clean apron over uniform.

6:30–8:00 a.m.—Takes assigned place on tray line and prepares trays for breakfast.

8:00–9:00 a.m.—Turns off machine which heats the dishes. Sets up delay trays as directed. (Delay trays are those needed for patients who must receive their meal later.)

91

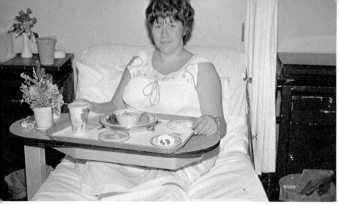

An attractive food tray with a prescribed diet is served to each patient.

9:00–10:00 a.m.—Cleans up equipment and area according to work schedule.

10:00–10:15 a.m.—Rest or coffee break.

10:15–11:00 a.m.—Prepares and delivers special nourishment orders.

11:00 a.m.–1:00 p.m.—Repeats same duties for noon meal as for breakfast meal.

1:00–1:30 p.m.—Eats lunch.

1:30–2:30 p.m.—Cleans up equipment and work area.

Learning to work well together, as these students are doing, is basic to success in food service.

Formula Room Worker

Hospitals have a formula room where milk formulas are prepared for new babies. This room is usually located near the maternity ward and the nursery. Hospitals vary in the operation of the formula room. It may be managed by the dietitian or by a registered nurse. The formula room is a divided room; one side is used for the preparation of formulas and the other for sterilization procedures.

Many hospitals now have pre-packaged, ready-to-use formulas in disposable bottles. However, there are still special baby formulas that have to be prepared according to doctor's orders.

Formula room workers assist in the preparation and sterilization of babies' formulas under the supervision of a trained nurse or dietitian. A nurse or the mother feeds the baby.

A formula room worker performs the following duties:

- Measures ingredients of formula accurately and according to directions.
- Prepares formula in quantity needed.
- Divides formula into the proper units, and bottles the formula correctly.
- Sterilizes equipment and bottles as directed.
- Cleans up and sanitizes work area, sinks, and refrigerator.
- Stores formula ingredients, bottles, and formula in appropriate area.

SUCCESS IN FOOD PREPARATION JOBS

At the beginning of this chapter, we discussed the success that many people find in food preparation work. If your ambition is to be a successful salad maker, baker, or chef, you will need to know the basic skills of food preparation. In addition to these skills, certain personal qualities are needed for success in food service. These were discussed in earlier chapters in this book. As you work on the job or in the classroom, you may want to check yourself on these qualities. Ask yourself these questions:

Personal Traits

- Are you interested in and friendly with co-workers?
- Are you cooperative with your employer?
- Are you at work on time and seldom absent?
- Do you practice good health habits?
- Do you speak pleasantly, using good English?
- Are you dependable and loyal?
- Are you clean and neat?
- Do you wear the correct uniform?
- Do you avoid eating or nibbling while working?
- Do you avoid gossiping about others?

Management Skills

- Do you keep to the time schedule given you?
- Do you practice and maintain the highest standards in sanitation when handling food?
- Do you use safety practices in your work methods?
- Do you learn and understand the work procedures?
- Do you conserve food, materials, and equipment?

93

H. J. Heinz Co.

This food service employee keeps in mind safe practice rules to avoid burns and fires.

Food service worker cleans off plates quickly and efficiently to help keep banquet on schedule.

Lyndenhurst Inn

This chef commands a well-paid job. Through study and experience, he has developed a high level of knowledge and skill in food preparation and service.
Institutions/VFM

- Do you know where supplies are kept, and replace them correctly?
- Do you use both hands when you work, making every motion count?
- Do you follow directions accurately?
- Do you see what needs to be done and do it?

Your success on the job depends entirely on you, your ability, and how well you perform your work. A knowledge of the basic skills needed for beginner's jobs can give you a good start towards such success. On-the-job training and work experience at school can be another step towards success.

Let's Think It Over

1. The food service business offers a variety of interesting food preparation jobs.

    - What are the beginning food preparation jobs?
    - What are the duties of a kitchen or cook's helper?
    - How can a kitchen helper succeed and advance on a job?
    - What is the job responsibility of a pantry worker?
    - What are the responsibilities and duties of a family meal aide?
    - Explain the duties of a tray-line worker, food checker, and formula room worker.

2. The successful workers in food preparation are those who have developed work skills and personal traits valuable to the business operation.

    - Make a list of the desirable personal traits that you feel can help a person succeed in a food preparation job.
    - Why do you think the following management skills could be important in food preparation work?
        Keeping to a time schedule.
        Practicing high standards of sanitation and safety.
        Knowing assigned work procedures.
        Following directions accurately.

3. Suggest several general ideas for saving time and energy in portioning fifty desserts for service.

Let's Investigate

1. Interview workers in food preparation jobs in your community. List and compare the benefits, advantages, and disadvantages of different jobs. Discuss in class.
2. Arrange to observe or interview a kitchen helper on the job. Describe the day's work. Analyze this work in relation to health requirements, your personal interests, future advancement, and earning possibilities.

Chapter **6**

Quantity Food

Methods

Food is prepared in food service kitchens by methods that differ from those used in your home kitchen. Why is there such a difference? In your kitchen, food is generally prepared for one family. Eating establishments must serve food to hundreds of people. Preparing food in quantity presents problems that do not occur in home preparation.

WORDS TO KNOW

Convenience foods	Safety guards
Standard recipes	Recipe costing
Portion control	Cost control

In this chapter, you will have an opportunity to understand these problems and to learn the basic principles of preparing quality foods in large quantities.

The food service industry has developed equipment and procedures to produce quantities of food quickly and economically. Guesswork is done away with. Special work methods and tested recipes, using accurate measurements and controlled temperatures, are necessary. All food production is carefully controlled, from purchasing through storage, preparation, and serving in order to produce attractive, nutritious, and delicious food.

As the trend toward eating out increases, the food service industry continues to grow. To meet the increased demand for good, nutritious food, the industry is constantly experimenting with new developments. As a result, new ideas in kitchen machines, equipment, and supplies have streamlined the jobs of food service workers.

The growing use of convenience foods is one of the changes which is helping food service managers provide quality foods for their customers.

CONVENIENCE FOODS

A convenience food is any partially prepared food product or ingredient that saves production time. For instance, a loaf of sliced bread is a convenience food because it saves the steps of mixing, baking, and slicing. Can you name others which have been in use for some time? As you can see, this is not such a new idea.

Today, an assortment of convenience foods is available to the food service industry. These include partially or completely prepared frozen foods, freeze-dried and dehydrated foods, and mixes. By using conveneince foods, the food service operator can eliminate some or all of the steps that would be involved if the recipe had been prepared in the kitchen. For instance, frozen pie shells require only filling and baking.

Frozen convenience foods include cooked or uncooked hors d'oeuvres; meat, fish, and poultry entrées; vegetables; and desserts. They may be packaged in quantity or portion-size disposable containers and need only reheating before being served. This saves time and labor, since there is no food preparation other than heating. If the food is served in the original disposable container, there is no need for dishwashing.

Foods used in preparation such as stew vegetables can be purchased cleaned and frozen. This eliminates the need for pre-preparing fresh vegetables in the kitchen. Freeze-dried and dehydrated foods are often used in the preparation of recipes. These foods, along with mixes, can greatly cut down on the amount of time needed in the kitchen to prepare a meal.

Some food service operators are using only convenience foods, thereby eliminating most of the food preparation. These are generally called convenience food flow systems. A large university using this system reported an immediate reduction in cost of utilities, preparation time, and food waste.

Other food service units use convenience foods to cut down on the steps involved in preparing a recipe and to reduce costs. However, they do not eliminate food preparation entirely.

Some large restaurants may prepare and freeze foods, thus producing their own convenience foods. Large chain restaurants may prepare, freeze, and distribute foods from a central commissary to individual restaurants. Many small establishments find it economical to prepare their own mixes during slack working hours.

DISPOSABLES

Disposables are supplies of all kinds which can be used and then thrown away. They may be constructed of paper, plastic, or aluminum foil.

Paper tablecloths, place mats, napkins, aprons, and uniforms, which are strong, and look and feel like cloth, may soon replace linens. Tableware of formed aluminum or plastic is attractive and is now being produced in all sizes, shapes, and colors. Plastic knives, forks, and spoons are already in use in airline, drive-in, and vending food services. Can you think of other examples? What are some advantages and disadvantages of using disposables?

With disposables, managers can save in the cost of clean-up labor, and the amount of storage space needed. Of course, they need to figure the cost of using disposables against the cost of the dish machine, detergents, and the wages of a dishwasher. There are also possible savings in equipment and maintenance, in cleaning agents, and in laundry of linens. Disposables are sanitary, light weight, and easy to handle. Their use, as compared to the use of china, reduces the noise level considerably. Airlines, hospitals, and schools, especially, are finding that the use of disposables is a way of overcoming increasing labor costs and space problems.

Alcoa Co.

Frozen entrées for restaurant use are available in disposable aluminum foil steam table pans.

Disposable aluminum foil containers with adjustable adapters can be used with any standard steam table.

Alcoa Co.

BASICS OF FOOD PRODUCTION

As a member of the food production team, one of your goals will be to prepare high-quality, appetizing food. To do this, you must:

- Conserve the nutritive value of the food.
- Cook food properly so it is not indigestible.
- Develop the flavor of the food.
- Make the food attractive in color, form, and texture.
- Be sure the food is safe to eat.

H. J. Heinz Co.

For accurate results, food must be cut exactly the way the recipe states— sliced, chopped, or diced.

Students learn the secrets of decorating and garnishing food.

BOCES, Ithaca, N. Y.

Brookline, Mass., Public Schools

Ingredients must be combined exactly as the recipe states. Here a student uses a wire whip to mix a sauce in a trunnion kettle.

For accurate results, the exact temperature called for in the recipe must be used.

Brookline, Mass., Public Schools

Food managers and workers take pride in producing quality food for the public. Quality food is most important to the health and pleasure of the customers and to the successful operation of the eating establishment.

As a rule, food service units feed hundreds or thousands of people at one meal. When food is prepared in such large quantities, it is necessary to achieve the same result each time a recipe is used.

Have you sometimes followed a recipe carefully only to find that your product was different from the product prepared by a friend using the very same recipe? Can you give a reason for the difference? How is it possible to produce uniform, appealing, and flavorful foods in large quantities? This is done by purchasing standard ingredients and using:

- Standard recipes.
- Standard weights and measures.
- Appropriate equipment, tools, and utensils.
- Exact portion control.
- Food cost control.
- Basic methods of preparation.

One of your responsibilities in food service is to learn and use the basic procedures for cooking and serving.

In the following pages, you will be introduced to the general principles and methods of quantity food production. Keep in mind, however, that specific procedures will differ from place to place.

Standard Recipes

What does a standard recipe mean? Much experimentation with various combinations of foods and cooking methods goes into the making of a good recipe. Records are kept, and the results are judged for nutritional value, taste appeal, quality, and cost. Once the amounts of ingredients and preparation techniques have been determined, the recipes must be followed exactly as written. It is essential to use standard recipes to maintain quality and cost control in quantity food production. Kitchens generally keep the recipes on file and use them over and over as needed.

Restaurants may develop their own recipes. They may also use standard recipes from quantity cookbooks.

Standard recipes are written in a predetermined pattern. The ingredients and steps are written in the order in which they are used. Cooks familiar with the recipe format can follow it efficiently and produce the same results each time. A standard recipe will include:

- Amounts of ingredients, either by weight or volume, in order of their use.
- Step-by-step method of combining ingredients.
- Temperature.
- Size of utensils.
- Volume or weight to be placed in a specific container.
- Size of each portion.
- Number of portions in each pan.
- Quantity yield in cups, quarts, or gallons.

Examine some of the recipes you are using. Do they contain all of this information? The recipe on page 100 illustrates one format in common use. Find examples of other standard forms.

CHICKEN À LA KING	**Approx. yield:** 50 servings **Serving size:** 227 g [8 oz.] ladle served over toast or patty shell	
Ingredient	**Amount**	**Directions**
Boiled chicken or turkey Green peppers Pimientos Mushrooms	4.5 kg [10 lbs.] 2.5 cm [1″] dice 0.45 kg [1 lb.] 1.3 cm [½″] dice 227 g [8 oz.] 1.3 cm [½″] dice 0.9 kg [2 lbs.] 1.3 cm [½″] dice	1. Dice cooked chicken or turkey into 2.5 cm [1″] cubes with French knife. 2. Dice the green peppers, pimientos, mushrooms into 1.3 cm [½″] dice with a French knife. 3. Cook the green peppers in a saucepan in salt water until tender. Drain and hold. 4. Sauté the mushrooms in a saucepan in 0.23 kg [½ lb.] butter until slightly tender.
Chicken stock Milk Cream, light Shortening or butter Flour	2.8 L [3 qts.] 2.8 L [3 qts.] 0.9 L [1 qt.] 0.9 kg [2 lbs.] 0.74 kg [1 lb. 10 oz.]	5. Prepare the chicken stock (See recipe #8) 6. Heat the milk and cream in saucepan and hold. 7. Make the roux: melt remaining 0.7 kg [1½ lbs.] butter or shortening in saucepan. Add flour; cook for 5 min., stirring with kitchen spoon. 8. Add hot chicken stock. Whip with wire whip until thick and smooth. 9. Add hot milk and cream. Continue whipping until sauce is smooth.
Sherry wine Yellow color as desired Salt to taste	0.45 L [1 pt.]	10. Add sherry wine. Tint sauce with yellow color, if desired. 11. Add the cooked green peppers, mushrooms, pimientos, chicken or turkey. Stir carefully with kitchen spoon to blend. Add salt if necessary.

A standard typical recipe.

Weights and Measures

(U. S. Standard and Metric Systems)

1 gram	0.035 ounces
1 kilogram	2.21 pounds
1 ounce	28.4 grams
1 pound	454 grams
1 teaspoon	4.9 millilitres
1 tablespoon.	3 teaspoons
	½ fluid ounce
	15 millilitres
1 cup	16 tablespoons
	½ pint
	8 fluid ounces
	240 millilitres
1 pint.	2 cups
1 quart.	4 cups
	2 pints
	0.9 L
1 litre.	1000 millilitres
	1.06 quarts
1 gallon	4 quarts
1 peck	8 quarts
1 bushel	4 pecks

Abbreviations

ounces	oz.	gallon	gal.
pound	lb.	peck	pk.
teaspoon	t.	bushel	bu.
tablespoon	T.	gram	g
cup	c.	kilogram	kg
pint	pt.	litre	L
quart	qt.	millilitre	mL

Temperature Equivalents

Fahrenheit = Celsius		Fahrenheit = Celsius	
F	C	F	C
0°F	−18°C	300°F	149°C
32°F	0°C	325°F	163°C
40°F	5°C	350°F	177°C
140°F	60°C	375°F	191°C
165°F	74°C	400°F	205°C
200°F	94°C	425°F	219°C
212°F	100°C	450°F	232°C
225°F	107°C	475°F	246°C
250°F	121°C	500°F	260°C
275°F	135°C	525°F	274°C

Equivalent of Weights and Measures of Common Foods

Food	Weight	Measure	Food	Weight	Measure
Bananas	1 lb.	3 large	Potatoes	1 lb.	4 med.
Butter, fats	1 lb.	2 cups	Rice	1 lb.	2 cups
Cheese, American	1 lb.	3 cups, diced / 4 cups, grated	Sugar, brown, firmly packed	1 lb.	2¼ cups
Cocoa	1 oz.	2 T. plus 2 t.	Sugar, confectioners'	1 lb.	3½ cups
Chocolate	1 oz.	1 square			
Dates	10 oz.	2 cups	Sugar, granulated	1 lb.	2¼ cups
Eggs, average	1 lb.	10 eggs			
Flour, bread	1 lb.	4 cups	Tomatoes	1 lb.	4 small

Weights and Measures

Notice on the sample recipe that an amount is given for each ingredient, either a weight or a measure. Weights indicate how heavy things are; measures indicate the volume or size. Be sure to learn the abbreviations and symbols for weights and measures, and the quantities they represent. The chart on page 101 will help you.

Since the United States is planning to go on the metric system, figures are given for both the United States standard and metric systems. A temperature chart is also included, showing the Celsius (C) or metric equivalents of commonly used Fahrenheit (F) temperatures.

In quantity food preparation, weights rather than measures are more commonly used because they are more accurate. If a recipe uses household measures of cups and tablespoons, the measures need to be converted into equivalent weights. Refer to the chart on page 101, which gives equivalent weights and measures for some of the common foods. Try converting some recipes in class. Check to see that your arithmetic is accurate.

To weigh ingredients, a balance scale is generally used. For example, if 1.9 kg [4 lb. 6 oz.] of flour is needed for a recipe, weights equal to 1.8 kg [4 lbs.] are placed on one side of the scale. The weight attached to the graduated

Ithaca, N. Y., Public Schools

Both of these scales have dials which show the weight in ounces and pounds.

The balance scale uses weights for accurate measurements.

Brookline, Mass., Public Schools

gram [ounce] measure on the front of the scale is placed at 170 g [6 oz.]. Flour is scooped and gradually spilled into the container on the side opposite the 1.8 kg [4 lb.] weights. When the weight of the flour equals 1.9 kg [4 lb. 6 oz.], the scale will balance; that is, it will fluctuate up and down.

Another type of scale shows the number of grams and kilograms [ounces and pounds] on a dial.

In large establishments, you may see a platform scale. Large and heavy objects are weighed on this. Bags of produce or large quantities of meat are put onto the platform which is only a few centimeters [inches] above floor level. Weights are balanced in the same manner as described for the balance scale.

TOOLS, UTENSILS AND EQUIPMENT

In addition to the kitchen tools and equipment similar to those used in a home, special tools, utensils, and equipment are used in quantity food production. Review home kitchen tools and equipment to be sure you know the name and use of each.

The ability to use tools and equipment skillfully is essential for success in food service work.

Dudley–Anderson–Yutzy

Learning to use a French knife is one of the first steps in becoming a chef.

Each knife is used for a specific kind of cutting or slicing. Here students learn to use a boning knife to bone chicken.

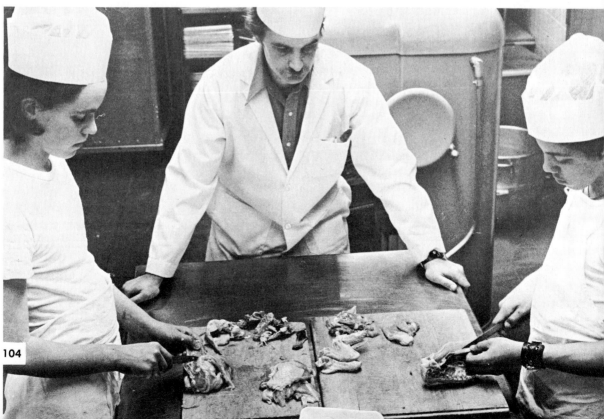

Tools

Long-handled spoons, either solid or slotted, are used for stirring and serving. *Wire whips* in various sizes are also used to stir as they are efficient in preventing lumping. *Large wire strainers* are used to drain vegetables and other foods.

Cutlery, a term applied to all cutting tools, is most important to any professional cook or chef. In fact, knives are so important that most chefs buy their own, which they cherish and care for. Each knife has specific uses and, for efficiency, must be kept sharpened. Knives should be protected by keeping them in a rack or in an individual sheath. Never throw knives into a drawer or drop them as they may become nicked.

Ladles of various sizes are used to transfer foods from one container to another. They are also used for measuring and serving. These are sized from 2 to 8 ounces each.

Measures vary from the 1 cup, graduated, to the 2 quart and gallon size, which are also graduated.

Openers of many types are used for containers and cans. A can opener may be a small hand type or a heavy-duty table model, either manual or electric.

Utensils

Utensils hold foods. Most well-equipped kitchens do not use many big pots. When filled, they are too heavy to lift. Large amounts of food are cooked in steamers instead of on top of a range. Sauce pots from 2–4 quarts in size are commonly used. Larger pots may hold 20 quarts, but they are extremely heavy.

Double boilers, roast pans, bun pans, sheet pans, bowls, and various *special pie, cake,* and *bread pans* are used. Examine these where you visit or work and become familiar with standard sizes and the different materials from which they are made.

Scoops are commonly used for serving. Each size scoop holds a portion of a cup. Remember, the higher the number of the scoop, the smaller the volume it holds. Here is the volume of commonly used scoops:

No. 6	$\frac{2}{3}$ c.	No. 16	$\frac{1}{4}$ c.
No. 8	$\frac{1}{2}$ c.	No. 20	$3\frac{1}{5}$ T.
No. 10	$\frac{2}{5}$ c.	No. 30	$2\frac{1}{5}$ T.
No. 12	$\frac{1}{3}$ c.	No. 40	$1\frac{3}{4}$ T.

The larger scoops may be used for plate servings of potatoes or vegetables. Scoops are used to portion hamburger for cooking if a special patty machine is not used. Smaller scoops are used for sauces or to portion drop cookies for baking.

Equipment

Equipment for quantity food production is designed to do a specific job quickly, safely, and efficiently. This equipment is expensive. It must be cared for with proper cleaning and maintenance to keep it functioning properly and to extend its life.

Machines save labor and thus reduce labor costs if they are operated at capacity. If they are used only occasionally, they are not fulfilling their purpose. The greater the volume of food production, the more the equipment will be used. Why? Could a company afford to buy a piece of equipment that would be used only a few hours a week?

There is a correct way to operate each piece of equipment for best results. Sometimes attachments are used on the basic machine to perform additional jobs. For example, a mixer may be fitted with a vegetable shredder. You will be given instructions for the correct method of using each machine. Follow directions carefully.

All cutting machines have *safety guards*. For your own protection, always use the guards and operate the machine as you have been instructed.

Commonly used equipment consists of *ranges* for top-stove cooking and *ovens* for baking or roasting. *Convection ovens* have a fan at the back to distribute heat. As a result, these ovens bake more quickly than the regular ones.

The *microwave oven* cooks food in about one-fourth the time of a conventional oven. A five-pound roast, for instance, is cooked in 35 minutes and a baked potato in five minutes. The microwave oven cooks by an entirely different method than the standard oven. Microwaves are developed by a tube located in the oven. In turn, the microwaves are absorbed by the food in the oven and cause only the food to heat. Therefore the oven remains cool during cooking. Microwaves are reflected by metal but pass through other materials such as glass, plastics, paper, and most ceramics. This means that metal, including aluminum foil, cannot be used in microwave ovens. Food can be cooked on china, plastic, or paper plates. The plates remain cool, except for a little heat that may be transferred from the food.

Sterno Co., Tapas Restaurant

Food service workers need to become familiar with the different types of hot food servers. Sterno heat is often used, as in these attractive buffet servers.

H. J. Heinz Co.

An assortment of pots and pans is conveniently arranged within reach of the workers.

A large, movable bowl is used to mix foods such as salad or meat loaf. Sanitary plastic mitts are used for hand-mixing food.

The baking pans on the rack are parallel with the oven racks so that they can be easily moved in and out of the convection oven.

A microwave oven cooks food quickly. It is especially useful in cooking frozen foods. Here the worker heats up a frozen entrée on a dinner plate.

A student uses a scoop of a specified size to portion cookie dough onto a baking pan.

107

A 40-gallon steam jacketed kettle is used for foods such as soups and stews. A wooden paddle or large wire whip is used to stir the food.

A compartment steamer cooks batches of food quickly.

Microwave cooking demands exact timing, so the ovens are equipped with a minute timer. When the doors are opened, the microwaves turn off automatically. Because foods cook quickly, these ovens are used where speed is essential. Microwave ovens will be found in kitchens as the cost becomes lower.

Steam is a quick method of cooking used in quantity cooking. The steam is generated by gas or electricity and is under pressure. Notice the gauge on steam equipment in the kitchen you work in or visit. This gauge tells the steam pressure in pounds.

A *steam jacketed kettle* is a large container that is constructed so steam can flow around it in an enclosure and thus heat the contents of the kettle. Foods such as soups, spaghetti, and stews are cooked in this kettle. *Upright or compartment steamers* are also used. The food is placed in a perforated or solid basket and put on a rack of the steamer. Vegetables, chicken, eggs, and many foods are cooked this way. Different types of steam cookers are available which vary in speed, size, and operation.

A *grill or griddle* is used for broiling and quick cooking. Steaks, hamburgers, and other meats and seafood are cooked on the grill. It is heated by gas or electricity. For grilling potatoes, steaks, and hamburgers, temperatures from 177°C to 232°C [350°F. to 450°F.] are used. A lower temperature is needed for eggs, sandwiches, and pancakes. Usually, signal lights indicate overheating. A built-in ventilation system draws off smoke and odors quickly. The grill must be kept clean at all times to prevent flavors from one food mixing with another. Fat is usually drained off at the sides and collected in a drip cup which must be cleaned frequently during use.

A *broiler*, either gas, electric or charcoal, is similar in some ways to a flat grill. However, it is usually operated at a higher temperature. The heat may be above or below the food to be cooked. Some broilers are upright and heat is applied to both sides of the food at once. Here care must be taken not to let fat catch on fire. The intense heat of a broiler sears the outside of meat, giving a pleasing color and flavor while retaining juices in the meat. As with a grill, ventilation is essential. All ventilating hoods must be kept free of grease which can cause a fire.

Whenever you work at a grill or broiler, be alert. Watch what you are doing every minute. In *short order cooking*, timing is important for good results. Care is necessary to prevent over cooking. Remember, the food that is generally cooked on a grill or broiler is expensive.

When using a grill or broiler, be careful—protect yourself from burns at all times.

Mechanical equipment in the kitchen may consist of a *chopper* for vegetable preparation. A round, rotating bowl is fitted with a guard to protect your fingers from the sharp blade. Learn to feed food into the chopper carefully. A *vertical cutter* is similar to a blender. It quickly shreds salad greens, makes mayonnaise, and does a variety of other tasks.

Vegetable peelers remove skins from potatoes and other vegetables by rotating them against an abrasive surface. Peelers are not as common today as they were in the past. Potatoes are now purchased peeled, sliced, shredded, and in many other semi-prepared forms.

Slicers are used to slice food such as meats and cheese. A gravity-feed slicer automatically feeds food to the blade. A gauge on the front regulates the thickness of a slice.

How to use a vertical cutter . . .

A vertical cutter is similar to a home blender. Here celery for a salad is put into the cutter, which contains water.

Timing is essential. If the cutter is allowed to run too long, vegetables can be turned into liquid.

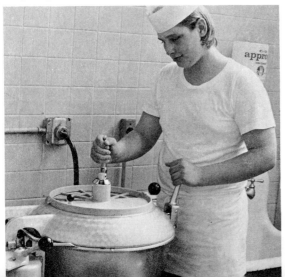

The chopped celery is lifted from the water with two wire baskets.

Chopped celery is placed in a perforated pan for further draining.

110

A new employee gets instructions in the use of the vertical cutter.

Student practices filling a cone with soft-serve ice cream.

Most quantity food kitchens have a *fryer*, heated by either gas or electricity. It has a thermostat to control the temperature of the fat to be heated. This equipment is used for French fries, chicken, fish, and, of course, doughnuts.

Machines to meet specific needs are also available. A machine to make soft-serve ice cream is one example.

Try to become familiar with all equipment in the kitchen. You will be a valued employee if you can operate the machines quickly and carefully and know how to clean each.

Food service workers must know how to use and clean specialized equipment such as this milk shake machine.

PORTION CONTROL

Portion control means that a specific size portion of each food is served. Without strict control, food may be wasted, money may be lost, and one customer may receive larger servings than another.

Portion control is based on the standard recipe, which tells exactly what the yield should be. This is stated by the size and number of cut pieces, or by the scoops or ladles used for serving. The recipe on page 100, for example, specifies 50 servings using an 8 oz. ladle. If the recipe is followed accurately, it should result in the same quality and quantity each time.

We have already mentioned scoops and ladles as a means of portion control. There are other specific tools to give uniform portions. On page 113 you see *wheel cutters* attached to a metal bar being used to cut brownies. One set cuts in one direction, then the pan is turned and the other set of cutters cuts across the pan. In this way, each portion is the same. Smaller, accordion-type wheels are used to mark sheet cakes so that they may be cut uniformly. Pies and round cakes are cut with round cutters divided into wedges. The cutter is pressed down to cut uniform servings. Similar devices are used to section fruit such as apples or pears. As you become familiar with portion control devices, you may be able to invent one that has not yet been thought of.

FOOD COST CONTROL

Food cost control is as important as portion control. All food service units operate within a strict budget. Management must know the average cost of all food items and meals served, and to control this cost at every step of preparation and service. How is this done?

One basic control method is recipe costing of each food item. This means figuring the cost of preparing and serving each item on the menu. This determines the price to charge customers in order to make a profit. The general formula for this is:

$$\frac{\text{Food} + \text{Labor} + \text{Overhead} + \text{Profit}}{\text{Number of Servings}} = \text{Selling Price}$$

Start with the recipe and determine the cost of each ingredient used. The price paid per can or per pound should be available either on an inventory card or purchase order. Divide the total cost of the recipe by the number of standard portions. This gives the food cost for each serving.

Other costs must be added before the price of a serving can be set. First, a labor cost must be added. It would be too time consuming to keep a record of the number of minutes and hours of labor that go into preparing a recipe. Therefore most units add a specific percentage to the food cost to cover labor costs. Let us take as an example a restaurant which has determined that adding 70 percent to the food cost would cover the cost of labor. Fifty percent must be added for overhead and 10 percent for profit. A recipe for 50 costs $6.00 for food. Add 70 percent or $4.20 for labor, 50 percent or $3.00 for overhead, and 10 percent or $.60 for profit. Add all costs—food $6.00, labor $4.20, overhead $3.00, and profit $.60— for a total of $13.80. This is cost for 50 servings, so divide $13.80 by 50—$.28 for one serving. Round off selling price to $.30.

Some food operators figure just the food cost of a recipe and multiply it by 3 to get the selling price. This is easier to do but may not be as accurate as adding the actual labor, overhead, and profit figures. If this method were used for the example given above, the price would be higher. Multiply the food cost of $6.00 by 3. This gives $18.00 for 50 servings or $.36 for one. This can be rounded off to a selling price of $.40. Can you see that 3 times the food cost is allowing for higher labor and overhead costs and profit?

On some jobs, you may be asked to help compile certain records or forms used in food cost control. No matter what kind of record you may be responsible for, be sure you are accurate and neat. Also be sure to write clearly. One way to increase your value as an employee is to help management keep these records accurate.

Florida Dept. of Citrus

The portion size in this molded chicken aspic is controlled by cutting between strips of green pepper.

A wheel cutter consists of circular blades attached to a metal bar. The spaces between the blades may be adjusted to control portion size.

Brookline, Mass., Public Schools

An accordian-type wheel marker is used to mark a sheet cake.

Brookline, Mass., Public Schools

113

À LA CARTE FOODS

À la carte foods are generally cooked to order.

Customers often question how long they will have to wait for their order. The cooking time varies with the size and thickness of the serving. The chart below gives the average length of time.

WORK SIMPLIFICATION

The purpose of work simplification is to get the best results with the least amount of effort. The supervisor or manager has probably set up

Approximate Cooking Times for Cooked-to-Order Foods	
Type of Food	*Minutes*
Broiled Chicken	25–30
Broiled Fish	10–15
Broiled Lobster	20–30
Fried Chicken	30–40
Fried Fish	15–20
Fried Oysters	10–15
Fried Scallops	15
Individual Steaks:	
Rare	10
Medium	15
Well-done	20
Lamb Chops	10
Oyster Stew	10
Pork Chops	15–20
Porter House Steak (for 2)	20–25
Sirloin Steak Planked (for 2)	25–30
Veal Chops	20

the most efficient work methods for each job. However, as you do your work, it is up to you to use these methods. How you work makes a great difference in how you produce, how tired you get, and how many accidents you may have.

Keep in mind that good posture helps you to work better and also helps to prevent fatigue. Learn to use your body correctly as you work. This helps you to accomplish more on the job with less weariness. If you stand tall with your head, chest, and hips aligned, you will need only a minimum amount of muscular control to keep your body in balance.

Poor work habits can also put unnecessary strain on your muscles. Some of these poor habits include bending the head forward, twisting the body, lifting incorrectly, or reaching beyond your arm span. It has been found that reaching out with the arms so that you have to stretch requires twice as much energy as reaching out comfortably at arm's length. Reaching below counter heights or to the floor uses many times the energy required to reach out at arm's length.

One way to simplify work procedures is to arrange the work area properly. There should be no need for unnecessary reaching or stretching. Utensils and tools should be placed so they are convenient to use and in logical order for the job to be done.

Proper work motions help you to do a better job and help you to work more comfortably. If you are active in any sport, you know that there is a correct way to hold and use the equipment. The same is true in the kitchen. There is a correct, efficient way to hold and use food preparation equipment and to perform each process.

When you first learn to use a tool or to perform a process, be sure to learn the right way. It may seem difficult or awkward at first, but stay with it. Concentrate on the right way until it becomes a habit with you.

You may hear your supervisor and other workers say, "Always use both hands when you work." Most people think of themselves as being left-handed or right-handed. Therefore it often comes as a surprise to learn that you *can* use both hands in food production. In making sandwiches, for instance, use both hands to put meat, cheese, or tomato slices on the bread—one slice with each hand. This way you can fill the same number of sandwiches in only half the amount of time it would take if you used just one hand. At first, this may seem difficult to do, but with practice it becomes easy. Can you see how much more you can produce by working with both hands? Using both hands is not only more efficient and speeds up production, but it is less tiring to the muscles since the body is kept in balance.

As you learn work simplification methods, think about what you are doing. You may be able to develop a method of your own that saves time and energy and still gives a good product. For example, whenever possible, combine two or more processes. Keep in mind that the purpose of work simplification is not only to produce good results and speed up food production—it also helps to keep you from becoming tired.

A student learns the proper techniques in using a steam jacketed kettle.

BOCES, Ithaca, N. Y.

Correct height of work area, proper equipment, and efficient work habits can help prevent fatigue.

Let's Think It Over

1. Convenience foods are often used in quantity food production.

   - Discuss the advantages and disadvantages in relation to:
     Cost.
     Time saving.
     Labor saving.
     Quality.
     Equipment needed.
     Specialties available.

- When might it be an advantage to prepare several specialties in quantity and freeze for later use?

2. Quality and cost control are important in food service.

   - Why is it essential to control quality and yield of a recipe?
   - Discuss basic procedures for:
       Selecting ingredients.
       Weighing.
       Scaling or portioning.

3. Many pieces of equipment can aid in fast, efficient food production.

   - Discuss the operation, principal uses, and care of the following:
       Broiler.
       Steam jacketed kettle.
       Fryer.
       Microwave oven.

4. When food is produced in large quantities, the results must conform to predetermined standards.

   - Name several procedures used by food managers to produce quantity foods that are both uniform and tasty.
   - Describe the general format of a standard recipe. Why are such recipes important to food preparation?
   - Discuss the meaning and importance of portion control.

5. The costing of recipes and pricing of food items is essential to business success.

   - Explain how a mistake of a few cents in costing can result in a large loss.

- Why do recipes need to be costed frequently? Discuss.

6. The way you work can control fatigue. Discuss how you can work efficiently in a kitchen without becoming fatigued.

Let's Investigate

1. Talk with managers of different types of food service units to learn their formula for pricing food. Discuss how methods will vary in each of the following:

   - A non-profit school lunch.
   - A hospital.
   - An in-plant lunchroom.
   - A hotel dining room.

2. Visit a quantity food kitchen. Observe the kinds of convenience foods that are used. Do these foods save time, labor, and money? Discuss.

3. Watch trained workers at any food production job. Observe how they have placed their tools and equipment, and how they work. Discuss in class how:

   - Rhythmically they worked.
   - They used their bodies when bending, reaching, or lifting.
   - Efficiently they produced.

4. Collect several quantity recipes. Analyze the format as to the amount of information given and the details of preparation. Discuss this in class.

5. Practice changing the weights and measures in a recipe to yield one-half the number of servings; one-fourth; double.

6. Figure the cost of a quantity recipe and the cost per portion.

Chapter **7**

Preparation

of Food

Since they have had both training and experience, chefs and cooks are highly skilled in cooking methods. By observing them, you can increase your knowledge of these methods.

Back-of-the-house food production involves hot and cold food preparation. Hot foods are those served warm or hot such as cereals, soups, meats, vegetables, and beverages. Cold foods, served at room temperature or chilled, include cereals, salads, sandwiches, juices, desserts, and fruits.

WORDS TO KNOW		
Boil	Roast	Cold soup
Braise	Steam	Proof box
Grill	Stew	Leavening
Fry	Emulsion	Vacuum
Stock	Thin soup	Batch
Bake	Thick soup	cooking

HOT FOOD PREPARATION

Hot foods must be prepared close to mealtime in order to be fresh, appetizing, and retain their nutrients. Food must also be kept hot during serving time, without continuing to cook. Overcooking causes the food to lose flavor and nutritive value. These problems of hot food preparation are controlled by *batch cooking* (cooking in smaller amounts at a time), not keeping food standing too long on the range or steam table, and using the correct cooking methods.

The following cooking methods are generally used in the preparation of hot food:

Bake. Cook in the oven in an uncovered pan without the addition of moisture; correct temperature must be used. Examples: cakes, pastries, breads, fish.

Boil. Cook in water or other liquid at 100°C [212°F.], causing bubbles at the surface. Other terms associated with boiling are: *Parboil*—boil until partially cooked; *simmer*—cook in a liquid just below the boiling point; *poach*—cook food such as eggs or fish in simmering water or other hot liquid; *scald*—bring to a temperature just below the boiling point.

Braise. Brown meat or vegetables in a small amount of fat at a high temperature, then simmer slowly in a small amount of liquid in a covered pan. Examples: pot roast, Swiss steak, braised lamb.

Broil. Cook quickly by direct flame or heat; sometimes called grilling. Examples: steaks, chops, fish fillets.

Fry. Cook in a small amount of fat until browned or done. Other methods of frying are pan-frying, sautéing, searing, and deep-fat or French frying. Examples: eggs, shrimp, meat, poultry, potatoes.

Grill. Cook on a griddle. Sometimes used interchangeably with *broil.*

Roast. The same as baking but applies to meats and poultry cooked by dry heat, uncovered, in an oven. Examples: turkey, prime ribs of beef.

Brookline, Mass., Public Schools

A compartment steamer provides moist heat for slow cooking of less tender cuts of meat such as chuck and rump roasts.

Students learn correct procedures for carving roasts.

Brookline, Mass., Public Schools

Steam. Cook food in a steam-filled container, either with or without pressure. The cooking temperature in steamers is above the boiling point, which shortens the cooking time. Steam is generated by the use of electricity or gas. Examples: meats, poultry, puddings, cereals, vegetables.

Stew. Boil or simmer in a small quantity of liquid below the boiling point in a covered container. Examples: meat stews, poultry, chowders, some vegetables.

Generally, six types of foods are prepared in the hot foods area. They are meat, fish, poultry, vegetables, cooked cereals, and eggs.

In selecting the best preparation method for each, certain basic principles of cookery must be considered.

Meat

Two cooking methods are generally used— moist heat and dry heat.

Moist heat is used with the less tender cuts of meat such as chuck, rump, and stew meats. The long, slow cooking by moist heat tends to break down connective tissue and make the meat less tough. Braising, stewing, boiling, and steaming are moist-heat methods.

Dry heat is used with the tender cuts of meat, such as steak, chops, and roasts. The methods include roasting, broiling, and frying. Relatively low roasting temperatures are used in order to prevent shrinkage. When meat is roasted, it should be juicy, tender, and appetizing.

Pork must be thoroughly cooked to an internal temperature of 85°C [185°F.], and never served underdone. Beef, however, especially

National Broiler Council

Chicken may be pan fried, sautéed, or deep fat fried.

steaks and prime ribs, may be served rare, medium, or well done.

A *meat thermometer* is used to measure the internal temperature of roasts. It is inserted into the thickest part of the meat. When the desired internal temperature has been reached, the meat is done.

Poultry

The age of the fowl determines the method of cooking. Young poultry such as a fryer is generally cooked with dry heat, while the older poultry such as stewing chicken is cooked with moist heat. Remember, poultry must be thoroughly cooked to be safe. Internal temperatures of 85–90°C [185–195°F.] indicate the poultry is cooked.

Before cooking, poultry should be carefully cleaned. The heart, liver, gizzard, and neck are removed and usually cooked separately. Poultry may be prepared in many ways— roasted, baked, broiled, fried in the oven or on top of the range, braised, fricasséed, simmered, or stewed.

Remove thigh and drumstick from back.

How to cut a broiler-fryer . . .

Separate thigh and drumstick.

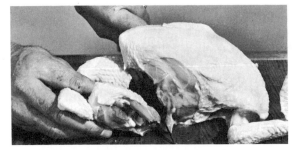

Separate half of lower back from breast.

Remove wings.

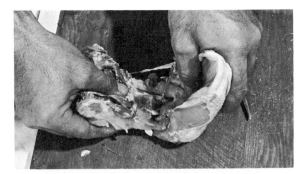

Separate remaining lower back from breast.

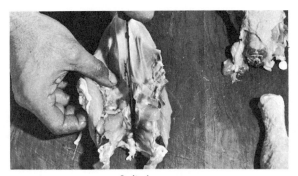

Split breast.

Ten cut-up pieces of chicken.

20

Fried chicken for carry-out service . . .

Photos this page courtesy of Kentucky Fried Chicken

This breading machine takes 180 servings of cut-up chicken through the batter mix at one time.

Five trays of breaded chicken (180 servings) are placed in an automatic chicken cooker. The cooker lowers the chicken into the fat, which is maintained at the proper frying temperature.

Breaded chicken is removed from the breading machine and arranged on portable tray trolleys to be transported to the cooker.

Thirteen minutes later, the five trays of deep-fat fried and drained chicken are ready for serving.

121

Brookline, Mass., Public Schools

This student has prepared fish fillets with a garnish of parsley and maître d'hôte butter. He is adding the finishing touches to the sauce accompaniment.

Fish

Many varieties of fish and shellfish are available in most areas of the country. The popularity of fish has increased greatly due to modern methods in catching, processing, transporting, and preparing this delicate, tasty food. Eating establishments often feature three or four choices of fish on their menu.

Fish and shellfish are usually tender because they do not have the heavy connective tissue found in meat.

The bland flavor of most fish can be enhanced with a well-seasoned sauce or with fresh lemon juice.

The size, shape, and thickness of the fish will determine the length of cooking time. When properly cooked, the flesh will flake easily and be moist and tender. A thermometer may be used to test fish for doneness. The fish is edible when the internal temperature reaches 140°F. This method is practical only with a thick portion.

Like other protein foods such as meat and eggs, fish will be toughened by high temperatures or excessive cooking. Overcooking will also cause dryness and loss of flavor.

Fish may be steamed, baked, boiled, broiled, fried, sautéed, and poached.

As said before, high heat will toughen fish. However, high temperatures are used for broiling and frying but only for a very short time, usually a few minutes.

If strong-flavored fish is fried, the flavor is transferred to the cooking fat. If the same fat is used to fry other foods, those foods will have a strong, unpleasant fish flavor. Therefore fat used for frying fish should not be re-used for other foods.

Vegetables

Cooked vegetables change in color, flavor, and nutritive value if overcooked or held too long at serving temperature. They should be cooked in small amounts or batches as close to mealtime as possible, preparing one batch after another. They should never be held more than twenty to thirty minutes at serving temperature.

United Fresh Fruit and Vegetable Assoc.

An assortment of garden-fresh vegetables, cooked and raw, makes an appetizing relish tray.

Idaho Potato Commission

Do you know how dutchess potatoes are prepared so they do not soak up juices or gravies from accompanying foods?

Tray 1. (top) Cooked potatoes are riced, seasoned, and shaped with a pastry tube.

Tray 2. Slices of cooked potatoes are prepared, which will hold the shaped dutchess potatoes.

Tray 3. The dutchess potatoes, on a slice of cooked potato, are placed on breakfast trays . . .

Tray 4. luncheon trays . . .

Tray 5. dinner plates.

The prepared trays can be frozen for transport to airlines or other food service units.

123

These vegetables have been cooked in small batches to help prevent over cooking and over holding.

Dudley–Anderson–Yutzy

Automatic deep fat fryers provide fast, scientific preparation of French fries. A computer sets the cooking time. When the fries are done, a buzzer goes off, alerting the crew to remove them from the fryer.

McDonald's

The method of cooking should be suited to the type of vegetable:

- Green vegetables are cooked in a small amount of boiling, salted water for a short time, or in a steam pressure cooker.
- Steaming is a good method to use for mild-flavored vegetables such as carrots, young cabbage, spinach, squash, and potatoes.
- Canned vegetables are heated in their own liquid, then seasoned and served.
- Yellow, red, and white vegetables (carrots, parsnips, beets, squash, sweet and white potatoes, onions) are more easily held at serving temperature for a longer time than green vegetables.
- Strong-flavored vegetables (onions, leeks) are best cooked in large amounts of boiling water, uncovered, for a long time with low heat.
- Varieties of cabbage are best cooked for a short time in boiling salted water.
- Cook vegetables only until tender. Do not overcook.

A nutritious, appetizing meal—broiled ham served with seasoned cooked spinach and garnished with egg slices.

Dudley–Anderson–Yutzy

- To preserve water-soluble vitamins, cook in as little water as possible and use vegetable water in soups or gravies.

Cereals and Cereal Products

Cereals such as rice, macaroni, barley, rolled oats, rolled wheat, cornmeal, hominy grits, and others require cooking. In general, they are thoroughly covered with water and simmered until tender. Cereals and pasta increase in bulk as they absorb water. When cooking cereals, remember these points:

- Measure water accurately according to the recipe, and add salt.
- Be sure water is boiling before adding the cereal.
- Measure or weigh cereal carefully.
- Stir cereal slowly into the boiling water to keep water boiling and prevent lumps.
- Continue stirring while cereal is cooking to prevent cereal sticking to the pan.
- Reduce heat, cover, and continue cooking for required time, stirring occasionally.

BOCES, Ithaca, N. Y.

Students learn to prepare cereal.

125

Poultry and Egg National Board

An egg omelet filled with corned beef hash makes a hearty main dish.

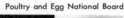

Poached eggs on toast with bacon are a favorite breakfast item.

Poultry and Egg National Board

Eggs

Eggs may be served as a main dish or used in other foods. It is important to purchase quality fresh eggs, especially for the breakfast service, to insure a good final product.

Eggs are cooked at low to moderate temperatures to keep them tender and tasty. Since eggs are usually cooked to order, small-quantity techniques may be used. Fried, shirred or baked, and scrambled eggs may be partially cooked, held for a short time in a warm oven, and then finished just prior to serving.

The basic principles of egg cookery may be summarized as follows:

- Eggs are refrigerated immediately and not washed until just before use.
- Egg is a protein food and heat causes changes in protein. Both the egg yolk and the egg white coagulate or thicken when heated. This means eggs can be used for thickening such foods as puddings and sauces.
- Low to moderate heat is used to cook eggs. High heat toughens and hardens them.
- Eggs add flavor and improve the texture in many dishes such as puddings, sauces, and cakes.
- When air is beaten into eggs, they act as a leavening agent. To *leaven* means to make a food light. Egg soufflé or egg meringues are examples.
- Eggs are used as a coating because they will hold bread crumbs, flour, or cornmeal together. Cutlets, fish fillets, and other foods are dipped into this coating mixture and fried.

126

- Eggs act as an emulsifying agent. An emulsion is formed when the albumin of the egg forms a film around globules of oil and keeps them suspended in a liquid. Mayonnaise is an example of an emulsion.

Soups

Soups are prepared mainly from the broth of meat, seafood, or vegetables. Light soups may be offered as an appetizer on the menu for the purpose of stimulating the appetite for the main dinner to follow. Hearty soups often serve as a main dish or complete meal. However, smaller servings of these hearty soups are also popular on the dinner menu as appetizers.

Most soups require long, slow cooking. In quantity production, they are usually prepared in a steam jacketed kettle. It is difficult to classify soups, since there are hundreds of soup combinations used by cooks and chefs. The main types more commonly used are *thin soups, thick soups, special soups,* and *cold soups.*

- *Thin soups* are prepared from *stock*, the clear, rich liquid derived from cooking meat, fish or poultry. Examples: bouillon, consommé, vegetable soup.
- *Thick soups* are prepared from a stock or milk base thickened by the addition of starch or starchy food such as potatoes, rice, barley, or macaroni. They can also be thickened with *roux*, a mixture of fat and flour. Examples: cream soups, chowders, bisques.
- *Special soups* include both thick and thin soups. There is a great variety of these soups, which have usually originated in a

Cape Coral Country Club, Fla.

Soups are prepared in large quantities in steam jacketed kettles such as this.

certain locale and may have a regional tradition. Examples: New England clam chowder, minestrone (Italy), onion soup (France), creole soup (New Orleans).
- *Cold soups* have become very popular in recent years, especially on summer menus. They are actually prepared as hot soups and served thoroughly chilled. Examples: jellied consommé, cold borscht, vichysoisse, jellied chicken broth, and gazpacho.

Sauces

Sauces are said to be the test of a great cook or chef. In a large hotel restaurant, there may be a special sauce chef who is noted for the delicious sauces he prepares.

127

Student prepares gravy in a tilting trunnion kettle.

A well-made sauce is smooth and perfectly seasoned to enhance the flavor of the food it will accompany.

In the general category of sauces are salad dressings, mayonnaise, gravies, marinades, and seasoned butters, as well as the sweet or dessert sauces.

Most sauces are thickened with flour, cornstarch, or eggs. In making gravies, a roux is used. A *roux* is a combination of fat and flour which is added to meat juices. It is cooked at low temperatures, stirring constantly, until the starch of the flour is thoroughly cooked and the gravy is thick and smooth. If you are asked to prepare or serve sauces, follow all directions carefully.

Temperature is important in making and keeping sauces. For instance, mayonnaise is not cooked but is a blend or emulsion of oil, eggs, and vinegar. This blend can be broken by excessive cold temperatures.

Sweet sauces based on sugar are simple to prepare. They are used on desserts such as puddings, ice cream, and cakes. Cornstarch and eggs are also used to thicken sweet sauces.

Tart flavors such as lemon are often used on very sweet desserts. Bland desserts are accompanied by sauces of distinct flavor.

Work Procedures

When working at a hot food station:

- Read recipe or directions carefully.
- Collect all tools and equipment needed.
- Assemble all ingredients in measured amount.
- Position food and equipment for fast work flow.
- Check large equipment for performance.
- Set temperature of oven or grill.
- Prepare pans and molds.
- Prepare food according to recipe.
- Use all safety guards as directed.
- Cook as directed.
- Cut or portion as directed.
- Store, refrigerate, or freeze as directed.
- Clean up work area, tools, and equipment.

When working with fat, follow directions carefully to get uniform results. Most foods are put into a basket and lowered into the deep fat. When the degree of doneness and brownness is reached, the food is removed and drained, usually on brown paper. Fried foods are usually cooked to order so that they can be served hot.

When cooking with fat:

- Drain thoroughly or pat dry any moist food.
- Crumb evenly.
- Control temperature.
- Lower food cautiously into fat to avoid splashing.

Food should be lowered into hot fat cautiously to prevent bubbling and splattering.

Fried chicken is stored in a heated cabinet, ready for fast service.

- Cook until brown.
- Drain excess fat.
- Keep equipment, especially exhaust flues, clean to prevent fat collecting and causing fire.

Overheating breaks down the fat, giving an objectionable flavor. Fat kept at controlled temperatures and kept clean may be used many times.

Keeping Food Hot

Each worker has a responsibility for serving the customer properly cooked food at the correct temperature. People are quickly dissatisfied if the hot food is only lukewarm or cold when they receive it.

Here are some practices that can help you to meet this responsibility:

- Heat the plates for hot foods.
- Take batches of hot food directly from the range to the steam table. Be sure steam table temperature is correct.

Good organization is needed so hot foods for one order are ready at the same time. A student prepares hamburgers and French fries at the fryer-grill.

A roast of beef is kept hot with overhead warmers during service.

129

- Pour hot coffee into heated pots. Serve immediately.
- Do not serve food which has been standing too long on the steam table. Meats shrink and vegetables lose flavor and color.
- Do not let your order of hot food stand on the counter while you do something else.

To make a citrus basket . . .

Florida Citrus Commission

Use a small, sharp knife. Cut a rounded slice off each end, as shown. Cut out pulp to form handle.

Fill basket with colorful flowers.

Food Accompaniments

It is the custom to serve traditional accompaniments and condiments with certain foods because the flavor and texture or color combinations are pleasing. This service helps to promote the popularity of the eating establishment. In the following chart, you will find a list of some of these traditional accompaniments.

Food Accompaniments	
Entrée	*Accompaniments*
Baked beans	Catsup, chili sauce, pickles, steamed brown bread.
Chow mein	Soya sauce.
Fish	Lemon, maitre d' hôte butter, tartar sauce, catsup.
Shellfish	Cocktail sauce, melted butter, lemon, mayonnaise.
Beef	Catsup, horseradish sauce, chili sauce, Worcestershire sauce, steak sauce, gravy.
Ham	Mustard, horseradish, raisin sauce, pineapple sauce.
Lamb	Mint sauce, mint jelly, currant jelly.
Pork	Apple sauce, cider sauce.
Chicken and turkey	Gravy, cranberry sauce, currant jelly.
Goose and duck	Orange sauce, glazed orange slices.

glazed, stuffed lobster with gelatin molds of eggs and black olives . . .

The art of garnishing . . .

Students learn the fine art of garnishing as they decorate baked ham with green pepper baskets, sliced peaches, and maraschino cherries . . .

poached fish with clear aspic and aspic molds . . .

chicken legs and wings garnished with foil collars and fruit for a children's party . . .

Beef Wellington with mushroom caps and braised celery and asparagus . . .

poached fish with aspic, shrimp, tomatoes, and mushrooms.

131

COLD FOOD PREPARATION

Much of the production of cold foods can be done ahead of time, and the ingredients stored or refrigerated. This is called pre-preparation. The final assembling of the ingredients is generally completed near serving time.

Salads and sandwiches are prepared in this area.

The basic principles of cold food preparation are discussed in the following pages.

Salads

There is such variety in salads today that it is difficult to give a definition. Generally, a complete salad will include an underliner (lettuce leaf or other greens), a body (main part of the salad), a spicy, sweet, or creamy dressing, and a garnish. Sometimes one or more parts are omitted.

Salads are usually grouped according to their main ingredient such as vegetable, fruit, meat, or seafood.

A variety of greens combined with pieces of vegetable such as tomato or cucumber is called a *tossed salad*. When *julienne* pieces of meat and cheese (cut in narrow strips), and sliced egg are added, the salad is usually called *chef's salad*.

Salads are generally good sources of minerals and vitamins. The fresh, crisp texture of salads offers a pleasing contrast to other foods in the meal.

In food service operations, salads may be used in any or all of the following ways:

- As an appetizer—crisp greens, vegetables, or tart fruits with a highly seasoned dressing. Example: fresh orange and grapefruit sections.
- As a main course—seafood, meat, vegetable, or cheese salads. These are usually featured with soup, beverage, and dessert. Examples: chicken salad, shrimp salad, or egg salad.
- As a side dish (accompaniment) to the entrée (main course)—smaller salads of greens, vegetables, fruits, or gelatin combinations. Examples: tossed salad, pineapple-carrot salad, or fruit in gelatin.
- As a refreshment or dessert—fruit salad or gelatin with a sweet dressing. Example: frozen fruit salad.

Grapefruit can be served in many ways as an appetizer—broiled, garnished with strawberries, frosted cherries, grapes, apple slices, sherbet, or coconut and orange sections, or stuffed with shrimp and fruit sections.

Dudley–Anderson–Yutzy

Some Facts about Salad Preparation

Salads must be fresh. Therefore, they are assembled as close to service time as possible. Salads should not stand unrefrigerated more than twenty minutes or they may lose crispness.

A variety of salad greens may be used, although head and leaf lettuce are most popular in food service operations. Salad greens should be crisp, clean, and chilled.

Potato, chicken, meat, seafood, and egg salads are potential carriers of food-borne illness. They must always be kept refrigerated at or below 7°C [45°F.] except during the time actually needed to prepare and serve them. When preparing these salads in quantities, all the ingredients except greens and dressing may be combined ahead of time and refrigerated. The greens and dressing are added at serving time.

Edible garnishes are used on salads. *Garnishing* means to decorate a food to make it more attractive. Nuts and cherries are appropriate for fruit salads. Poultry, meat, fish, and vegetable salads may be garnished with green pepper rings, stuffed olives, pimiento strips, carrot curls, cucumber rings, egg slices, celery fans, onion rings, or radish roses.

Salad Dressings

There are three basic types of salad dressings. *French* dressing is made of oil and vinegar or lemon juice, and seasonings. It is usually used with salad greens and on vegetable and fruit salads. *Mayonnaise* is made of vegetable oil, vinegar or lemon juice, egg, and seasonings. It is used with meat, fish, chicken, cooked

Canteen Corp.

Efficient, well-arranged equipment is essential in salad production. Salad girls use hand tongs to assemble salads as directed. Note recipe cards on counter at eye level. Scales are available for checking portions. When they are completed, salads will be refrigerated until serving time.

vegetables, and some fruit salads. *Cooked dressing* is made of liquid (water or milk), a thickening agent (starch and egg), seasonings, an acid such as lemon juice or vinegar, and fat, usually a small amount of butter. It is often used with fruit salads.

Many varieties of these dressings such as blue cheese, cheddar, thousand island, sour cream, Italian, and other specialties are featured in restaurants.

Assembling Salads

When you work in food service, you may be responsible for assembling a large number of salads in time for the meal. It is important that you do this efficiently and in line with the policies of the house. Generally, salads are assembled as follows:

- Collect all the tools and equipment needed.

133

- Assemble pre-prepared salad ingredients from the refrigerator and place conveniently on work surface.
- Pre-position the specified number of trays on the work space.
- Place cold plates, platters, or dishes on trays in rows.
- Arrange salad greens on each of the plates of the tray nearest you, using both hands.
- Place the salad foods, cold foods, mixes, or combinations neatly in the center of the salad green. Use the correct portion scoop or serving utensils.
- Check to be sure portions are uniform.
- Garnish each item according to directions.
- Slide the completed tray onto serving cart or into refrigerated unit or cold table, as directed.
- Repeat process until all trays of salads are completed.
- Clean up work area, tools and equipment.

Sandwiches

The popularity of sandwiches has increased rapidly in recent years. Business people, workers, teenagers, and travelers enjoy the variety as well as the fast service available at sandwich counters, vending machines, and drive-ins throughout the country. Sandwiches are often served with other foods such as French fries, vegetables, or salads, to complete a nutritious meal.

When you prepare sandwiches, remember they should have a fresh, attractive appearance. The bread needs to be firm, neither stale nor soft, with a well-flavored filling of tender texture that is easy to eat. About one-third to one-half of the sandwich's total weight should be composed of filling. Sandwiches should be cut evenly with no ragged edges, and no filling spilling out. Always serve cold sandwiches cold and hot sandwiches hot.

What types of sandwiches are there?

- Cold sandwiches with sliced, chopped, or ground fillings, with or without lettuce.
- Grilled or toasted sandwiches.
- Open-faced sandwiches, either hot or cold.
- Small fancy sandwiches for special occasions.

Sandwich Preparation

In table and counter service restaurants, drug stores and snack bars, sandwiches are usually made up on order. A well-organized

An ideal sandwich counter for a restaurant. All supplies are within easy reach of the work area—bread to the left, sandwich fillings above, and plates to the right.

American Institute of Baking

and equipped sandwich preparation center which can produce variety and volume is used.

Neatness, speed, and high standards of sanitation are required in making sandwiches, both in quantity or on order.

Sandwich spreads or fillings are the important part of the sandwich. These are usually prepared in advance and stored in the refrigerator or cold room. Fillings should be soft and easily spread, but of proper texture for good eating. All sandwich ingredients should be of top quality and fresh. These foods should not stand at room temperature for more than three hours. Remove only enough from refrigerator to use up promptly.

A variety of breads such as whole wheat, rye, pumpernickle, raisin, sour dough, or French add variety to sandwiches. Rolls, both hard and soft, plain or sesame seed, round or frankfurter type, add greatly to the appeal of a sandwich.

Garnishes used with sandwiches should be suitable in texture, form, color, and flavor. For example, soft sandwiches such as egg salad could be served with celery, which is crispy. The shape of a pickle, a tomato slice, or an olive is a contrast in form to the sandwich. Color may be added with vegetables such as carrot sticks. Bland foods such as ham or egg need the sharp taste of pickle or relish as a garnish. A cream cheese and date sandwich, although bland, would not be served with a pickle but an apricot half or pineapple stick could be used.

Cold sandwiches may be served wrapped or unwrapped, depending on the type of operation. Vapor-proof and moisture-proof wrappings may be used for some sandwiches. The unwrapped sandwiches can be covered with

BOCES, Ithaca, N. Y.

A student worker prepares peanut butter and jelly sandwiches for the cafeteria line. What quantity methods of preparation is the student using?

moisture-proof wrap paper and stored in refrigerator. Sandwiches can be held under refrigeration for approximately twelve hours at 4°C [40°F.].

Food service units may make sandwiches in quantity for service to large groups, vending machines, or snack counters. Some types of sandwiches can be frozen.

Making Sandwiches in Quantity

- Collect all tools and equipment needed and place within easy reach.
- Assemble on trays the pre-prepared sandwich fillings and spreads from refrigerator, and breads from storage.
- Slit wrappings on bread, but leave wrapper on bread until ready to use.
- Arrange trays of bread (usually six to eight loaves to a tray) on left of work space, so you will be working from left to right.

135

Wrapped and labeled sandwiches, along with other packaged foods, are ready for delivery to snack shops and vending units.

Garnishes—pimiento strips, egg slices, olives, pickle strip, radish rose, and tomato wedge—add to the appeal of this open-faced chicken salad sandwich. What other garnishes can be used?

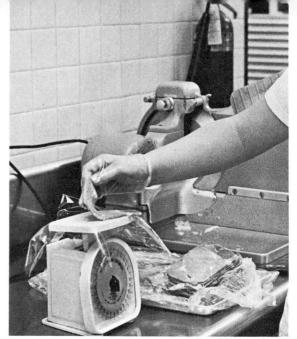

For uniform servings, sandwich meat is portioned by weighing.

- Line up spreads and fillings within 36 cm [14-inch] reach and in sequence of use.
- Pick up three or four slices of bread in each hand and place on work surface or bread board. Repeat to form four rows with three or four slices in each row.
- Spread softened butter or margarine on all bread slices, with spatula in right hand. Use one motion.
- Place filling on center of all bread slices with portion scoop.
- Use one motion of spatula to spread filling evenly to edges of bread.
- Use both hands to put bread slices on top of filled slices. Match edges of bread.
- Cut sandwiches as directed.
- Wrap sandwiches in moisture-proof wrapping, in sandwich bags, or store in covered pans as directed.
- Clean up work areas, tools, and equipment before beginning next assignment.

Other assembly type methods can be organized to suit the needs of the establishment.

136

Making sandwiches in quantity . . .

Pick up three or four slices of bread in each hand. Line up slices to form two vertical rows on work surface. Repeat to form a square of four-by-four slices.

Scoop fillings onto bread slices in the two center rows. Spread the two outside rows with softened butter or margarine. This step is not necessary if all-in-one spreads, which combine butter and fillings, are used.

Be sure to spread fillings to edges of the bread, using the two-stroke technique.

Using both hands, cover filling with bread slices from outside rows, butter side toward filling. Repeat entire process two more times so that finished sandwiches in center are stacked three high.

Cut the stacked sandwiches as desired.

Cut sandwiches should be wrapped neatly and securely for protection and display purposes. Sandwiches should be labeled for identification.

137

Canteen Corp.

Baker's helper puts rolls in oven to be heated while baker prepares pies in background. Notice the ovens, utensils, mixer, equipment, and ample work space needed for quantity baking.

This student learns to measure accurately by weight for large-quantity food preparation.

Ft. Myers Tech. School, Fla.

BAKE AREA

The bake area or bake shop, as it is often called, may be a section of a large kitchen or it may be in a different room. Except in very large establishments, the bake shop produces not only baked goods but also gelatin and frozen desserts, and puddings. Fruit and ice cream desserts may be assembled at the bake station or in another area near the dining room.

Breads and pastries prepared on the premises are the responsibility of a baker especially trained for this work. In small establishments, some special pastries may be purchased, or semi-prepared products such as frozen bread dough may be used.

Breads

There are two basic types of breads—quick breads and yeast breads. *Quick breads* such as muffins, popovers, and biscuits use baking powder as a leavening agent. *Yeast breads* are leavened by the action of yeast, either dry or in the moist, compressed form.

Whether baking powder or yeast is used, the leavening is accomplished by the formation of carbon dioxide gas. As the gas forms, the mixture rises, and is then set by the heat of baking.

Breads are made from flour, leavening, seasoning, sugar, and liquid. The mixture may be soft such as doughnuts or baking powder biscuits or stiff such as a regular bread dough.

Before yeast breads are baked, they must rise. Temperature is important in this step. Usually, room temperature or above is desirable. In quantity preparation, allowing the dough to rise is called *proofing*. A *proof box*

138

or *proofer* is a piece of equipment designed to hold the dough at a controlled temperature so it can rise.

Special breads add to distinctive dining, since customers enjoy them. The reputation of a restaurant can be heightened by serving hot breads or special yeast breads.

Batters and Soft Doughs

Batters are thinner than dough and may be poured. Popovers are poured into hot muffin pans. Pancakes are poured onto a griddle.

A soft dough may be dropped onto a griddle, but more often into hot fat. A soft dough is used for fritters.

If you are assigned to help with griddle cakes or waffles, you must learn to pour the exact amount of batter each time so that uniform portions will result. Sometimes a funnel device with a plunger is used. By moving the plunger up and down at controlled speed, a measured portion of batter is released. The grill or waffle iron temperature must be controlled for even cooking and browning.

Desserts

Usually, dessert served at the end of the meal is a sweet such as a pastry, pudding, ice cream, or cake. These foods may also be served as between-meal or snack foods. Desserts may be served hot or cold and with or without a sauce, topping, or accompaniment.

Sheridan Vocational Center, Fla.

The final glaze is brushed on an edible basket made of yeast dough.

A proof box holds temperatures between 90 and 100°F. (32 and 38°C) so yeast dough can rise.

Hample Equipment Co.

139

Dudley-Anderson-Yutzy

Be an artist in the kitchen! This chef proudly displays some of his decorative desserts, which are so appealing to customers. Many opportunities to be creative and to develop new dishes are available to food service workers.

Pies are popular. They have a crust of pastry made from flour, shortening, and water, and baked. They may also have a crust made of cracker or cookie crumbs pressed together with butter or margarine and refrigerated. Pies may have one or two crusts and be filled with fruit, a gelatin mixture, or a cream filling. They may be round or square and served in wedges or squares.

Cakes are usually of two types: Butter and sponge or angel food. They, too, come in an endless variety. Cakes may be frosted or iced, sprinkled with powdered sugar, filled, or served plain. Sizes and shapes vary from cupcakes to multi-layered tortes.

Butter cakes are made with butter or shortening. The sugar and shortening are creamed, or mixed together until soft and well blended; then eggs are added. The flour, baking powder, and seasoning are added alternately with liquid to the creamed mixture. The mixture is then baked.

Sponge and angel food cakes are leavened only with egg whites. A sponge cake also uses the yolks of eggs. Because of the high egg content, these cakes are baked slowly in a tube pan. They may be iced, split into layers and filled, or served with a dessert sauce.

Puddings are varied. They may be steamed or baked and served hot or cold. They may be light and airy such as a soufflé. They may be thickened with egg or cornstarch, or made firm with gelatin. They may be whipped or plain. Many puddings are made with a custard base and varied with chocolate, butterscotch, fruit, or a sauce. If you are helping to make a custard, remember that eggs toughen with high heat. Keep the temperature low both for soft custard or baked custard.

Gelatin is usually softened in cold water and dissolved in a hot liquid. As a gelatin cools, it begins to set or become firm. At this stage, it can be whipped until light. Sometimes it is combined with cream, custard, or beaten egg whites. Gelatin is colorful and may be used to decorate less colorful desserts. It may be served plain, or garnished with fruit and topped with whipped cream.

Ice cream and sherbets are popular and come in an endless number of flavors. Restaurants may make their own ice cream, but it is usually purchased from an ice cream manufacturer. Frozen desserts may be molded into fancy shapes, served with sauces, fruits, nuts, or liqueurs, and often topped with whipped cream.

Desserts are generally prepared in advance and refrigerated, frozen, or stored under cover until serving time. As a food service worker, you will probably help the cook prepare the desserts. You may also be asked to assemble and serve a variety of these desserts.

Serve desserts as instructed, using serving spoon or scoop, and a dish, plate, or glass as required. Cold dishes should be used for cold desserts. Be careful to add the sauce or other topping attractively and garnish as directed. If a wafer or cookie is to accompany the dessert, it may be placed on the underliner.

Fruit Desserts

Fresh fruits damage easily and spoil quickly, so they must be handled with care. They should be carefully washed and stored in a cold room or refrigerator.

Fruits such as bananas and apples darken when sliced and exposed to light. Citrus juice (lemon or orange) can be poured over the cut surface to help prevent darkening.

Fruits with heavy outside skins such as apples and pears hold steam. Therefore they bake well and keep their shape. To preserve the shape of fresh fruits, add sugar at the beginning of the cooking periods. For fruit sauces, add sugar later in the cooking period, after the fruit is soft.

Dried fruits may need to be soaked for several hours and then cooked in the same water. Some are purchased tenderized and ready for cooking without soaking. If sugar is needed, it is added in the last five minutes of cooking.

Bake Shop Procedures

When working in the bake shop:

- Read recipe carefully.
- Collect all tools and utensils needed.
- Assemble all ingredients.
- Check large equipment for performance.
- Set temperature of oven or refrigerator.
- Prepare pans and molds.
- Measure accurately.
- Follow techniques outlined to combine ingredients.
- Use equipment such as mixer to combine, knead, or beat.
- Use equipment and body motions properly to reduce fatigue.
- Bake, fry, refrigerate, or freeze as indicated.
- Cut, scoop, or portion prepared food as directed.
- Store or deliver to needed serving area.
- Clean up work area, tools, and equipment.

BEVERAGES

The most popular beverage in American restaurants is coffee. Milk, tea, cocoa, and chocolate are also available in most restaurants. Food service operators know the importance of beverages as part of the meal. They want to satisfy their customers by having consistently good beverages at all times.

There are some important points to remember if you are responsible for preparing beverages: Be sure to follow the procedure that has been given you. Keep coffee makers and tea makers immaculately clean. For best quality, serve coffee and tea immediately after it has been made. Coffee should not be allowed to stand, or be reheated, as it will acquire a bitter taste. For a flavorful beverage, good quality coffee and tea must be purchased.

The beverage station may be located in or near the cold food or pantry station. Some eating establishments provide several beverage pick-up stations which may be located in the dining area as well as in the pantry. It is important that the service workers have quick, easy access to the beverages.

Coffee

Urns or vacuum coffee makers are most commonly used in food service. The multiple vacuum coffee makers (2–4 vacuum coffee pots on hot plates) provide a continuous supply of fresh coffee.

To make coffee in an urn:

- Fill the hot water urn with fresh cold water, turn on the heat, and heat to boiling.

- Rinse coffee urn with hot water before using. Turn on the heat.
- Place filter into coffee basket or fit clean bag into urn. Fill the coffee bag, spreading the coffee evenly.
- Draw the hot water from water urn into the measure and pour it over the coffee bag. Use a steady circular motion. Repeat this until correct quantity has been added.
- Remove coffee bag when the liquid has drained through it.
- Cover the urn.
- Keep coffee temperature at 85°C [185°F.].

To make coffee in a vacuum maker:

- Place fresh water in lower bowl to proper level. Place it on the heat.
- Rinse a clean filter in cold water (some do not require a filter) and place it over filtering device.
- Place the filter device into the upper bowl. Add the proper amount of coffee into the upper bowl.
- Insert the top bowl into the lower bowl after the water begins to boil.
- Turn off the heat when the water has filled the top bowl. Stir the water in the upper bowl. Allow the brew to filter back into bottom bowl.
- Remove top bowl with coffee grounds. Empty grounds and clean top.

Instant Coffee

Instant coffee, often decaffeinated, is served in individual packages.

- Open package and place in cup or pot.
- Add hot water and mix well.

Tea

Usually, tea is prepared individually in small tea pots and served at once. The same techniques can be used for small or large quantities.

- Rinse tea pot or container with hot water.
- Use quantity as directed and place the tea (tea bag, tea leaves, or instant tea) in the pot.
- Add boiling water in correct quantity.
- Serve the tea pot on an underliner. This method is called wet service. It is not correct to serve the tea bag on the side of saucer or plate as the wet bag drips onto the saucer and may get onto clothing.

Hot Chocolate or Cocoa

Most food service units use individually packaged mixes of chocolate or cocoa.

- Open package and place in a cup or individual pot.
- Add hot water and mix well.
- Whipped cream is usually added to each cup as it is served.

Iced Tea and Coffee

Iced tea and coffee are generally served during hot weather.

- Prepare tea or coffee three times its usual strength.
- Fill the glasses with crushed ice or ice cubes.
- Pour the freshly made tea or coffee over the ice until glasses are full.

- Serve on an underliner. Lemon wedges and/or mint leaves are served with iced tea.

Let's Think It Over

1. Basic principles are involved in cooking different types of foods.

   - Explain the principle of cooking:
     Protein.
     Starch.
     Vegetables.

   - Explain the following basic cooking methods and give an example of a food prepared by each method.

Bake.	Grill.
Boil.	Fry.
Braise.	Roast.
Broil.	Steam.
	Stew.

   - What general principles are important in the preparation of the following cold foods?
     Salads.
     Sandwiches.
     Desserts.
     Fruits.

   - Explain the difference between a batter and a dough; a soft dough and a stiff dough. Give an example of each.

2. Leavening means to make light.

   - What ingredients are used to leaven:
     Muffins?
     Bread?
     Sponge cake?
     Butter cake?

3. Beverages, especially coffee, add to the satisfaction of a meal.

   - Discuss the following:
     Quality of beverage.
     Methods used.
     Cleanliness of equipment.

Let's Investigate

1. Visit a quality restaurant or hotel kitchen. Observe the food preparation methods used by chefs and bakers. Discuss in class the:

   - Variety of procedures used.
   - Kinds of sauces prepared.
   - Different methods used to cook meat and fish.
   - Bake shop production.
   - Beverage making.
   - Garnishing.

2. Visit a school or commercial cafeteria. Observe the procedures used in quantity sandwich and salad preparation. Report to the class on efficient methods used.

3. Visit a commercial bakery to observe their production methods. Discuss:

   - Quality control of ingredients.
   - Machines and equipment.
   - Production steps.

4. Collect and study several restaurant equipment booklets. Identify and list the appropriate tools and utensils to use in preparing large quantities of: soups; meat roasts; chicken à la king; fresh or frozen vegetables; whipped potatoes; baking powder biscuits; cakes.

Chapter **8**

Menu Strategy

When you read a newspaper, what attracts your attention first? Probably the headlines, the big news of the day. Notice how easy it is to locate what you are looking for in the advertisements, the comics, or the sports pages. It is easy because the paper's layout is carefully planned and organized to give you, the reader, information, pleasure, and satisfaction.

This is exactly what a menu does. The menu is often called the newspaper of the food service operation. It tells the customer what food is available, how it is prepared and served, and how much it costs.

Like a newspaper, the menu is planned so the customer can find the food items easily and see the prices clearly.

The menu is the hub of the entire food service operation. Why? The food preparation and service activities revolve around the demands of the menu.

The food listed must be attractive, well prepared, and ready on time to sell to customers. Food service operators, therefore, plan the menu carefully—it affects every operation. The amount of labor needed, the way equipment is utilized, and the profit, all depend upon the menu.

Employees need to be well informed on all details of the menu. This information is important for both front-of-the-house and back-of-the-house workers. Why is this important to you?

There are many foods listed on a menu. What will you need to know? Think about:

- Organization and use of menus.
- Nutrition in menu planning.
- Kinds of meals.

Food Service Careers

If your job in food service is to wait on customers, you will probably be asked questions about the menu such as:

"Are the clams fresh?"

"How is Beef à la Stroganoff prepared?"

"What is Sauce Béarnaise?"

"Is the fruit cup made of fresh or canned fruit?"

"What do you recommend today?"

Could you answer these questions? Knowing about the product that you help prepare or sell is a big step toward success in food service work. You will feel proud to have the answers to customers' questions.

Good restaurants always offer customers a variety of appetizing and nutritious foods so that a well-balanced meal may be selected.

WORDS TO KNOW

À la mode	Gourmet
Nutrition	Basic Four Food Groups
Carte du jour	À la carte
Accompaniment	Table d'hôte
Entrée	Appetizer
Canapé	Hors d'oeuvre

GOOD NUTRITION IN MENU PLANNING

The menu is planned to offer the customer a selection of nutritious foods which will satisfy his appetite and meet his budget needs.

Therefore a knowledge of good nutrition is an essential part of menu planning. Do you have this knowledge? Could you suggest a balanced food selection from the menu, if asked? What does good nutrition mean to you?

Nutrition refers to the food a person eats and how the body uses that food. Good nutrition usually results when a person normally selects the right food in the proper quantities needed by the body each day.

All people need the same nutrients to be healthy, but in different amounts. The nutrients can be obtained by eating a variety of foods. The important point is to meet the body's nutrient needs by selecting a *variety* of well-prepared foods in the day's meals. How is this accomplished in menu planning?

Nutritionists tell us that the best way to have a good daily food selection is to follow the pattern of the *Basic Four Food Groups*. What does this mean?

Foods have been grouped according to the nutrients they supply. The four groups are: *Milk Group*, including milk, cheese, ice cream, and other milk products; *Meat Group*, which includes meats, fish, poultry, eggs, dry beans and peas, and nuts; *Fruit-Vegetable Group;* and the *Grain Group*, including breads, cereals, and other grain products.

Guide to Good Eating

A Recommended Daily Pattern

Milk
Group

Calcium
Riboflavin (B₂)
Protein

**2 Servings/Adults
4 Servings/Teenagers
3 Servings/Children**

Foods made from milk contribute part of the nutrients supplied by a serving of milk.

Meat
Group

Protein
Niacin
Iron
Thiamin (B₁)

2 Servings

Dry beans and peas, soy extenders, and nuts combined with animal protein (meat, fish, poultry, eggs, milk, cheese) or grain protein can be substituted for a serving of meat.

Fruit-Vegetable
Group

4 Servings

Vitamins A and C

Dark green, leafy, or orange vegetables and fruit are recommended 3 or 4 times weekly for vitamin A. Citrus fruit is recommended daily for vitamin C.

Grain
Group

Carbohydrate
Thiamin (B₁)
Iron
Niacin

4 Servings

Whole grain, fortified, or enriched grain products are recommended.

National Dairy Council

The Basic Four Food Groups.

147

Each day you should have four servings (at least two for adults) from the Milk Group, two servings from the Meat Group, four servings from the Fruit-Vegetable Group, and four servings from the Grain Group. Selecting foods from each of these groups daily should give you a balanced diet.

When choosing fruits and vegetables, be sure to include dark green or yellow vegetables and a citrus fruit or tomatoes each day.

Foods which are low in nutrients and high in calories such as fats, sugar, and baked products made with unenriched flour are not included in the Basic Four. Generally they are used to provide additional flavor and calories.

Become familiar with the Basic Four Food Group pattern. It is not only important for your own health, but also for your job. With this knowledge, you can help customers select balanced meals. If you have the opportunity, you can also help by making menu suggestions to your employer.

Restaurant operators understand the value of nutrition. They use the Basic Four Food Groups as a guide in planning their menus. Generally, a variety of foods from each of the Basic Four Groups is included in the menu. From these menu offerings, customers can select flavorful, nutritious meals. Restaurants also offer complete, well-balanced meals with special prices to encourage customers to select nutritious meals.

CUSTOMER FOOD CHOICES

Of course, it would be ideal if people would naturally like and eat the foods from the Basic Four Food Groups. However, most people have definite feelings about food—they usually develop eating patterns which give them the greatest personal satisfaction. Do you have certain likes and dislikes concerning food? What causes these eating habits?

Personal Preferences

People may avoid certain foods for many reasons. For instance, strong personal dislikes of certain foods may be caused by poor cooking methods. Thus a child who is served overcooked, soggy vegetables may develop a dislike for all vegetables.

Young people often tend to imitate their parents. Therefore if the father does not like a particular food such as salads, the children generally will also dislike that food.

Sometimes people may hesitate to try an unfamiliar food. A man may prefer green beans, carrots, and peas because he is accustomed to their flavor, but may refuse to try other vegetables which he has never tasted.

Adults often hesitate to drink milk—they think of it as a food suitable only for babies and children.

How can the nutritional problems caused by personal opinions and misinformation be handled in menu planning? Menus should include nutritious foods prepared in many different ways. Customers should have a wide choice from which to select. For instance, those who refuse salads may be offered additional vegetables or fruits. Milk may be used in cream soups and desserts.

Cultural Patterns

Families generally develop certain eating habits as part of their culture. Often these

Ethnic foods such as spaghetti and meatballs are popular items in many restaurants.

habits have been repeated within the family for generations and have become family customs. Sometimes these eating patterns are in conflict with good nutrition. For some families, clinging to their established eating patterns gives them a feeling of stability in a changing world.

How do these cultural patterns come about?

National backgrounds may influence eating patterns. For instance, people of Italian origin generally like spaghetti, lasagna, and greens cooked in oil. Chinese enjoy rice, egg rolls, and soya sauce. Those of German background like sausage, sauerkraut, and sauerbraten. Can you think of others?

Many restaurants feature specific nationality foods. Chinese and Italian eating places are very popular. In larger cities, you will find restaurants specializing in French, English, Mexican, Polynesian, Japanese, and other international foods. As a result, many people are familiar with international foods and have developed a taste for them.

Eating habits may also be affected by religious dietary laws. Some Jewish people eat only *kosher foods*—those prepared according to strict, religious dietary laws. Catholics have religious traditions which limit the kinds and quantities of food they eat at certain times. Although many of these laws and traditions are changing with the times, they are deep-rooted customs which many people continue to follow. You may wish to discuss these dietary restrictions in class and trace their origins.

There are also regional eating patterns in the United States that may be part of a person's cultural background. Certain foods are favorites in the southern United States, but are not well known in the north and west. For

instance, many southerners like hominy grits for breakfast and fried chicken with black-eyed peas or collards for dinner. Baked beans and brown bread are a favorite of New Englanders. People in some parts of the country like clam chowder made with milk (New England clam chowder) while others like it made with tomatoes and no milk (Manhattan clam chowder).

Menu planners know that regional favorites are generally expected on a menu. A restaurant near the ocean may specialize in seafood, while a restaurant in a cattle area will feature a variety of steaks.

The amount of money available for food also influences food selection. If money is limited, usually food selection is also limited. Thus a

A restaurant in a coastal city offers an assortment of seafood salads—avocados filled with crabmeat salad, tomatoes stuffed with shrimp salad, and cucumbers spread with lobster salad.

H. J. Heinz Co.

During hot weather, customers may prefer chilled foods such as salads.

Although hot, hearty meals such as beef stew are popular the year 'round, some customers may prefer them only during cold weather.

Dudley–Anderson–Yutzy

person who has never enjoyed a wide variety of foods is apt to prefer a few basic foods. Transportation and food processing have so improved that a great variety of foods at reasonable prices is now available. This tends to encourage people with limited income to try different foods.

Seasonal Preferences

The foods customers select at different seasons of the year also influence menu planning. This is especially true of areas where noticeable climate changes mark the seasons. During hot weather, people may prefer light meals and chilled foods. However, as the weather gets colder and freezing rain and snow become common, most people want hot foods and hearty meals. Thus seasonal changes have an effect on menu planning in many parts of this country.

Some foods are associated with certain holidays and are served regardless of the climate. For instance, warm-weather states such as California, Texas, and Florida offer traditional foods at holiday time—pumpkin pie for Halloween, and roast turkey with trimmings and mincemeat pie for Thanksgiving and Christmas. Can you think of other examples?

Age Group Preferences

Teenage customers generally have eating patterns which tend to be similar in many regions of the United States. They usually want foods such as hot dogs, hamburgers, French fries, and a beverage. Teenagers as a rule have little interest in such dishes as Alaskan Crab Meat or Shrimp à la Creole. Therefore, a restaurant wishing to attract teenagers may feature specialties such as giant hamburgers, cheeseburgers, submarine sandwiches, or other local favorites.

Adults, on the other hand, may enjoy a sophisticated restaurant featuring international foods, or perhaps a family-style restaurant where they can take their children. Elderly people who live on fixed incomes often prefer cafeterias. There they can select foods that not only fit their diets but are economical as well.

PLANNING THE MENU

The menu that you present to the customer is not just a list of any food the manager happens to feel like offering that day. A great deal of thought and careful planning goes into its organization.

Usually, all menus are carefully planned to meet the specific needs of eating establishments and their customers. As said before, the foods offered generally give the customers an opportunity to select nutritious, enjoyable meals.

A different menu may be planned for each meal, each day, or for a week or longer. Some food operations never change their menus. For example, a drive-in may keep the same menu, year in and year out.

Some restaurants prefer simple menus with very little selection. A steak house, for instance, may offer three or four types of steaks accompanied by baked potato, specific vegetable, and salad. The customer can select from an assortment of steaks but has no choice of accompaniments. Other restaurants may feature elaborate menus with a great variety of selections.

National Broiler Council

A restaurant specializing in Polynesian foods offers foil-fried chicken on its menu.

A German-style restaurant features an elaborate buffet of roast duck and pork, sweet-sour red cabbage, sausage on hot potato salad, vegetables, and rye bread and assorted rolls.

Accent International

151

A sandwich shop may offer an assortment of appetizing, nutritious selections. Here a chicken salad sandwich is served open faced, garnished with egg slice, pimiento strips, tomato wedges, and black olives.

A tea room may offer a menu of dainty sandwiches, salads, pastries, and beverages. After-theatre supper restaurants generally feature a late-evening snack menu.

Some restaurants have special children's menus. These offer small portions of the regular menu selections and special combinations at lower prices.

Some menus are specialized. A school lunch menu must be nutritious and still sell at a low price to students. In-plant cafeterias generally must offer meals and snack foods to meet the needs of both the industrial and office workers. Hospitals and nursing homes may stress special diet foods. In addition, they generally have regular meals and snacks for patients and staff members.

Generally, there are separate menus—one each for breakfast, luncheon, and dinner. Depending on the type of restaurant, there may also be a wine list, which names the types of wines available. There may also be a cocktail menu, which lists the alcoholic beverages. Some restaurants have special dessert menus, which are presented when the customers are ready for the final course.

As a rule, the menu organization and the variety and number of selections are based on the following:

Type of service. Counter, drive-in, and vending food service units usually have spe-

Restaurants may specialize in preparing baked potatoes in a variety of ways, such as stuffed baked potatoes with cheese, chives, bacon, or mushrooms.

152

Jimbo Restaurant, Cape Coral, Fla.

Note how counter service provides food accompaniments and menu within easy reach. Well-planned equipment back of the counter provides fast service.

Canteen Corp.

Menus in vending units are generally limited to foods that keep well and are easy to serve.

cific, limited menu selections because food items need to be quick to prepare and easy to serve. On the other hand, cafeteria and table service, which means more leisurely eating, will offer greater menu variety.

Size of the operation. Small operations often lack space or facilities and must offer a limited variety of menu selections. Large operations, however, can feature a greater variety and may offer special menu selections.

Kind of equipment. If equipment is well planned to produce efficiently, greater food selection is possible.

Number and abilities of employees. When food service workers are well trained and supervised, it is possible to increase the variety and quality of foods offered.

The larger the cafeteria, the greater the variety of food it will offer on its menu.

H. J. Heinz Co.

153

Market price and availability of food. When foods are high in price, they are used less frequently on the menu. Generally, high prices are caused by a short supply of that food.

The foods on the menu are generally grouped according to courses: appetizers, soups, main dishes or entrées, vegetables, salads, breads, desserts, and beverages.

Appetizers

An appetizer is a small amount of food served to stimulate the appetite. It may be served as a first course at the table for breakfast, lunch, or dinner.

Fresh fruits in season can be served as appetizers at any meal. The natural sweetness and acidity of the fruit help to stimulate the appetite. A slice of melon served with a lemon or lime wedge, fresh fruit cups with pleasant color contrast, fruit juice, and fruit frappé (fruit juice with a scoop of sherbet) are popular items.

The colors of fruits and fruit combinations should be natural, clear, and bright.

Fruits may be served in glass sherbet dishes and fruit juices in parfait glasses or fruit juice glasses. An underliner is generally used.

Combinations of vegetable juices may be used as appetizers to give variety to the menu. In some areas, it is customary to serve a tossed green salad as an appetizer.

Seafood appetizers include oysters and clams on the half shell, and flaked fish or seafood cocktail with a spicy cocktail sauce. Marinated herring with sour cream is also popular.

Chopped chicken livers with a lemon wedge are frequently featured.

Crackers, wafers, and breads may accompany appetizers served at the table.

For special occasions, appetizers may be served to guests before they are seated. In this case, the appetizers are usually hors d'oeuvres and canapés, served with an alcoholic or non-alcoholic drink.

An *hors d'oeuvre* may be any small, tasty piece of food, served hot or cold, before a meal. Following are some examples of hors d'oeuvres served in restaurants and at social gatherings and cocktail parties:

Cold Hors d'Oeuvres

- Celery sticks stuffed with cheese.
- Raw cauliflower buds with a dip.
- Small pieces of cheese, smoked oysters, clams, meat, fish, or sausages.
- Tiny éclairs filled with a salad mixture.
- Finger foods such as chips and crackers to dip into tangy mixtures.
- Pickled foods.

Hot Hors d'Oeuvres

- Tiny hot croquettes.
- Deep-fried clams, frog legs, shrimp.
- Hot cocktail sausages with dip.
- Oysters broiled in bacon wrap.
- Small meatballs in a tangy sauce.

A *canapé* can be described as a small, open-face sandwich. The base may be a small piece of bread, toast, cracker, or pastry. This can be covered with a tasty spread, meat, fish, or vegetable, and garnished in many ways. Canapés are finger foods and may be served as appetizers before a meal. However, they are more popularly served at large receptions or parties.

Both hors d'oeuvres and canapés are usually served on attractive trays, glass plates, or silver platters. Plastic or wooden picks are usually inserted into hors d'oeuvres so that guests may pick them up easily. The foods should be well prepared, give a pleasing decorative effect, and have good flavor, form, and texture.

Soups

Soups may be served as the first course of a meal. They can be either hot, cold, or jellied, depending on the season and the menu.

Hearty soups such as beef-vegetable and split pea may also be served as the main course, especially at lunch. They are generally accompanied by a salad, beverage, and dessert.

Soups are served in bouillon cups, soup cups, or soup bowls, with the appropriate spoon.

Cold and jellied soups should be chilled in their serving cups until service time. Hot soups should be served steaming hot (77°C) [170°F.], never lukewarm.

Garnishes may be added to soups just prior to service. These include parsley, watercress, croutons, minced olives, thin slices of lemon or egg, shredded vegetables, pimiento strips, chopped bacon, grated cheese, sour cream, or whipped cream.

Crackers, toast, cheese straws, or breads are generally served with soups.

Entrées

The menu term *entrée* refers to the main dish of the meal. Entrées are the meat, poultry, fish, and egg dishes listed on a menu. These

Ramada Inn

For special parties, many restaurants offer a buffet.

An elegant appetizer tray featuring eggs stuffed with crabmeat salad, carrot sticks, celery sticks, black olives, stuffed green olives, and radish roses.

Poultry and Egg National Board

Corning Glass Works

A tempting entrée of golden-brown fish fillets with egg sauce and vegetables. What foods would you add to make this a complete dinner?

main dishes are clearly described, including the method of preparation, the accompaniment, and the price.

Variety in the dinner menu is achieved by a wide selection of entrées. Menus usually feature a choice of eggs, seafoods, poultry, veal, pork, lamb, beef, and cheese.

The entrée description on the menu and the way it is served is determined by the type of restaurant operation. For example, a typical restaurant may offer a choice of favorite American entrées such as steak, roast turkey, fried chicken, hamburgers, and others. A distinctive atmosphere restaurant may offer unusual entrées such as roast duckling and London broil along with a selection of familiar entrées. These may be served with special sauces, garnishes, and accompaniments.

Many foreign terms, especially French, are used for entrées. These indicate the way that they are prepared or served. A study of menus,

the use of a menu dictionary, and on-the-job training will help you become familiar with these terms. Refer to the menu terms at the end of this chapter.

Entrées must be served at the correct temperature and not allowed to stand at room temperature. Special service equipment such as banquet covers for plates, (used to keep the temperature constant), sizzling platters, wooden planks, and heated dishes are used to bring the entrées to the table at the correct serving temperature.

Vegetables

Choices of vegetables on the menu are planned to offer contrast in color, flavor, and texture, and to complement the entrée. Avoid serving two similar vegetables such as cauliflower and broccoli, or creamed onions and creamed potatoes.

The shape as well as the preparation of vegetables is varied to please customers. For example, carrots may be cooked whole or cut in halves, quarters, strips, slices, or cubes. They may be cooked in water and served in assorted sauces, or they may be baked or glazed. Some restaurants may feature fresh vegetables while others may use frozen, canned, dried, or freeze-dried vegetables. Customers will often ask whether vegetables are fresh and how they are prepared.

High-quality, well-cooked vegetables will have a natural flavor, neither bland nor strong. They should have a tender, firm, sometimes crisp texture, and an attractive, clear, natural color. Only quality vegetables should be purchased and correct cooking methods used, as described in Chapter Seven.

Vegetables may be served on the dinner plate or in individual heated vegetable dishes. If family style service is used, the vegetables are placed in serving dishes, to be passed by the guests. Cooked vegetables should be served well seasoned, appropriately garnished, and piping hot.

Salads

A salad may be served as an appetizer to a meal or as an accompaniment. In formal meals, the salad is sometimes served as a course either before or after the entrée.

Accompaniment salads are planned to complement the entrée with which they are served. They should offer a contrast in flavor, appearance, and texture. For instance, the tangy flavor and bright color of fruit salad go well with poultry and pork.

Salads may be served in bowls or on plates. After they are prepared, they should be chilled so that the greens remain crisp. Salads are generally garnished to make them more attractive.

Accent International

For texture contrast, a crisp tossed salad is served with a seafood casserole.

Restaurants with buffet service may offer a large assortment of salads for guests to serve themselves.

Corning Glass Works

The popular Caesar salad is generally prepared at the guests' table by either the maître d' or the waiter or waitress.

Dudley–Anderson–Yutzy

157

Breads

Many restaurants offer an assortment of rolls, muffins, and breads. Others may have only a limited selection of rolls—generally one with a soft crust and one with a crisp crust.

In some restaurants, breads and rolls are kept in warming ovens so that they are at the correct serving temperature.

Hot breads and rolls are generally served in a basket covered with a napkin to retain the heat. They can also be served direct on the bread and butter plates.

Some distinctive atmosphere restaurants feature small loaves of hot bread which are served on cutting boards with knives. Guests help themselves by cutting the bread and passing the slices around on the board.

Desserts

The dessert is a sweet food which usually completes the meal. The number and kinds of desserts found on the menu will depend on the type of food service operation. Desserts generally include cakes, cookies, pastries, puddings, fruits, and ice cream.

Desserts should have good flavor and texture and an attractive appearance. They are generally garnished to present a colorful, final touch to the meal. Hot desserts such as cobbler should be served hot. Cold desserts such as cheese cake should be served chilled.

Food service operators generally plan a varied, daily pattern of desserts. Light, simple desserts such as sherbet or fruit gelatin are best suited for heavy entrées. Hearty, rich desserts such as pie or cake are suitable for light entrées.

Regional and seasonal favorites—Key Lime pie or fresh strawberry shortcake—are usually popular with customers.

Often, a restaurant will include a specialty dessert of the house, which may be an unusual cake, pie, or sundae.

Desserts should be attractively arranged and garnished, and served in appropriate dishes. A chocolate mint parfait, for example, should be served in a parfait glass on an underliner and garnished with perhaps a maraschino cherry or a sprig of fresh mint. A dish of ice cream is generally served with cookies. Pies and cakes are usually served on dessert plates. Pie served with a scoop of ice cream is called *pie à la mode*. One-crust pies are frequently garnished with whipped cream. Apple pie is often served warm with a slice of sharp cheese.

Some restaurants present an attractive variety of cakes, pies, and fancy pastries on a dessert cart or tray, which gives style to their service.

Following are descriptions of some of the popular dessert items:

Baked Alaska—A block of ice cream on a sponge cake base, covered with meringue and browned in the oven.

Peach Melba—A peach half topped with a scoop of ice cream, melba (raspberry) sauce, and whipped cream.

Fruit Mousse—A frozen dessert of whipped cream, gelatin, and fruit.

Meringue—Baked meringue shells made from egg whites, sugar, and flavoring and topped with ice cream and sauce or other fillings.

An assortment of breads and rolls adds variety to a meal. Here you see French, Boston brown, raisin, date-orange, cinnamon, date and nut, whole wheat, white, and cracked wheat breads, along with sesame, kaiser, hard, hamburger, and frankfurter rolls.

A warming oven keeps breads and rolls warm for serving. Note bread baskets and napkins on top of the oven for quick service.

Charlotte Russe—A mold lined with ladyfingers and filled with a thickened, flavored cream mixture; served with sauce and whipped cream.

Bavarian Cream—A molded, thickened mixture made with egg whites, milk, gelatin, whipped cream, and flavoring.

Puff Pastries—Made from a rich pastry which rises into a flaky, tender, and crisp product.

Beverages

Food service units offer coffee, tea, and milk as beverages. Carbonated beverages and fountain specialties may also be served.

Guests seated at their tables may select elegant desserts from the dessert or pastry cart such as cheese cake, strawberry tarts, coconut cream pie, chocolate mousse with sauce, or chocolate éclairs.

C.C. Coffee Shop, Cape Coral, Fla.

Good coffee is an important part of any restaurant menu. Coffee makers, such as this, prepare coffee which is fresh, hot, and ready at all times.

Beverages may be served with the meal or after, depending on the customer's preference. Some people like to drink their beverage after they have finished eating. In this case, the beverage, especially if it is hot, should not be served until the customer is ready for it.

Many restaurants offer cocktails and wine with meals. Keep in mind that the person serving alcoholic beverages must have reached a minimum age specified by law. Check the laws in your state. If you are below the age limit, the hostess or another service worker will generally serve the alcoholic beverage for you.

Menus usually reflect the decor and atmosphere of the restaurant.

USING THE MENU

The menu for the day is often called *carte du jour* (kahrt-du-joor), which is a French term meaning menu or bill of fare for the day.

There is a standard arrangement for most menus. Foods are listed, with the prices beside them, in the order in which they are generally served and eaten. Soups or appetizers are listed first, then entrées, vegetables, salads, breads, desserts, and beverages.

The menu must be suitable for the operation of the food service unit and for its customers. The same menu may be offered every day, or there may be a different one for each day of the week. A card showing the special for the day is often attached to the menu. Holiday menus are generally featured at appropriate times of the year.

There are two types of menus that a food service unit may generally use. One is called the standard or *à la carte* (ah-lah cart) menu. This means that each food item is priced separately.

The second type of menu is the *table d'hôte* (tabluh-dote). It generally features complete meal combinations at set prices, which are listed with the entrées. On a breakfast menu, the table d-hôte meals are usually listed under *club breakfasts*.

Many restaurants have a combination menu which includes both à la carte and table d'hôte prices. Usually a note states that the appetizer, dessert, and beverage are included in the table d'hôte price.

Since the menu is used by the customers, it must be clean, attractive, accurate, and easy to read. It is the show window of the restaurant and helps sell the food.

160

EXAMPLE OF AN À LA CARTE MENU

Appetizers

Choice of Chilled Juice 50
Chopped Chicken Livers 1.50
Fresh Jumbo Shrimp Cocktail 2.50

Soups

French Onion Soup and Croutons 75
Consommé 65
Soup du Jour 65

Entrées

Broiled Lamb Chops with Apple Mint Jelly 7.50
Boneless Breast of Chicken with Rice 6.95
Broiled Chopped Sirloin Steak with Mushroom Sauce 7.50
Broiled Lobster Tail 10.00
French Fried Jumbo Shrimp 5.95

Vegetables

Whipped Potatoes 75
Buttered Green Beans 75

French Fried Potatoes 75

Sandwiches

Ham and Cheese 1.75
Chicken Salad 2.25
Sliced Turkey 1.95

Salads

Green Salad Bowl 2.25
Tomato with Chicken Salad 2.50

Desserts

Warm Apple Pie 1.25
Assorted Ice Creams 75

Beverages

Coffee 30
Tea 30
Milk 40
Cocoa 40

EXAMPLE OF A TABLE D'HOTE MENU

Appetizers

Cream of Chicken Soup

Chilled Fresh Fruit Cup

Chicken Liver Canapé

Iced Tomato Juice with Lemon Wedge

Marinated Herring

Entrées

Roast Prime Ribs of Beef au Jus 8.95

Roast Turkey, Sausage Dressing 7.50

Roast Loin of Pork, Apple Sections 7.50

Lamb Chop Grill with Bacon and Tomato 8.50

Fresh Mountain Trout, Sauté Amandine 6.95

Deep Sea Scallops, Tartar Sauce, Lemon Garnish 6.95

Vegetables

Baked Idaho Potato

Buttered Green Beans

Whipped Potato

Creamed Tiny Onions

Chef's Salad

Dinner Rolls

Coffee, Tea, Milk

Desserts

Pecan Pie

Éclair with Sauce

Pineapple Sherbet

Blueberry Pie

Strawberry Shortcake

Baked Apple

Chocolate Mint Parfait

Dinners

Your dinner includes:

Oven fresh Rolls and Blueberry Muffins • Potato and Vegetable • Salad Bar • Coffee or Tea or Milk

Continental Specialties

Chicken Cordon Bleu 5.95
Pan fried breast of young chicken stuffed with proscuitto ham and gruyere cheese and served with a supreme sauce.

Veal Scaloppine Marsala 6.95
Slices of milk-fed veal sauteed in olive oil and butter, with mushrooms, lemon and Marsala wine

Shaslik Flambe 6.95
Tenderloin of beef chunks on a skewer with peppers, onions, mushrooms and tomatoes, broiled and flamed at your table.

Broiled Spring Lamb Chops 6.75
Tender, juicy loin lamb chops served with mint jelly

Veal Parmigiana 5.95
Thinly sliced cutlet with provolone cheese and tomato sauce served with spaghetti.

Fisherman's Platter 7.50
Golden fried oyster, shrimp, scallops, fillet of flounder, crab cake and clams.

Beefeater Selections

Aged beef broiled to your taste and served with crisp onion rings.

Filet Mignon, 8 oz. 9.95
Petite Filet Mignon, 6 oz. 7.75
New York Strip Sirloin, 12 oz. 9.95
Petite Sirloin Strip Steak 8 oz. 7.75

Beverages

Coffee	.35	Sanka	.35
Tea	.35	Hot Chocolate	.50
Iced Tea	.35	Irish Coffee	1.75
Milk	.50	Sodas	.50

American Favorites

Sauteed Calves Liver 5.50
Sauteed with bacon or smothered onions.

Crabmeat au Gratin 6.95
Alaskan crabmeat sauteed with a rich cheese sauce and served in a casserole with toast points.

South African Rock Lobster Tails 10.95
Broiled petit tails served with drawn butter.

Broiled Cape Scallops 5.95
Cape scallops broiled in lemon butter.

Baked Stuffed Flounder 6.50
Fillets of flounder stuffed with crabmeat baked to a golden brown.

Rainbow Trout 5.95
Broiled or Pan Fried, Almondine.

Grilled Pork Chops 5.95
Juicy center cut chops grilled to perfection.

Sirloin Chopped Steak 4.95
Served with a mushroom and wine sauce or with sauteed onions.

SURF and TURF

A petit filet mignon and a South African Rock Lobster Tail served with drawn butter.

10.95

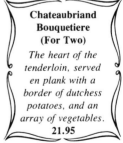

Chateaubriand Bouquetiere (For Two)

The heart of the tenderloin, served en plank with a border of dutchess potatoes, and an array of vegetables.
21.95

Sharaton Inn

The entrées on this menu are described in terms likely to create an appetite for the food. Accompaniments and prices are clearly stated for the convenience of the guests.

Poultry and Egg National Board

Club breakfast menus feature nutritious meals, usually at less cost than à la carte selections. This hearty club breakfast includes two eggs with sausage, fresh fruit, rolls, and coffee.

A well-designed menu that is colorful gets attention. Have you noticed any particularly interesting menus when eating out? Some are huge, some are small. Some have unusual shapes. Others tell interesting facts about the restaurant or region. It is fun to collect menus, and most establishments are glad to give you one as a souvenir. They consider it good advertising. Bring menus to class to compare and analyze the type, format and arrangement. Which have the most appeal? Why?

Merchandising or promoting foods through the menu is done by appealing to the senses. Descriptive terms such as golden brown, piping hot, succulent, young and tender sound good and may stimulate appetites and sales. Describing the ingredients in a food item also helps—a customer rarely orders an unfamiliar food. The way the foods are listed for easy reading is important.

Pricing has appeal also. Specials of the day or of the house, if attractively priced, usually result in volume sales.

You, too, if you are waiting on the customer, can help sell by making suggestions. Sometimes just the mention of a dessert or specialty food will be enough to encourage the customer to buy.

Helping guests select from the menu and answering their questions correctly is one of your responsibilities if you are in a food service job that involves waiting on customers. You should know:

- The day's menu.
- The choices offered.
- The prices.
- How the dishes are prepared.
- The meaning of commonly used foreign menu terms.

THE BREAKFAST MENU

The breakfast menu pattern will probably be similar wherever you work because customers tend to prefer certain foods for breakfast throughout the country. As a rule, these foods include fruits and juices; cereals with cream or milk; eggs; meats such as bacon, ham, and steak; pancakes, waffles, and French toast; hot breads and rolls; and beverages. In some areas, foods such as grits, hashed brown potatoes, and refried beans are also served.

Food service units may use an à la carte or a club breakfast menu or a combination of both.

Menu items are usually served in the following order: fruits and juices; cereals and cream; eggs, meats, and specialties; breads and jams; and beverages. Compare this pattern of service with the two breakfast menus shown.

Sometimes guests do not always notice the club combinations on the menu. They appreciate it when you bring this to their attention, or point out specials, or recommend an appetizing food. A special may be fresh strawberries, melon, or other seasonal foods.

À LA CARTE BREAKFAST MENU

Fruits and Juices

Chilled Orange Juice 40	Chilled Vegetable Juice 40
Chilled Tomato Juice 40	Chilled Prune Juice 40
Apple Sauce 40	Stewed Prunes 35
Sliced Bananas with Cream 45	Stewed Apricots 45

Cereals with Cream

Cream of Wheat 65	Oatmeal 65
Shredded Wheat 65	Toasted Corn Flakes 65
Special K 65	Rice Krispies 65

Breakfast Features

Griddle Cakes with Genuine Vermont Maple Syrup, Broiled Sugar Cured Bacon . . .1.75
Broiled Ham and Fried Egg 1.85
Small Steak. 3.00
Poached Eggs on Toast . . . . (one) .85 (two) .95
Scrambled Eggs . . . . (one) .85 (two) .95
Boiled Eggs . . . . (one) .60 (two) .90
Fried Eggs. . . . . (one) .60 (two) .90
Omelet: Plain 1.35
Broiled Sugar Cured Bacon . . . . (half order .90) 1.15

Hot Breads

Raisin Bran Muffins 40	Corn Toastee 40
Rolls and Butter 35	Special Muffins 40
Toasted English Muffins 40	Doughnuts. 35
Danish Pastry 50	Dry or Buttered Toast 30

Orange Marmalade or Currant Jelly served with above

Beverages

Tea (pot) . . . . . .30 Coffee (cup) . . .35 Sanka (cup) . . . .30 Milk 40

Many people prefer a continental breakfast—juice, rolls, and coffee.

Sheraton Inn

CLUB BREAKFAST MENU

Fruits and Juices

Orange Juice
Stewed Prunes
Stewed Apricots
Tomato Juice

Prune Juice
Apple Sauce
Sliced Bananas
with Cream

Club Breakfasts

1—Choice of Fruit or Juice and Hot Bread,
One Egg—Boiled, Poached or Fried 1.85
2—Choice of Fruit or Juice,
Hot or Cold Cereal with Cream,
Danish Pastry. 1.65
3—Choice of Fruit or Juice and Hot Bread,
Griddle Cakes with Genuine Vermont Maple Syrup
(Served with Crisp Bacon .90 additional) 1.95
4—Choice of Fruit or Juice and Hot Bread,
Broiled Sugar Cured Bacon with a Fried Egg. 1.95
5—Choice of Fruit or Juice and Hot Bread,
Scrambled Eggs with a Toasted Bacon Roll 2.15
6—Choice of Fruit or Juice and Hot Bread,
Broiled Ham with Fried Eggs 2.85

Hot Breads

Toasted English Muffin
Buttered Toast

Corn Toastee
Hot Muffin

Orange Marmalade, Currant Jelly or Honey

Coffee, Tea, or Milk

Cereal served in place of fruit or juice .10 additional

Today's Menu Suggestions

Home Style Soup W/Crackers Cup.. 50¢ Bowl.. 70¢
Iced Tea W/Lemon Wedge.....30¢   Coffee.....30¢

1. FRIED CHICKEN LUNCHEON................. 2.50
       3 Pieces Southern Fried Chicken
          French Fried Potatoes — Cole Slaw
             Roll & Butter

2. SWISS STYLE STEAK LUNCHEON............ 2.75
       Tender Swiss Steak — Vegetable Gravy
          Whipped Potatoes — Choice of Vegetable
             Roll & Butter

CRISP TOSSED SALAD — A LA CARTE .... .50

$2.50   TODAY'S LUNCHEON SPECIAL $2.50
   SPAGHETTI W/MEAT SAUCE — Parmesan Cheese
      Roll & Butter — Choice of Beverage
         Gelatin W/Whipped Topping Or
            Ice Cream W/Chocolate Sauce

---

3. SHOPPER'S DELIGHT..................... 1.50
       Cup of Soup — Grilled Cheese Sandwich
          W/Potato Chips — Choice of Beverage

4. HOT TURKEY SANDWICH................... 2.25
       All White Meat Turkey On Two Slices Bread
          Creamy Whipped Potatoes — Turkey Gravy
             Chilled Cranberry Sauce

TODAY'S DESSERT FEATURES

Selected Fruit Pies ...50¢ Layer Cake........65¢
Cream or Custard Pie ..50¢ Gelatin W/Topping..40¢
Delicious Home Made Ice Box Cheese Cake ......75¢
      Pie or Cake With Ice Cream 10¢ Additional

#8

Restaurants may use a daily, mimeographed insert, similar to this, and clip it to the à la carte menu. This helps guests to select complete, nutritious meals.

THE LUNCHEON MENU

Luncheon menus are designed to meet many needs. For instance, business people generally have limited lunch periods. Shoppers or travelers may be in a hurry. Others, however, may wish a more leisurely lunch. Some customers like a hearty lunch similar to a dinner, while others prefer a light lunch. How does the luncheon menu provide for these needs?

Some restaurants offer a variety of à la carte foods, entrées, and both hearty and light lunch specials. Other restaurants, catering to people with limited time, may feature a few à la carte foods, sandwiches, salads, and several plate lunches. The plate lunch is similar to the table d'hôte menu. It offers a complete meal at a specific price. Distinctive atmosphere restaurants, designed for leisurely meals, may offer a selection of gourmet foods. *Gourmet* (goor-may) is a French word meaning top quality food prepared and served in the finest manner.

Look at the examples of lunch menus from different restaurants. Notice that an entrée may offer the guest a substantial meal such as breaded veal cutlet accompanied by French fries and green peas. A guest wishing a light lunch may select from salads, sandwiches, or soups. Heartier foods are offered for those who want a heavier meal. Menu planners use a variety of names for their luncheon special. These featured luncheons may be given such headings as *chef's special, table d'hôte, shopper's special, today's special, today's feature,* or *dieter's lunch.* How many can you find on the menu examples?

Usually the arrangement of the luncheon menu follows the commonly accepted sequence of courses:

Appetizers—relishes, hors d'oeuvres, soups.
Entrées—eggs, seafood, meats, casseroles.
Vegetables.
Salads.
Sandwiches—usually listed as club or three-decker sandwiches, hot sandwiches, and cold sandwiches.
Desserts—fruits, puddings, cakes, pastries, ice creams, cheese and crackers.
Beverages.

Open-faced sandwiches are popular. For this one, split and toasted hot dog buns are placed open on a plate and topped with bacon strips, onion rings, sliced eggs, and Thousand Island dressing.

Poultry and Egg National Board

168

🌹 LUNCH 🌹
Includes Soup du Jour

HAMBURGER • Our fresh-ground-daily hamburger with French fried onion rings   **3.00**

DOWN UNDER DIET PLATE • Hamburger patty, cottage cheese, sliced tomato and heart of palm   **3.50**

COLD SHRIMP BOWL • With hardboiled egg, tomato wedges and Russian dressing   **4.75**

BRUTUS SALAD • Our answer to the Caesar salad—Bibb lettuce, crisp bacon, croutons, tomatoes, with our own "Caesar" dressing. Et tu Brute!   **3.50**

FRESH SMOKED IDAHO RAINBOW TROUT • With horseradish cream sauce   **4.75**

TERRINE DE MAISON • Cold slices of the chef's special mixture of game, pork and veal seasoned and baked. Garnished with pickles and tomatoes   **3.00**

CRIPPEN SALAD • Watercress, raw mushrooms, hearts of palm, sliced almonds with a vinaigrette dressing   **3.50**

FRESH CRAB AND SHRIMP PLATE • Green Goddess dressing   **5.50**

AVOCADO AND FRESH LUMP CRAB • Green Goddess dressing   **5.75**

COLD LOBSTER • Fresh Florida lobster tails, Green Goddess or Russian dressing   **5.25**

CHEF CHRISTIAN'S NEW ORLEANS' SEAFOOD GUMBO • Our own inspired version of the half soup, half stew made famous in the French Quarter's great restaurants—served with salad   **4.00**

The Down Under Restaurant

This luncheon menu offers hearty lunches especially appealing to men.

Our History-making Sandwiches

(1) The "Wilbur Wright"
*Corned Beef, Swiss Cheese and Cole Slaw
on Pumpernickel* $2.25

(2) The "Wrong Way Corrigan"
*Danish Ham, Swiss Cheese, Tomato,
French Dressing (we make it the right
way—on Rye)* $2.25

(3) The "Eddie Rickenbacker"
*Choose Roast Beef, Tuna or Ham for
this three-decker* $1.95

(4) The "Spirit of St. Louis"
*Crisp Bacon, Lettuce and Tomato, three-
decker* $1.50

(5) The "Red Baron"
A great big Roast Beef beauty on a bun .$1.50

(6) The "Howard Hughes"
A cheeseburger worthy of the name ...$1.35

(7) The "Orville Wright"
The Ultimate Ham Sandwich $1.35

(8) The "Amelia Earhart"
*We made a Beefburger big enough so
you won't lose it* $1.25

(9) The "Wiley Post"
Tuna Fish Salad, plain or toasted $1.25

(10) The "Billy Mitchell"
Give our Grilled Cheese a trial $1.00

Accompaniments

A Cup of Soup......................... 50¢

A Bowl of Soup .... 70¢

Salads .... 50¢

French Fries .... 50¢

The Airport Lounge

This menu features an assortment of hearty sandwiches with accompaniments.

Luncheon menus may include all or some of these courses, depending on the needs of the customers. However, sandwiches and salads are generally the most popular luncheon foods.

Sandwiches

The sandwich is probably one of the most frequently served food items in America today. This is apparent when you see the thriving business done at hot dog and hamburger stands. Sandwich vending machines are becoming more popular. Sandwiches continue to be best-sellers in snack bars and cafeterias.

Sandwiches vary from the typical two slices of bread with filling to hearty three deckers or dainty tea sandwiches. Some hearty sandwiches form the major part of a meal such as hot roast beef sandwich. Others such as ham and cheese on rye can accompany a salad or soup. Most food service operations offer the following types of sandwiches on their menu:

Type	Example from Menu
Regular Cold	Tuna salad.
Three Decker	Three slices of bread with sliced turkey, grilled bacon, lettuce, and tomato.
Regular Hot	Hot beef barbecue.
Broiled	Steak sandwich.
Grilled	Grilled cheeseburger.
Deep Fried	Fish fry.
Baked	Open-faced ham and chicken with cheese sauce.

170

COLD LARDER

ALL-FRESH FRUIT SALAD
Served with Pot Cheese or Sour Cream.................................. 2.75

CHEF'S SALAD BOWL
Julienne of Turkey, Ham, Tongue, Imported Swiss Cheese,
Mixed Greens 3.00

FRESH COLD SEAFOOD PLATTER
Cold Half Lobster, Jumbo Shrimps, Potato Salad, Cole
Slaw, Sliced Tomatoes, Black & Green Olives.................... 5.40

DICED FRESH WHITE MEAT CHICKEN SALAD,
With Tomato Wedges, Hard-Boiled Egg, Mayonnaise........... 3.50

GULF OF MEXICO SHRIMP SALAD
Quartered Egg, Tomato Wedges.................................... 3.85

WHITE MEAT TUNA FISH—Individual Can
Quartered Egg, Olives, Lettuce, Tomato, Mayonnaise or
Russian Dressing... 3.25

THE CATTLEMAN'S COLD PLATTER
Sliced Ham, Breast of Turkey, Tongue, Imported Swiss
Cheese, Cole Slaw, Potato Salad.................................. 3.60

AVOCADO WITH CRAB MEAT AND SHRIMP
Avocado Pear generously filled with Lump Crab Meat and
Tiny Shrimp, Topped with Our Chef's Own
Chutney Dressing.. 4.75

Cattleman Restaurant, N. Y., N. Y.

This menu accurately describes the main dish luncheon salads. Guests may select a light or heavy meal, as desired.

Corning Glass Works

A luncheon featuring rolled roast beef slices and cole slaw. If you were to serve these same items for dinner, what foods would you add to complete the menu?

Food service managers plan varieties of sandwiches, new and unusual combinations, interesting garnishes, and accompaniments, as a means of increasing sales. Giant-size sandwiches usually served on crusty bread or roll under various names such as submarine, hero, or longboy are especially popular with teenagers.

Salads

Luncheon menus usually feature main dish salads, most of which include some form of meat, fish, egg, or cheese. Can you explain why? Refer to the discussion of the Basic Four Food Groups. There are three basic types of main dish salads—vegetable, fruit, and combination.

The *vegetable salad* consists of salad greens and raw vegetables such as carrots, cucumbers, radishes, celery, and tomatoes. Cold, cooked vegetables such as beans and peas may also be used. The salad is tossed with a dressing and

This special, listed on the menu as Chef's Turkey and Ham Platter, is described as an open-faced sandwich with sliced breast of turkey and Virginia ham rolls served with potato chips and sour cream dip.

Dudley–Anderson–Yutzy

172

generally topped with egg slices and strips of cheese and cooked meat. This type of salad is often called a chef's salad. Frequently, a restaurant may feature its own version of a chef's salad with a unique combination of vegetables or a special dressing.

The *fruit salad* is an attractive arrangement of fresh, frozen, and canned fruits on a bed of salad greens, with cottage cheese or sherbet in the center. A special fruit salad dressing is generally served. Small sandwiches made with fruit and nut breads and cream cheese fillings often accompany this type of salad.

The *combination salad* consists of cooked meat, seafood, or poultry, usually cut in bite-size pieces, combined with fruits or vegetables and a dressing. The salad may be served on a bed of greens. Often, however, it is attractively arranged on fruit such as a half of pineapple, avocado, or melon.

Salads are popular luncheon items, especially with people who are weight conscious or those who prefer light meals.

Rolls, breads, and crackers, and a beverage are generally served with main dish salads.

THE DINNER MENU

It is generally the custom for people to relax, socialize, and enjoy a leisurely evening meal. Usually the day's work is over, and people are not in a hurry. Thus, the dinner menu in restaurants and institutions is planned by courses, which may vary in number from the simple two- or three-course dinner to the eight-course formal dinner. Dinners are designed to be nutritious and balanced in texture, color, and form and to offer a variety of choices to the guest.

As said before, the foods on the menu are listed by courses in order of service:

- Appetizers—oysters, clams, shellfish cocktail, fruit juices, hors d'oeuvres, canapés, fruits.
- Soups—listed separately or with the appetizers.
- Fish—offered as a separate course only on the more formal menus found in the distinctive atmosphere restaurants.
- Entrées—main course meats, poultry, and fish.
- Vegetables—listed below the entrées. Some menus may list vegetables à la carte.
- Salads—listed with a choice of dressings below the vegetables or under the à la carte section.
- Desserts—featured near the bottom of the menu or on a separate dessert menu.
- Beverages—listed at the bottom of the menu.

Although restaurant menus vary greatly, let us look at two typical dinner menus. The first is the usual à la carte dinner menu. From this, the guests may select an entrée with vegetables for the price opposite the entrée. If they select an appetizer and a dessert, they pay the price shown for each additional item.

Some menus may feature one-course dinners of charcoal broiled or grilled meats or fish, which are prepared to order.

Distinctive atmosphere restaurants often feature a special dessert menu, which is presented to customers when they are ready for the last course. Notice the unusual items featured on the dessert menu on page 177. Would you be interested in trying any of them?

À LA CARTE DINNER MENU

Chilled Tomato Juice 60   Fresh Fruit Cocktail. 85

Soup de Jour 75   French Onion Soup au Gratin 90

* * * * * * *

Entrée includes potato, salad, and beverage.

Broiled Half Young Chicken, Spiced Watermelon Rind. 4.95

Broiled Chopped Sirloin Steak, French Fried Onion Rings 4.50

Broiled Jersey Pork Chops, Spiced Apple Ring 5.95

Broiled New York Strip Sirloin Steak for Two 14.00

Broiled Filet Mignon, Mushrooms 8.95

Baked Potato, Sour Cream   French Fried Potatoes

Creamy Mashed Potatoes

Au Gratin Potatoes

Tossed Garden Salad   Choice of Dressing

Coffee   Tea   Sanka   Milk   Iced Beverage

From the Sea

Broiled Alaskan King Crab Legs, Lemon Butter Sauce. 7.95

Frog Legs, Fried Golden Brown, Lemon Tartar Sauce 5.50

Fresh Lobster à la Newburg en Casserole, Toast Points 8.50

Golden Fried Ipswich Clams, Coleslaw. 5.95

Broiled Red Snapper, Butter Sauce, Lemon Garni 6.25

Desserts

Fresh Strawberry Shortcake . . . . . 1.25   Ice Cream or Sherbet 50

Homemade Pies . . . . 1.00   Crême de Menthe Sundae 1.25

Italian Spumoni 75   Chocolate Sundae 1.25

TABLE D'HÔTE DINNER MENU

Appetizers

Selection of One

Homemade Chicken Noodle Soup   Chilled Juices:
Baked French Onion Soup   Orange, Pineapple, Vegetable, Tomato

*   *   *   *   *   *

Entrées

Fresh Lobster à la Newburg en Casserole, Sherry Wine 8.50
Fried Deep Sea Scallops, Tartar Souce, Lemon Garni 6.50
Baked Canadian Lake Trout, Lobster Newburg Sauce 6.50
Roast Prime Ribs of Beef, au Jus 8.75
Roast Long Island Duckling, Dressing, Apple Sections 7.50
Fried One Half Premium Spring Chicken, Pineapple Fritter 5.95
Grilled Certified Ham Steak, Spiced Fruit Sauce 5.25
Brisket of Corn Beef and Cabbage 4.90
Choice German Pot Roast of Beef with Buttered Noodles 4.90

From Our Charcoal Broiler

New York Cut (Aged) Sirloin Steak, Fried Onion Rings 8.50
Prime Tenderloin Steak, Sautéed Mushroom Caps 9.00
French Cut Lamb Chops, Mint Jelly 7.95
Land and Sea (Rib Eye Steak and Broiled Lobster Tail) 10.00

Assorted Salad Tray

Roquefort Cheese Dressing . . . . .50 extra

Potato   *Vegetable*

Baked California Long Whites   Buttered Home Grown Sweet Carrots
Whipped   Baked Summer Squash

Desserts

Choice of Homemade Pastry or Ice Cream: Vanilla, Chocolate, Strawberry, Butter Pecan

Your customer has ordered this meal of baked pork chop, baked potato, asparagus, sesame roll, and coffee. He asks you to recommend a dessert. What would you suggest?

Corning Glass Works

What foods would you select to make this entrée of broiled lobster tails a complete dinner?

Corning Glass Works

A nutritious dinner selected from a cafeteria menu. What Basic Four Food Groups are represented?

Dudley–Anderson–Yutzy

176

Desserts such as this charlotte russe are popular menu items. A charlotte russe has a base or crust made of ladyfingers with a whipped cream or custard-gelatin filling.

Dudley–Anderson–Yutzy

DESSERT MENU

Danish Honey Wine Parfait
Strawberry Parfait
Baked French Custard à la Mode with Red Raspberries
Strawberry Rhubarb Pie
Georgia Pecan Pie
Strawberry Cheesecake with Whipped Cream
Hawaiian Pineapple Chunks in Cointreau Liqueur
Bavarian Crême-Filled Chocolate Éclair à la Mode
Butter Pecan Ice Cream
Angel Food Cake à la Mode with Hot Chocolate Fudge
Freestone Peaches in Port Wine
Hot Butterscotch Sundae

❧ LUNCHEON ❧
Includes Soup and Salad

LOBSTER CARDINAL • Fresh Florida lobster with a light lobster cream sauce **5.75**

FRESH IDAHO TROUT MEUNIERE OR AMANDINE 6.75

OYSTERS ROCKEFELLER • Baked oysters with chopped spinach and Pernod **4.00**

OYSTERS KIRKPATRICK • From New Orleans' Commander's Palace. Baked oysters
with tomato sauce, bacon and Parmesan cheese **4.00**

OYSTERS SAVANNAH • Baked oysters with chopped shallots, bacon,
green pepper and pimiento **4.00**

MUSHROOMS CREAM GEORGE • Fresh mushrooms cooked with butter, sherry, cream
and seasonings. Served over toast **3.00**   Served with hamburger patty **4.25**

STEAK GEORGE • A small strip sirloin with our Mushrooms Cream George **7.75**

FRESH CHICKEN LIVERS AND MUSHROOMS SAUTÉ 4.00

VEAL CURRY INDIENNE • Cubes of veal in a French cream-curry sauce served
with rice and chutney **5.50**

SWEETBREADS FINANCIÉRE • Sautéed with fresh mushrooms, olives and
Madeira wine, then simmered in *espagnole* sauce **6.00**

EGGS BENEDICT 4.50

QUICHE MICHELE • Our original egg custard pie filled with Cheddar cheese,
fresh mushrooms and ham **3.25**

HARDING'S CORNED BEEF HASH WITH POACHED EGGS 4.50   With *hollandaise* **5.00**

SAUERBRATEN • Served with fresh red cabbage and dumplings **4.25**

CREPE PRINCESSE • French pancake filled with chicken and baked au gratin **4.00**

CHICKEN GEORGE • Boneless chicken breast covered with our
Mushrooms Cream George **4.00**

BENGAL CHICKEN CURRY • An authentic Indian curry dish. Hot, spicy. Served
with chutney, rice and cucumber **4.25**

CANNELONI VIEILLE MAISON • Our French version of an Italian favorite. A delicate
crepe filled with ground veal and spinach, topped with fresh tomato sauce **4.50**

VITELLO TONNATO • The Italian classic cold-sliced braised veal napped with a tuna sauce **5.00**

ONION TART NICQISE • Onions, tomatoes and ripe olives baked in a crust **3.00**

COFFEE • TEA • MILK .75

The Down Under Restaurant, Ft. Lauderdale, Fla.

A luncheon menu from a French restaurant. Notice the use of descriptive French words.
Look up the meanings of those you do not understand.

ENTRÉES

COQ AU VIN • Chicken cooked in red wine with fresh mushrooms, shallots and herbs **7.75**

CHICKEN MADAGASCAR • Chicken sauteed with green peppercorns, brandy, *demi-glace* and cream, served with our homemade *spätzle* **8.00**

BENGAL CHICKEN CURRY • An authentic Indian curry dish. Hot, spicy. Served with chutney, rice and cucumber **7.75**

CANARD À L'ORANGE • The French classic roast duck with orange sauce and wild rice **9.00**

CANARD AU POIVRE VERT • Braised duck simmered in green peppercorn cream sauce. Wild rice **9.50**

VEAL CORDON BLEU • Thin slices of ham and Swiss cheese layered between veal cutlets, lightly breaded and sautéed in butter **9.75**

VEAL CURRY INDIENNE • Cubes of veal in a French cream-curry sauce served with rice and chutney **8.50**

VEAL PICATTA • Medallions of the finest *plume de veau* sautéed in lemon butter **8.75**

VEAL NAPOLITAINE • Veal with fresh tomato sauce and spaghetti **9.75**

SWEETBREADS FINANCIERE • Sautéed with fresh mushrooms, olives and Madeira wine, then simmered in *espagnole* sauce **9.00**

SAUERBRATEN • The German classic marinated beef served with homemade dumplings and fresh red cabbage **7.75**

FRENCH-CUT LAMB CHOPS • Mint or béarnaise sauce **9.25**

TENDERLOIN TIPS STROGANOFF 8.00   WITH WILD RICE 8.75

BEEFSTEAK TARTARE 8.00

STEAK GEORGE • A strip sirloin accompanied by fresh mushrooms in cream sauce **8.75**

TOURNEDOS CHORON • Twin filet mignons served with an artichoke bottom filled with asparagus tips and topped with choron sauce. (Béarnaise and tomato purée lightly whipped) **11.00**

FILET MIGNON, BÉARNAISE SAUCE, FRENCH FRIED ONION RINGS 11.00

NEW YORK SIRLOIN, BÉARNAISE SAUCE, FRENCH FRIED ONION RINGS 11.00

THE DOWN UNDER'S BEEF WELLINGTON • A filet mignon larded with Strasbourg liver pate, topped with a mushroom puree, encased in a pastry crust and baked **12.00**

ESQUIRE'S CARPETBAG STEAK • A 14 oz. New York strip sirloin, with a pocket of herb-marinated fresh oysters and broiled; it is served with a classic *sauce diable*, wild rice, and a broiled tomato *provençale* **12.00**

The Down Under Restaurant, Ft. Lauderdale, Fla.

You may enjoy studying the entrée descriptions from this French restaurant menu. Look up the meanings of the menu terms you do not understand.

MENU TERMS AND THEIR MEANINGS

Many foreign terms are used in describing food items on the menu. You should know the correct meanings of these terms so that you will be able to answer customers' questions. Commonly used menu terms are:

Term	Pronunciation	Meaning
à la	(ah-lah)	After the style or fashion.
à la carte	(ah-lah-cart)	On the bill of fare; prepared as ordered.
à la king	(ah-lah-king)	Served in a cream sauce containing mushrooms, green peppers, and pimientos.
à la mode	(ah-lah-mode)	Usually means a scoop of ice cream served on or alongside a piece of pie.
anchovy	(an-cho-vee)	A small salted fish used for appetizers.
antipasto	(an-tee-pas-to)	Relishes and other foods used as a first course with Italian dinners.
au beurre	(oh-burr)	Cooked in butter.
au gratin	(oh-grahtin)	Baked with a sauce and cheese.
au jus	(oh-ju)	Served in its natural juice.
au lait	(oh-lay)	With milk.
barbecue	(bar-be-kyou)	Cooked in a sauce of tomato, vinegar, and seasonings.
béarnaise	(ber-nays)	A light, fluffy sauce made of eggs, butter, onion, and seasonings.
béchamel	(bay-sha-mell)	A basic white sauce made of chicken or veal stock and milk or cream, thickened with flour and butter, and seasoned.
bisque	(bisk)	A thick cream soup, usually made of shellfish.

bouillabaisse	(boo-ya-bays)	A thick fish soup or stew.
canapé	(can-a-pay)	A small piece of bread, toast, or cracker spread with savory foods and served as an appetizer.
carte du jour	(kahrt-du-joor)	Menu of the day.
compote	(kom-pote)	Fruit stewed in syrup.
consommé	(kon-so-may)	Clear meat stock; hot or jellied.
créole	(kray-ol)	Prepared with tomatoes, green peppers, and onions.
croissant	(krwa-san)	Crescent-shaped rolls.
croutons	(kroo-tons)	Small pieces of fried or toasted bread used as accompaniments for soups or salads.
demitasse	(deh-mee-tahs)	Small cup of coffee; after-dinner coffee.
duchess potatoes	(doo-ches)	Mashed potatoes that contain egg yolk and squeezed through a pastry tube for decoration.
éclair	(ay-klair)	French pastry filled with custard or whipped cream; may be iced.
en brochette	(ahn-bro-shet)	Broiled on a skewer.
entrée	(ahn-tray)	The main dish such as meat or fish.
en casserole	(ahn-kahs-e-rol)	Served in the dish in which it was baked, generally an individual casserole or ramekin.
fillet	(fee-lay)	A boneless loin cut of beef, veal, or pork, or a boneless strip of fish.
fricassée	(free-kah-say)	Meat or chicken stewed and served with white sauce.
garnish		An edible food used to decorate another.

glacé	(glah-say)	Frosted, glazed, or iced.
hollandaise	(hol-lan-days)	Sauce made of egg yolks, butter, lemon juice and seasonings.
hors d'oeuvre	(ohr-derv)	Savory food served as appetizers.
Italienne	(ee-tal-ee-yen)	Dishes using Italian sauces and cheeses.
jardinière	(zhar-din-eeyair)	A mixture of garden vegetables.
julienne	(zhu-lee-yen)	Cut in thin strips.
lyonnaise	(li-a-nays)	Heavily seasoned with onions and some parsley.
maison (à la)	(may-zon)	Specialty of the house.
mayonnaise	(may-on-ays)	A salad dressing made of egg yolk, oil, and lemon juice or vinegar, beaten together and seasoned.
melba sauce		Cooked, thickened raspberry sauce served over ice cream. Called Peach Melba, if ice cream is on peach half.
mignon fillets	(min-yon)	Small, tender fillets from beef tenderloin.
meringue	(meh-rang)	Egg whites and sugar beaten stiff. Used to make small shells which are filled; also spread on pies and browned.
newburg	(nu-berg)	Cream sauce thickened with eggs and flavored with sherry.
oeuf	(uff)	Egg.
parfait	(par-fay)	Ice cream and sauce arranged in layers in a parfait glass and frozen; garnished with whipped cream.
paté	(pah-tay)	A fine paste mixture.

purée	(pu-ray)	A thick, sieved vegetable or fruit; a thick soup made of sieved vegetable pulp.
ragout	(ra-goo)	A rich stew of highly seasoned meat and gravy.
ramekin	(ram-eh-kin)	A small, individual heat-proof dish in which food is baked and served.
rissolé	(ree-soh-lay)	Browned.
sauté	(saw-tay)	Cook in small amount of fat.
soufflé	(soo-flay)	A light, puffy, baked egg mixture served as an entrée. When sweetened, can be served as a dessert.
table d'hôte	(tabluh-dote)	A meal served in several courses at a set price.
vichysoisse	(vee-shee-swaz)	Cold cream of potato soup, seasoned with onion or leeks.

Let's Think It Over

1. The menu not only sells the foods, but also controls the entire food service operation. Thus, it must be planned, organized, and used with skill and care.

   • What three things does the menu tell the customer?
   • Name five specific points you should know about the menu in order to answer customer's questions.
   • How do the following basic factors affect menu organization?
     Number and abilities of employees.
     Kind of equipment.
     Size of operation.
     Type of service.
     Market price.

2. Knowledge of nutrition plays an important part in menu strategy.

   • List the four basic food groups, with their daily requirements, and explain how menu planners use this nutrition guide.
   • How do the following affect eating habits and therefore the planning of restaurant menus?
     Family customs.
     Personal opinion.
     Religious beliefs.
     Family economics.
     Regional foods.

3. Various types of menus are used in food service operations.

- Explain each of the following:
  À la carte.
  Carte du jour.
  Table d'hôte.
  Club.
  Combination.
- How and why do luncheon menu offerings differ from a dinner menu in most restaurants?
- Describe the courses a restaurant might serve in an eight course formal dinner.
- If a customer asked you the meaning of the following menu terms, how would you answer?

Hors d'oeuvre.	À la mode.
Canapé.	À la king.
Entrée.	Au gratin.
Au jus.	Au beurre.
Bisque.	Brochette.
Glacé.	Lyonnaise.

Let's Investigate

1. Study a collection of menus from local restaurants, coffee shops, drive-ins, and cafeterias. Analyze these menus and report your findings in relation to the following:

- Ways the menu provides for an easy selection of balanced, nutritious meals.
- Meanings of menu terms that are new to you and the class.
- Styles of menu presentation and types of meals served.

2. Select a typical breakfast, luncheon, or dinner from a restaurant menu. List the type of kitchen equipment that would be necessary to prepare the food.

3. Interview the manager of a food service unit in your community or nearby areas. What menu planning strategy is used to meet customer needs and increase their business? Consider such items as local menu favorites, food combinations, prices, seasonal preferences, and descriptions on the menu. Report your findings to the class.

Chapter 9

Catering

What does catering mean? To cater means to provide food and service for social functions for clubs, private parties, businesses, and community organizations. The person who provides this service is a *caterer*.

A caterer may operate from his home kitchen or use an available community, school, or commercial kitchen. Well-known restaurants may also provide catering services.

Catering differs from a restaurant operation. The caterer is mobile and does not have a daily routine schedule of meals. He provides food and service wherever needed, both indoors and outdoors. He needs to adapt readily to differing situations. To be successful, he must have a good understanding of food merchandising.

Catering is an excellent way to start a business of your own with minimum overhead expenses. You will probably find both professional and amateur caterers in your community. How do they differ? How do they operate?

WORDS TO KNOW
Caterer
Catering
Special occasion caterer
Food specialist
Amateur caterer
Overhead expenses
Yield

PROFESSIONAL CATERING

In Chapter Two we discussed food service jobs. Catering is another interesting career possibility. Catering differs in every locality, and caterers have many specialities. There are basically four kinds of professional caterers.

The Food Specialist prepares sandwiches, canapés, hors d'oeuvres, or single food items in quantity. These are usually prepared in his own home and priced in bulk such as sandwiches priced by the dozen. He may deliver or the customer may have to pick the food up. He does not provide table service.

The Prepared Meal Expert prepares and sells casseroles, boxed meals, cold plates, salad plates, buffet, and dinner party specialties. He usually delivers the food, but provides no table service. He charges either by the dozen or by the number of servings for such foods as casseroles.

The Special Occasion Service Caterer provides party meals for large functions such as weddings, receptions, political rallies, picnics, and anniversaries. The customer selects the meal from a sample menu. The caterer prepares the meal in his own kitchen, delivers the food, supplies buffet or table service, and may even supply serving equipment and dishes. His prices are based on the number of people served.

Elaborate buffet service such as this is available from professional caterers. Special decorative themes, unique foods, and complete service are often included.

Dudley–Anderson–Yutzy

The Caterer Director provides a detailed, elaborate, and extensive catering service. He can plan and carry out the details of the invitations, decorations, menu service, and entertainment. He often creates the theme of a party and secures the dining room or banquet hall. He specializes in such novelties as carved ice centerpieces, foods prepared in special shapes, and elaborate desserts and cakes. He must be an expert in all types of entertaining. A flat fee is charged for this service. This means the caterer charges or fixes a certain price for each type and size of service.

AMATEUR CATERING

Many adult and youth community groups include the service of food in their programs. A good meal is an excellent way to bring people together for sociability or business and perhaps some profit. This food service area is generally called amateur or non-professional catering because men, women, and youth work on a volunteer basis. Members of the organization give their time and labor freely as their community contribution. Food may also be donated by members and friends.

When amateur catering is done for profit, it is usually for a specific goal such as new athletic equipment, renovation of a building, or official trips for group members.

Have you ever helped in amateur catering? You may find many opportunities within your community to develop your skill in food service through volunteer work. You might help in the food preparation and service. You might even help plan and organize large group feedings for the organizations to which you belong.

187

Harry Hooper, Cape Coral, Fla.

Clubs and organizations often prepare and serve a public meal to earn money for special projects.

A caterer arranges a simple buffet of finger foods for a home reception, including crackers and cheese and roast beef to be sliced for sandwiches.

Meils

Salvation Army Nutrition Program

Hot food prepared in this central kitchen is packed in insulated containers to be transported to a senior citizen center.

Sandwiches, wrapped in plastic for a catered picnic.

Edison Community College, Ft. Myers, Fla.

What groups provide amateur catering in your community? Churches, volunteer fire departments, senior citizen groups, community centers, Scouts, and school and youth clubs frequently provide food service. This may be as simple as a coffee hour or as complex as a dinner. For small groups, food may be prepared by members at home and brought to a central meeting place. Pot luck suppers are one example of this method. For larger groups, food may be purchased and prepared by members either in their homes or in a community or school kitchen.

Roast turkey, chicken, baked ham, international foods, fish dinners, clambakes, and pancake-and-sausage breakfasts are popular in many localities. The menus may feature such favorites as homemade fruit pies, locally produced maple syrup, and homemade rolls and cakes.

When profit is the aim, community organizations may schedule their public meals for special occasions that will attract people such as holidays, voting days, community bazaars or outings, and football games and other sporting events. Some organizations catering public dinners will advertise, "All you can eat for $2.50," or "Children under ten free if accompanied by parents." This has a strong sales appeal to individuals and families who are eating out.

Organize the Work

When you are involved in an amateur catering project, careful planning is needed. Food should be served efficiently and economically. The project should be an enjoyable experience for both workers and guests.

188

These modular mobile units fit together for complete cold and hot food setups. They offer great flexibility in catering various events.

Skillful management during preparation and service can help make up for lack of equipment, supplies, and work space. Improvising equipment and utensils may also help. *Improvising* means to make do with whatever is at hand. For example, Scouts, when camping out, may improvise eating and cooking utensils from tin cans. For amateur catering projects, large cooking containers may be made from oil drums, galvanized pails, and buckets. These would have to be well-cleaned and sterilized with boiling water. If a double boiler is needed, place a kettle on a rack inside a larger kettle or pan containing water.

Amateur catering is generally organized by dividing the work among committees. A *planning committee* usually has the responsibility for selecting the menu and the standardized quantity recipes. It determines the number of people to be fed and the amount of food to be prepared, makes the market order, estimates the meal cost and price to be charged, and decides on the method of service. A *kitchen committee* may buy the food and prepare it and wash the cooking utensils. A *dining room or service committee* may set up dining or buffet tables and serve the food to guests, with the assistance of the kitchen committee. A *cleanup committee* washes the dishes and does other cleanup. A *publicity committee* prepares publicity, takes reservations, and sells tickets.

Plan the Menu

Success in amateur catering depends a great deal on a carefully selected menu. The menu should be well-balanced, offer contrasts in color, texture and flavor, and appeal to the

group served. What do you need to consider when you plan a menu for large groups?

Choose seasonal foods which are plentiful and low in cost.

Select foods according to the people in the group. If the group is made up of families, select foods enjoyed by all ages and include a variety of beverages. Serve hearty foods for active people and lighter, nutritious foods for less active groups and senior citizens.

Keep in mind the size of servings you want for each guest and the cost. Extras such as relishes, large servings, and second helpings raise food costs.

In planning the menu for a catered event, select foods that are easy to prepare and serve such as a roast. Here a student displays his carving skills at a banquet.

Choose foods that are easy to prepare, especially for large group meals. Remember, the amount and variety of food you can serve depends on the preparation and serving equipment and the number of experienced workers available. For example, you may want to serve foods such as chicken or potato salad. Do this *only* if you have enough refrigeration space to keep the food at a temperature below 4°C [40°F.]. Otherwise, harmful bacteria, which cause food poisoning, may develop.

Plan menus that are appropriate to the occasion and the method of serving. For outdoor catering and buffet service, choose foods which do not spoil easily, and which retain an appetizing appearance if allowed to stand several hours before being eaten. Select foods which can be easily served and which guests can eat even when holding the plates on their laps.

For camping or hiking, choose foods that can be safely packed and carried without spoiling quickly. Dehydrated foods, because of reduced volume and weight and ease of storage and transportation, are excellent for camping trips.

Festive foods and special garnishes are especially appropriate for indoor banquets.

Estimate Quantity of Food Needed

You need to know the number of people to be served and the size of the servings. It is usually a good idea to plan on extra servings, also. This is difficult to know beforehand, especially when guests serve themselves, as in buffet service. The size and number of servings can best be controlled by preparing individual plates rather than letting guests help themselves.

Past records, the experience of other groups, and advance ticket sales or reservations will help you to estimate the number of guests to be served. The amount of food to be prepared and purchased will depend on this figure.

Keep the following in mind as you plan the food preparation and the market order:

- Remember, the workers will have to eat, too. Add the number of workers to the number of guests you expect to get the total number to be served.
- Decide on the size of serving for each food.
- Decide whether or not second servings of food or beverages will be offered.
- Select and use standard quantity recipes. Some sources of standard quantity recipes are listed under *Student Resources*. Family-size recipes cannot be increased easily to large quantities. If you use family-size recipes, you will have greater success if you prepare them in small batches.
- Increase the size of the standard quantity recipe, if needed, to give the correct number of servings.
- Prepare the market order by listing all the food and supplies needed to prepare and serve each food on the menu. Remember to include garnishes, butter or margarine, cream or coffee lightener, sugar and artificial sweetener, coffee, tea, milk, lemon slices, salt, pepper, detergent, paper supplies, and other miscellaneous items.

The charts on pages 199–208 show the amounts of food to buy for fifty servings. This can help you to make market orders once you have the menu planned.

Figure the Cost of the Meal

List the total cost of the food, whether purchased or donated. If the meal is being served for profit and some people donate food, the cost of this food should be included as it represents time and money. The people who donate food may then be reimbursed or given the meal free. However, if a meal is being planned for members of an organization and each family donates food, the cost of the meal for each person is usually reduced so that just enough money is taken in to meet expenses.

If wages are paid to workers, labor costs must be included. Workers sometimes donate their time in amateur catering projects so that an organization can make more money. In such cases, there are no labor costs.

Add any miscellaneous expenses to the total cost of the meal. These may be flowers or other decorations, paper goods, rental or laundering of linens, rental of a building, room, or equipment, and cleaning supplies.

The steps in figuring the cost of the meal are:

- Price the cost of the foods on the market order. Total their cost.
- Estimate the cost of labor and miscellaneous expenses. Add these to the food costs.
- Divide the approximate total meal cost by the number of people to be served. This will give you the approximate meal cost for one person.

Decide on the Price of the Meal

If you are serving meals for profit, one way to set the selling price is to multiply by two

United Fresh Fruit and Vegetable Assoc., Stouffer

If refrigerated equipment is available on a catering job, fruit and other deserts may be prepared ahead and stored on a cold table, ready for service.

the estimated cost per person. For example, if the cost of the meal per person is $1.50, charge $3.00 per person. Sometimes your figures may result in odd cents, such as $2.23 or $3.13. It is simpler to make change if the selling price is set so that it can be divided by 25. So, instead of $2.23 or $3.13, set the selling price at $2.25 or $3.50.

If you do not wish to make a profit, add 25 percent to the estimated food cost. For example, the food cost is $.80. Multiply that by 25 percent, which gives $.20. Add $.20 to $.80 and charge $1.00. This will allow for changes in food costs and will help prevent a loss of money if fewer people attend.

Sheridan Vocational Center, Fla.

Be sure to have adequate refrigeration for foods that must be chilled such as salads. If not, plan to serve foods that do not require refrigeration.

SANITARY FOOD HANDLING

Sanitary food handling is extremely important in amateur catering. Outbreaks of bacterial food poisoning are often traced by health officials to community or public meals. Generally, these outbreaks are caused by carelessness in food handling. This may be due to the lack of or the limited equipment and facilities and the use of untrained workers.

Since amateur catering tends to be informal, people are not always as careful in handling food as they should be. Study Chapter Thirteen, which treats the cause and prevention of foodborne diseases, before you prepare and serve meals to any groups.

The precautions below apply specifically to amateur-catered meals.[1]

- Practice good housekeeping and maintain high standards of personal hygiene.
- Use safe water from a municipal supply or a good quality source.
- Buy federally or locally inspected meats. Buy oysters, clams, fish, and poultry from approved sources only.
- Buy sanitary, individually packaged foods when possible. Such items might be milk, cream, sugar, condiments, and ice cream.
- Use only pasteurized milk, cream, ice cream, butter, and cheese.
- Provide refrigeration below 4°C [40°F.] for food in which harmful bacteria may grow. These include the following: salads that use salad dressing, mayonnaise, or cream dressing; salads with eggs, fish, poultry, or meat; sandwich fillings such as ham, turkey, or egg salad; cream puddings; cream puffs; cream pies; and pies with a custard base including pumpkin and squash pies.
- Cook pork and pork products to an internal temperature of 85°C [185°F.].
- Avoid using home-canned, non-acid foods such as peas, string beans, corn, and meats. If you must use them, boil them for 15 minutes before serving.
- Do not stuff turkeys. Prepare the dressing, refrigerate it, and bake in shallow pans as near serving time as possible. Roast turkey whole without stuffing. To save time, cut turkey in pieces and roast.

[1] Adapted from information prepared by the New York State College of Human Ecology, Cornell University, Ithaca, New York.

- Dispose of garbage and other wastes after each meal by municipal collections, burying, or burning. Keep waste receptacles clean.
- Do not allow anyone with an open cut or wound on the hands to touch the food. Harmful bacteria from the wound can become mixed with the food and cause food-borne illness if anyone eats it.

OUTDOOR AMATEUR CATERING

Outdoor cooking is especially popular during the good-weather months. Youth groups such as Scouts plan and prepare food for hiking and camping trips. Both adult and youth organizations make money for special projects by serving outdoor chicken barbecues, beef barbecues, clambakes, fish fries, and other picnic meals. Some groups sell foods such as hamburgers, hot dogs, candy, ice cream, and beverages at local sport events, field days, or fairs.

Outdoor meals are casual and informal. People do not expect the special service and convenience of restaurant dining. Thus, outdoor cookery and service are somewhat easier for amateur groups to manage. Usually, such meals are simpler than those organized by professional caterers. For example, a typical chicken barbecue menu planned by a community group might include barbecued chicken, potato salad, cole slaw, baked beans, rolls, coffee or milk, and pie or cake.

For amateur catering, use individually packaged foods such as condiments, coffee whitener, sugar, and milk. Disposable paperware cuts down on cleanup.

Dudley—Anderson—Yutzy

193

Salvation Army Nutrition Program

Note the emphasis on sanitary food handling in this program. The hot food, prepared in this kitchen, is carefully covered and packed in insulated food carriers. The caterer can then transport it to another destination safely.

Outdoor chicken barbecue for a group . . .

Supplies for outdoor catering are often brought in and used out of a truck.

The barbecue pit is made from sheet metal sections. These are fastened together to provide enough space for barbecuing large numbers of chicken broiler halves. The pit is usually placed on a road or pathway, not on the grass. It is fired with charcoal briquettes which are allowed to burn until there is a good bed of red-hot coals.

A table for supplies is convenient in outdoor cookery.

The grates on which the chicken will be placed are made of wire mesh. Handles on both ends make it easy to turn the grates. Here the grates are being placed on the flaming fire pit to burn off any residue that might remain from previous use or storage.

The chicken broiler halves were kept packed in ice in crates until ready to use. They are lined up on the grates which are then placed over the fire.

A clean pail makes a handy container for barbecue sauce. The sauce is brushed on the chicken halves continually during the cooking process.

Pans such as these are used to carry the barbecued chicken to the serving area.

A quantity of chicken is turned easily at one time by turning the grate.

195

Clambake . . .

The fire for the clambake is made by resting a large piece of sheet metal on six upright concrete blocks. Firewood is spread under the metal between the block. Here you see the loaded pit, ready to be fired.

The lobsters, clams, and corn are covered with mesh and then with damp seaweed.

To load the pit, food is arranged over a layer of damp seaweed covered with mesh—lobsters in the center, clams in mesh bags around the lobsters, and ears of corn on top.

After the top layer of seaweed is placed on the food, the fire is started. The food will be ready for service in 1-1/2 to 2 hours.

196

Hot food is generally prepared with somewhat limited equipment over barbecue pits, grills, and open fireplaces. Paper and plastic supplies, pre-packaged condiments, relishes, and foods such as packaged potato chips, ice cream cups, and cookies may be used. Each person picks up his food from a buffet table and eats at a picnic table or sits on the grass.

Perhaps a brief description of a typical outdoor meal prepared by a professional caterer will help you to understand the work involved. Let us use a clambake as an example. These popular events are generally served picnic style. Fraternal organizations, labor unions, clubs, and businesses often promote all-day clambakes. Usually, some form of entertainment or sports is provided. Guests can eat as much and as often as they wish.

The menu may include a great variety of food such as raw and steamed clams, clam chowder, hot sausage sandwiches, steak sandwiches, sweet potatoes, chicken, hot dogs, Swedish meat balls, cold shrimp, assorted relishes, salads and cheeses, corn on the cob, and cold and hot beverages.

The price of such a clambake depends on the number and variety of foods ordered by the organization and the number of people served. Generally, the clambake will be priced from $7 to $10 per person for 100 to 150 guests. The number of workers needed to prepare the food will depend on how much pre-preparation can be done and the equipment available. Some caterers use three to five workers for 150 guests and approximately 12 workers for 500 guests.

Although some foods such as salads and baked beans are prepared indoors, the majority of the hot foods are prepared outdoors over wood or charcoal-fired fireplaces, grills, or pits. Large steamers and copper wash tubs with wooden slats on the bottom are used for steaming clams, chicken, shrimp, corn, and sweet potatoes. Pits, fired with charcoal briquettes, and turning racks are used for barbecuing chickens. Paper and plastic supplies are used for the food service. Caterers will usually set up two to three grill and serving areas so that guests can be served efficiently.

A caterer from a seashore area, specializing in outdoor shellfish bakes, may use a different preparation method. Fresh lobsters (one or two to a person), two dozen clams in individual mesh bags, and corn on the cob are placed in layers over a wood-fired pit. Each layer is separated by aluminum foil. A thick layer of wet seaweed is placed on top. The moisture from the seaweed on the hot coals produces steam, which cooks the food. Approximately ten minutes after the seaweed stops dripping, the meal is ready to serve.

This method of cooking has been used in many parts of the world. Tourists to Hawaii often enjoy a luau where a small suckling pig is cooked in a pit. The pig is wrapped in ti-plant leaves, and water is thrown on the hot rocks to form steam. If fish is cooked this way, it is called a hikilau.

Since outdoor catering in northern states occurs only during the summer months, you may find an opportunity here for work experience during your vacation.

CAREERS IN CATERING

If you have an interest in food and enjoy people, catering can be challenging and creative work for you. It gives you the opportunity to work at parties, special celebrations, and festive occasions. A caterer must supply excellent food, serve guests graciously and efficiently, and handle all details for the customer. This helps to build a good reputation.

You may even be looking ahead to a future as a caterer with a business of your own. Whether or not you are, your work as a caterer's helper or at community meals will give you an opportunity to practice quantity food preparation. You will probably have a chance to learn menu planning and efficient work methods and to observe how orders of different sizes are handled. You will also have an opportunity to understand the methods used, the stamina needed, and the value of a creative food style.

FOOD TO BUY FOR 50 SERVINGS[2]

The foods listed in the chart below are those most likely to be used in amateur catering projects. You can obtain additional information from college and university extensions services, institutional management colleges, hotel and restaurant schools, or quantity food preparation books.

Here are suggestions for using the information in the chart:

- The amount to buy is for 50 servings of the size stated, not necessarily for 50 people. If your servings are larger than the ones specified, the amount listed to buy

[2]*Ibid*

will not be enough for your particular situation.
- Although these charts give the amount of food to buy for 50, they can also be used to plan purchases when you need less or more than 50 servings. For example, if you need 25 servings, divide the amount to buy by 2; if you need 100 servings, multiply the amount to buy by 2; if you need 150 servings, multiply the amount to buy by 3.
- To determine the amount to buy for an exact number of servings, such as 180, use these steps:

Divide the number of servings (180) by 50.

$$
\begin{array}{r}
3 \\
50\overline{)180} \\
150 \\
\hline
30 = 3^{30}/_{50} \text{ or } 3\frac{3}{5}
\end{array}
$$

Multiply the quotient (final number) in the above step $(3\frac{3}{5})$ by the amount to buy for 50 servings such as 20 pounds of beef.

$$
\begin{array}{r}
3\frac{3}{5} \times 20 \text{ (pounds)} = 20 \\
\times 3\frac{3}{5} \\
\hline
60 \\
12 \\
\hline
72 \text{ pounds—} \\
\text{amount} \\
\text{to buy for} \\
180 \text{ servings.}
\end{array}
$$

AMOUNTS TO PURCHASE FOR 50 SERVINGS
Canned Fruits and Vegetables, No. 10 Cans[1]

Fruits	Servings per Can	Size of Serving	Cans to Buy for 50 Servings
Apples (pie pack)	3 pies	$\frac{1}{6}$ or $\frac{1}{8}$ pie	2 to 3
Applesauce	25	120 mL [$\frac{1}{2}$ c.]	2
Apricots, halves	25 to 30	3 or 4	2
Cherries, sweet	30	120 mL [$\frac{1}{2}$ c.] (10 to 12 cherries)	2
Fruit cocktail	25	120 mL [$\frac{1}{2}$ c.]	2
Peaches, halves	24 to 27	$1\frac{1}{2}$ or 2	2
Pears, halves	24 to 27	$1\frac{1}{2}$ or 2	2
Pineapple slices	25 to 28	1 or 2	2
Plums, purple	25 to 30	2 or 3	2

Vegetables	Servings per Can	Size of Serving	Cans to Buy for 50 Servings
Beans, green or wax	20 to 23	85–100 g [3 to $3\frac{1}{2}$ oz.]	$2\frac{1}{4}$ to $2\frac{1}{2}$
Beets	22 to 26	85–100 g [3 to $3\frac{1}{2}$ oz.]	2 to $2\frac{1}{4}$
Corn, cream style	27 to 30	100–115 g [$3\frac{1}{2}$ to 4 oz.]	$1\frac{3}{4}$ to 2
Corn, whole kernel	22 to 26	85–100 g [3 to $3\frac{1}{2}$ oz.]	2 to $2\frac{1}{4}$
Peas	25 to 29	70–85 g [$2\frac{1}{2}$ to 3 oz.]	$1\frac{3}{4}$ to 2
Potatoes, sweet			
Syrup pack	20 to 25	115–140 g [4 to 5 oz.]	2 to $2\frac{1}{2}$
Dry pack	20 to 25	115–140 g [4 to 5 oz.]	2 to $2\frac{1}{2}$
Tomatoes	25 to 29	100–115 g [$3\frac{1}{2}$ to 4 oz.]	$1\frac{3}{4}$ to 2

Fresh Fruits

Kind and Unit of Purchase	Weight, Measure or Count per Unit	Approximate Size of Serving	Amount to Buy for 50 Servings	Additional Information
Apples Pound	2 to 3 medium apples per 0.45 kg [1 lb.]	120 mL [$\frac{1}{2}$ c.] sauce	7–9 kg [15 to 20 lbs.] for sauce or pie	0.45 kg [1 lb.] before peeling yields 720 mL [3 c.] diced or sliced; 1–1.2 L [$4\frac{1}{2}$ to 5 c.] pared, diced, or sliced weigh 0.45 kg [1 lb.]; 1 peck (5.4 kg) [12 lbs.]
Peck	1 peck weighs 5.4 kg [12 lbs.]			
Bushel	1 bushel weighs 21.8 kg [48 lbs.]			

[1] Weight: 2.7 kg to 3 kg [6 lbs. 2 oz. to 6 lbs. 12 oz.]. Measure 2.8 to 3 L [12 to 13 c.]. If more than one but less than two No. 10 cans are required, use No. $2\frac{1}{2}$ cans to provide the extra amount needed.

Fresh Fruits (Continued)

Kind and Unit of Purchase	Weight, Measure or Count per Unit	Approximate Size of Serving	Amount to Buy for 50 Servings	Additional Information
Apples (cont.) Box	1 box contains from 80 to 100 large or 113 to 138 medium apples			makes 4 to 5 pies, 3.8 to 4.7 L [4 to 5 qts.] of sauce, 6.6 to 7.6 L [7 to 8 qts.] of raw cubes.
Cranberries Pound	0.45 kg [1 lb.] measures 0.95 to 1.2 L [1 to 1¼ qts.]	60 mL [¼ c.] sauce	1.8 kg [4 lbs.] for sauce	0.45 kg [1 lb.] makes 720 to 840 mL [3 to 3½ c.] of sauce or 660 mL [2¾ c.] of jelly.
Strawberries Quart		120 mL [½ c.]	9.5 to 12.3 L [10 to 13 qts.]	0.95 L [1 qt.] yields 720 mL [3 c.], hulled; 0.9 L [1 qt.] yields from 5 to 6 servings of fruit.
		80 mL [⅓ c.] for shortcake	7.5 to 9.5 L [8 to 10 qts.]	0.9 L [1 qt.] yields 0.47 L [1 pt.] hulled and crushed, which yields 6 servings of sauce for shortcake.

Fresh Vegetables

Kind and Unit of Purchase	Weight, Measure or Count per Unit	Approximate Size of Serving	Amount to Buy for 50 Servings	Additional Information
Cabbage Pound		Raw: 30 to 60 g [1 to 2 oz.]	3.6 to 4.5 kg [8 to 10 lbs.]	0.45 kg [1 lb.] raw yields 0.9 to 2.4 L [4 to 6 c.] shredded. 1.8 L [2 qts.] raw, shredded, weight 0.45 kg [1 lb.]
		Cooked: 70 to 85 g [2½ to 3 oz.] or 120 mL [½ c.]	5.4 to 6.8 kg [12 to 15 lbs.]	
Carrots Pound	6 medium carrots per 0.45 kg [1 lb.]	Cooked: 70 to 85 g [2½ to 3 oz.] or 120 mL [½ c.]	6.4 to 7.2 kg [14 to 16 lbs.]	0.45 kg [1 lb.] yields 480 mL [2 c.] cooked and diced.
		Raw: 2 to 7.5 cm [2- to 3-inch] strips	0.9 to 1.1 kg [2 to 2½ lbs.] for raw strips	840 mL [3½ c.] diced, raw, weighs 0.45 kg [1 lb.]

Kind and Unit of Purchase	Weight, Measure or Count per Unit	Approximate Size of Serving	Amount to Buy for 50 Servings	Additional Information
Cucumbers Single	1 cucumber weighs 284 to 397 g [10 to 14 oz.]	Raw: 5 to 7 slices (60 mL) [¼ c.]	8 to 9	1 medium yields 420 to 480 mL [1¾ to 2 c.] of peeled slices.
Celery, Pascal— Bunch	1 medium bunch weighs 0.9 kg [2 lbs.]	Cooked: 70 to 85 g [2½ to 3 oz.] or 120 mL [½ c.] Raw: 1 or 2 pieces	7 to 10 bunches 3 to 4 bunches	1 medium bunch yields 1.3 L [1½ qts.] raw, diced.
Lettuce Head	1 medium head weighs 0.7 to 1.1 kg [1½ to 2½ lbs.] before trimming	Raw: ⅙ to ⅛ head	6 to 8 heads for salad 4 to 5 heads for garnish	10 to 12 salad leaves per head; 1 head un-trimmed yields 1.3 to 1.9 L [1½ to 2 qts.] shredded.
Onions Pound	4 to 6 medium onions per 0.45 kg [1 lb.]	Cooked: 85 to 100 g [3 to 3½ oz.] or 120 mL [½ c.]	6.4 to 7.2 kg [14 to 16 lbs.]	0.45 kg [1 lb.] yields 600 to 720 mL [2½ to 3 c.] chopped.
Parsley Bunch	1 bunch weighs 28 g [1 oz.]			1 medium bunch yields 60 mL [¼ c.] finely chopped.
Peppers Pound	5 to 7 peppers 0.45 kg [per lb.]			0.45 kg [1 lb.] yields 480 mL [2 c.] finely diced.
Potatoes: Sweet Pound	3 medium pota-toes per 0.45 kg [lb.]	100 to 115 g [3½ to 4 oz.]	7.7 to 9 kg [17 to 20 lbs.]	
White Pound	3 medium pota-toes per 0.45 kg [lb.]	115 to 130 g [4 to 4½ oz.] or 120 mL [½ c.] mashed or creamed	6.8 to 9 kg [15 to 20 lbs.]	0.45 kg [1 lb.] yields 540 mL [2¼ c.] diced.
Spinach Bag Bushel	285 to 570 g [10 to 20 oz.] per bag	Cooked: 85 to 100 g [3 to 3½ oz.] or 120 mL [½ c.]	7.7 to 9 kg [17 to 20 lbs.] of homegrown; 12 to 15 285 g [10-oz.] bags, cleaned	1 285 g [10-oz.] bag yields 2.8 L [3 qts.] raw, coarsely chopped for salad.

Fresh Vegetables (Continued)

Fresh Vegetables (Continued)

Kind and Unit of Purchase	Weight, Measure or Count per Unit	Approximate Size of Serving	Amount to Buy for 50 Servings	Additional Information
Squash: Summer Pound Winter Pound		Cooked: 70 g [2½ oz.] or 120 mL [½ c.] Cooked: 85 g [3 oz.] or 120 mL [½ c.] mashed	5.9 to 7.2 kg [13 to 16 lbs.] 11.4 to 13.6 kg [25 to 30 lbs.]	
Tomatoes 454 g [Pound]	3 to 4 medium	Raw: 3 slices	4.5 kg [10 lb.] fresh for slicing	0.45 kg [1 lb.] yields 480 mL [2 c.] diced or wedges.

Frozen Fruits and Vegetables

Kind	Size of Serving	Amount to Buy for 50 Servings
Frozen fruits Frozen vegetables	120 mL [½ c.] 80 mL [⅓ c.] (70 g) [2½ oz.] 120 mL [½ c.] (85 g) [3 oz.]	4.5 kg [10 lbs.] 3.4 kg [7½ lbs.] (three 1.1 kg [40-oz.] packages) 4.5 kg [10 lbs.] (four 1.1 kg [40-oz.] packages)

Note: Frozen fruits and vegetables are available in paper packages or tin cans of varying sizes. New types and sizes of containers are continually being developed to meet market demand. Buy frozen fruits and vegetables by the kilogram [pound] regardless of the size of the package.

Meats[2]

Kind	Size, Weight, Measure or Count per Unit	Approximate Size of Serving	Amount to Buy for 50 Servings	Notes
Beef: round steak		115 to 130 g [4 to 4½ oz.] boneless meat uncooked	7.8 to 9 kg [17 to 20 lbs.]	Bottom round requires longer cooking than top round.

[2] Unit of purchase: kilogram [pound].

Meats (Continued)				
Kind	*Size, Weight, Measure or Count per Unit*	*Approximate Size of Serving*	*Amount to Buy for 50 Servings*	*Notes*
Pork: roast loin, trimmed	4.5 to 5.5 kg [10 to 12 lbs.]	70 to 85 g [2½ to 3 oz.] cooked	9 to 11.4 kg [20 to 25 lbs.]	
Ham: Fresh (bone in)	4.5 to 5.5 kg [12 to 15 lbs.]	70 to 85 g [2½ to 3 oz.] cooked	9 to 11.4 kg [20 to 25 lbs.]	Smoked shoulder may be substituted for ground or cubed ham in recipes.
Smoked, tenderized (bone in)	4.5 to 5.5 kg [12 to 15 lbs.]	85 to 100 g [3 to 3½ oz.] cooked	7.8 to 9 kg [17 to 20 lbs.]	
Canned, boneless ready-to-eat	0.9 to 4 kg [2 to 9 lbs.]	85 g [3 oz.] cooked	4.5 to 5.5 kg [10 to 12 lbs.]	
Meat cakes	0.45 kg [1 lb.] of raw meat measures 480 mL [2 c.] of meat, packed	115 to 130 g [4 to 4½ oz.] uncooked; 1 to 2 cakes	7.8 to 9 kg [17 to 20 lbs.]	One kind of meat only or combinations may be used such as 4.5 kg [10 lbs.] of beef and 2.2 kg [5 lbs.] of veal or pork, or 4.5 kg [10 lbs.] of fresh pork and 2.2 kg [5 lbs.] of smoked ham.
Meat loaf or extended meat patties	0.45 kg [1 lb.] of raw meat measures 480 mL [2 c.] of meat, packed	115 to 130 g [4 to 4½ oz.] cooked meat loaf	5.5 to 6.8 kg [12 to 15 lbs.]	
Sausage: Links	8 to 9 large per 0.45 kg [lb.]	3 links	7.8 to 9 kg [17 to 20 lbs.]	Yield varies with proportion of fat that fries out in cooking.
Cakes		170–230 g [6 to 8 oz.] raw meat = 2 cakes	9 to 11.4 kg [20 to 25 lbs.]	
Wieners	8 to 10 per 0.45 kg [lb.]	2 wieners	4.5 to 5.2 kg [10 to 11½ lbs.]	

Seafood			
Kind	Size, Weight, Measure or Count per Unit	Approximate Size of Serving	Amount to Buy for 50 Servings
Clams		1 to 2 doz.	50 to 100 doz.
Fresh or frozen fish fillets		115 to 150 g [4 to 5 oz.]	6.4 to 7.7 kg [14 to 17 lbs.]
Lobster (fresh)		1 to 2 lobsters	50 to 100 lobsters
Oysters:			
For frying	24 to 40 large per L [qt.]	4 to 6 oysters	6.6 to 7.6 L [7 to 8 qts.]
For scalloping	60 to 100 small per L [qt.]	4 to 6 oysters	3.8 to 4.7 L [4 to 5 qts.]
For stew	60 to 100 small per L [qt.]	4 to 6 oysters	2.8 L [3 qts.]

Poultry			
Poultry Eviscerated, Ready-to-cook	Weight, Each	Approximate Size of Serving	Amount to Buy for 50 Servings
Chicken:			
Fryers	0.8 to 1.1 kg [1¾ to 2½ lbs.]	¼ fryer to ½ fryer	11.4 to 13.6 kg [25 to 30 lbs.]
For fricassée	1.1 kg to 2 kg [2½ to 4½ lbs.]	115 to 180 g [4 to 6 oz.] including bone	11.4 to 13.6 kg [25 to 35 lbs.]
For dishes containing cut-up cooked meat		30 to 60 g [1 to 2 oz.] of boneless meat	5.9 to 7.7 kg [13 to 17 lbs.]
Turkey	4.5 to 11.4 kg [10 to 25 lbs.]	60 to 70 g [2 to 2½ oz.] of boneless meat	11.4 to 13.6 kg [25 to 35 lbs.]

NOTE:

Chicken: 1.4 kg [3 lbs.] of eviscerated chicken yield approximately 0.45 kg [1 lb.] of cooked meat removed from the bone.

Turkey: Yield of meat depends on type and size of bird. Broad-breasted birds yield a larger amount of boneless meat than the standard-type bird. Larger birds yield a greater amount of boneless meat than smaller birds.

Staples		
Items	*Equivalent Weights and Measures*	*Proportions for Use*
Baking powder	28 g [1 oz.] measures 38 mL [2½ T.]; 0.45 kg [1 lb.] measures 600 mL [2½ c.]	
Chocolate	1 bar equals 8 28 g [1-oz.] squares	
Cocoa	240 mL [1 c.] weighs 112 g [4 oz.]; 0.45 kg [1 lb.] measures 960 mL [4 c.]	480 mL [2 c.] of cocoa for 50 c. of beverage or 9.5 L [2½ gals.]
Cornmeal	0.45 kg [1 lb.] measures 720 mL [3 c.]	
Cornstarch	28 g [1 oz.] measures 45 mL [3 T.]; 0.45 kg [1 lb.] measures 720 mL [3 c.]	120 mL [½ c.] to thicken 0.9 L [1 qt.] of liquid for pudding.
Flour:		
White	240 mL [1 c.] weighs 112 g [4 oz.]; 0.45 kg [1 lb.] measures 960 mL [4 c.] or 0.9 L [1 qt.]	
Graham or whole wheat	240 mL [1 c.] weighs 137 g [4⅘ oz.]; 0.45 kg [1 lb.] measures 800 mL [3⅓ c.]	
Gelatin:		
Granulated	28 g [1 oz.] measures 45 mL [3 T.]; 0.45 kg [1 lb.] measures 720 mL [3 c.]	30 to 45 mL [2 to 3 T.] per 0.9 L [1 qt.] of liquid
Flavored	28 g [1 oz.] measures 38 mL [2½ T.]; 0.45 kg [1 lb.] measures 600 mL [2½ c.]	240 to 300 mL [1 to 1¼ c.] per 0.9 L [1 qt.] of liquid
Rice	0.45 kg [1 lb.] raw measures 510 mL [2⅛ c.]; 0.45 kg [1 lb.] after cooking measures 1.7 L [1¾ qts.] and yields 20 No. 16 scoops (60 mL) [¼ c.] or 15 No. 12 scoops (80 mL) [⅓ c.]	1.1 to 1.4 kg [2½ to 3 lbs.] for 50 servings
Shortening, vegetable	0.45 kg [1 lb.] measures 600 mL [2½ c.] (560 mL [2⅓ c.] firmly packed)	
Sugar:		
Light brown Packed to hold the shape of the cup	0.45 kg [1 lb.] measures 480 to 540 mL [2 to 2¼ c.]	It is difficult to measure brown sugar accurately.
Confectioners'	240 mL [1 c.] weighs 149 g [5⅓ oz.]; 0.45 kg [1 lb.] measures 720 mL [3 c.]	Used for frosting.

Staples (Continued)		
Items	*Equivalent Weights and Measures*	*Proportions for Use*

Sugar (Cont.):
  Cube
 	
  Granulated
	0.45 kg [1 lb.] equals 50 to 60 large or 100 to 120 small cubes
	240 mL [1 c.] weighs 196 g [7 oz.]; 0.45 kg [1 lb.] measures 510 mL [2⅛ c.]
		
		0.3 to 0.45 kg [¾ to 1 lb.] to sweeten 50 c. of coffee or 8 mL [1½ t.] per 240 mL [1 c.]

Miscellaneous Foods

Items	*Equivalent Weights and Measures*	*Amounts for 50 Servings*
Bread: White and whole wheat	1 0.45 kg [1-lb.] loaf = 18 slices; 1 0.9 kg [2-lb.] club loaf = 24 slices; 1 0.9 kg [2-lb.] Pullman (sandwich) loaf = 36 slices	Usually allow 1½ slices per person to accompany meal.
Crumbs, fine, dry	0.45 kg [1 lb.] measures 1200 mL [5 c.]	
Soft, chopped	0.9 L [1 qt.] weighs from 168 to 196 g [6 to 7 oz.]; 0.45 kg [1 lb.] measures 2.3 L [2½ qts.] or approximately 1440 mL [6 c.]	
Butter or Margarine:	0.45 kg [1 lb.] measures 480 mL [2 c.]; 28 g [1 oz.] measures 30 mL [2 T.]	0.45 to 0.7 kg [1 to 1½ lbs.] (available in wholesale units cut into 48 to 90 pieces per 0.45 kg [1 lb.]; 60 count gives average size cut) **OR** allow 57 to 114 g [⅛ to ¼ lb.] for each table.
For table	0.45 kg [1 lb.] cuts 48 to 60 squares	
Cheese: Cheddar or American	0.45 kg [1 lb.] chopped measures 0.9 L [1 qt.] or 960 mL [4 c.]	
Brick	1 brick weighs 2.3 kg [5 lbs.]; 0.45 kg [1 lb.] yields 16 thin slices (28 g [1 oz.] each) 0.45 kg [1 lb.] cuts 20 cubes for pie—22 g [⅘ oz.]	1.6 kg [3½ lbs.] sliced for sandwiches 1.1 kg [2½ lbs.] for pie.

Miscellaneous Foods (Continued)		
Items	*Equivalent Weights and Measures*	*Amounts for 50 Servings*
Cottage	0.45 kg [1 lb.] measures 480 mL [2 c.]; 0.45 kg [1 lb.] yields 8 to 9 No. 10 scoops (84 to 112 g [3 to 4 oz.] servings); 12 to 13 No. 16 scoops (56 to 63 g [2 to 2¼ oz.] servings); 25 No. 30 scoops (28 to 42 g [1 to 1½ oz.] servings)	2.7 kg [6 lbs.] for 50 average servings (No. 10 scoop, approximately 120 mL [½ c.]
Coffee:		
Ground	0.45 kg [1 lb.] drip grind measures 1200 mL [5 c.]	0.45 kg [1 lb.] coffee and 9.5 L [2½ gals.] of water for 50 servings.
Instant		600 mL [2½ c.] of instant coffee and 9.5 L [2½, gals.] of water for 50 servings.
Eggs, medium	Whole = 6 per 240 mL [1 c.]; Yolks = 14 per 240 mL [1 c.]; Whites = 9 per 240 mL [1 c.]; 1 doz. hard-cooked and chopped measures 840 mL [3½ c.]	1 case = 30 doz.
Fruit or vegetable juice	1 1228 mL [46-oz.] can measures approximately 1.35 L [1½ qts.]. 1 can, No. 10, measures 3120 mL [13 c.] or 2.9 L [3¼ qts.]	4⅓ 1288 g [46-oz.] cans, or 5.9 L [6½ qts.]; 119 mL [4-oz.] glass or 120 mL [½ c.] per serving.
Honey	0.45 kg [1 lb.] measures 320 mL [1⅓ c.]	2.3 kg [5 lbs.] (30 mL [2 T.] per serving).
Ice Cream:		
Brick	1 0.9 L [1-qt.] brick cuts from 6 to 8 slices	7 to 9 bricks (may be purchased in slices individually wrapped).
Bulk	3.8 L [1 gal.] yields from 25 to 30 servings dipped with a No. 10 scoop	7.6 L [2 gals.]
Lemonade		9.5 L [2½ gals.] (25 to 30 lemons for 1.1 L [1¼ qts.] of juice).
Milk:		
Powdered or dry:		
Instant	320 mL [1⅓ c.] instant and 900 mL [3¾ c.] water make 0.9 L [1 qt.] re-liquified milk	

Miscellaneous Foods (Continued)

Items	Equivalent Weights and Measures	Amounts for 50 Servings
Regular	240 mL [1 c.] (113 g [4 oz.] and 0.9 L [1 qt.] water make 0.9 L [1 qt.] reliquified milk	
Peanut butter		1.8 kg [4 lbs.] for sand-wiches.
Potato chips	0.45 kg [1 lb.] measures 4.5 L [5 qts.]	0.9 kg [2 lbs.], 21 to 28 g [¾ to 1 oz.] per serving.
Puddings		5.7 L [6 qts.], 120 mL [½ c.] per serving.
Rolls		6 to 6½ doz., 1½ rolls per serving.
Salad mixtures		6.6 to 7.6 L [7 to 8 qts.], 120 mL [½ c.] per serving.
Salad dressings: 　Mayonnaise		0.9 to 1.4 L [1 to 1½ qts.] for mixed salads. 720 to 960 mL [3 to 4 c.] for garnish, 15 mL [1 T.] for each salad.
French		0.7 to 0.9 L [¾ to 1 qt.]
Sandwiches: 　Bread	1 0.9 kg [2-lb.] loaf (35 cm [14-inch]) cuts from 30 to 35 medium or from 35 to 40 very thin slices.	3 35 cm [14-inch] loaves.
Butter		340 g [¾ lb.] to spread 1 slice of 50 sandwiches; 0.7 kg [1½ lbs.] to spread both slices.
Fillings		1.7 to 1.9 L [1¾ to 2 qts.], 30 mL [2 T.] or 1 No. 30 scoop per serving; 2.4 to 2.9 L [2½ to 3 qts.], 45 mL [3 T.] or 1 No. 24 scoop per serving.
Soups		11.4 L [3 gals.] or 48 serv-ings
Tea	0.45 kg [1 lb.] measures 1440 mL [6 c.]	Hot—50 individual tea bags or Iced—85 g [3 oz.] bulk tea to 9.5 L [2½ gals.] of water and chipped ice.

Let's Think It Over

1. Catering is providing food and services to groups. How are the following alike and different?

   - The food specialist.
   - The prepared meal specialist.
   - The special occasion caterer.
   - The caterer director.

2. Explain how a meal price is arrived at for:

   - A nonprofit meal.
   - A profit meal.

3. How would you organize a club group to serve a nonprofit dinner for 50 people in your school cafeteria? Discuss:

   - The menu.
   - Type of service.
   - Amount of food to order.
   - Cost of meal.
   - Working committee duties.

4. What sanitary precautions must be observed to serve a chicken barbecue at a picnic area? Discuss:

   - Personal hygiene.
   - Refrigeration.
   - Cleanliness.
   - Disposal of waste.

Let's Investigate

1. Interview an amateur or a professional caterer in your area. Tell the class about him:

   - Type of business specialty.
   - How he got started.
   - Volume of business.
   - Job opportunities for beginners.
   - Advantages and disadvantages of his job.

2. Interview someone who specializes in outdoor barbecuing or clambakes. Ask him what jobs you might expect to do as his helper. Report to the class.

3. Discuss opportunities to start a catering business in your school or area that would take little money. Consider what might be involved in each of these:

   - A concession at the football games.
   - Serving a simple meal to a club.
   - Selling fancy cakes, sandwiches, and cookies.

Chapter **10**

Service Jobs

When you work in service jobs in the food industry, you are in direct contact with the public. Since you serve or wait on customers, you can help to influence the sale of the food. In some operations you may also assemble salad plates and fruit or shrimp cocktails.

Do you enjoy all kinds of people? Do you like to meet strangers? Do you think you can serve customers willingly and courteously? If so, you may find service jobs satisfying. It is exciting to organize your work, serve people efficiently, and know that they are pleased. As we discussed earlier, the aim of food service operators is to satisfy the customer. That is why you hear it said, "The customer is always right."

WORDS TO KNOW	
Service jobs	Room service
Fringe benefits	Drive-ins
Counter worker	Policy of the house
Runners	Floaters
Split shift	Snack bar
Bus service	Carry-out worker
Gratuities	Carhop

TYPES OF SERVICE JOBS

The jobs available depend on the kind of service provided. Following is a list of jobs in different types of food service units:

Waiter or waitress.
Dining room helper (busboy or busgirl).
Counter worker.
Food runner.
Carry-out worker.
Fountain worker.
Carhop.

As said earlier, most restaurants provide on-the-job training. This is necessary so that each worker will understand the expected standards and will carry out the policies of management.

However, if you know the basic skills and duties needed for the job, as well as the duties of each worker, you will have more to offer an employer and will be happier in your work.

REQUIREMENTS FOR SERVICE JOBS

When you have a service job, you have to be on your feet, standing or walking, much of your working day. Equipment is generally designed for use by workers of average size. Therefore the very tall or very short worker will often find service work tiring and difficult. Employers also find that overweight people tire more easily. As a result, employers generally prefer workers of average size—medium height and weight.

Other requirements employers look for are:

- General good health and stamina.
- No offensive habits.
- Clear skin.
- Well groomed appearance.
- Feet and legs in good condition.
- Ability to read and speak English correctly, write legibly, and add sales checks correctly.

- High school diploma.
- Training in food service.
- Physical examination.
- Age range from 18 to 50 years, male or female, according to the policy of the food service unit.

SALARY AND ADVANCEMENT

The wages you will be paid will depend on the policy of the establishment in which you are working and on the current Minimum Wage Law. Food service operators are allowed to pay less than the minimum wage to waitresses and waiters if meals are provided and tips received. For example, if the current wage is $2.30 an hour, you may receive $1.80 an hour. Remember, states differ in minimum wage regulations for food service workers, so inquire locally to learn the wage rate paid in your state or community. As you gain ability and experience, your wage will usually increase to a maximum determined by your employer.

Tips or *gratuities* received may range from $50 to $100 a week, again depending on the type and size of the unit. Usually more tips are received in resort areas and distinctive atmosphere restaurants. Tips are usually given direct to waiters, waitresses, and carhops. However, some places collect the tips as a percentage added to the customer's bill and then divide this between waitresses, waiters, and carhops. You are required by law to declare the total amount of your tips on your federal income tax return.

All workers have fringe benefits, which may include paid sick leave, full pay or extra pay for holidays, group insurance and pension

H. J. Heinz Co.

Waiter-trainee gets instructions on how to serve dessert course for formal dinner.

Waitress-trainee learns where supplies are stored.

H. J. Heinz Co.

plans, meals and coffee breaks, and uniform and/or uniform laundering.

The good waitress or waiter who proves his skill and ability and shows interest in doing his job well will be able to advance to a better job. The line of advancement is from busboy or girl to special server or waiter; waiter to captain or host; waitress to head waitress or hostess; host or hostess to service supervisor; service supervisor to assistant manager or manager.

Counter workers receive fewer tips and therefore may receive a higher wage. There is great variety in counter jobs. Opportunities for advancement are also available, depending on the size of the operation. In restaurant counter service units, you may advance from counter worker to head counter worker, to counter supervisor, to checker or cashier.

BEGINNER'S SERVICE JOBS

Now let us take a close look at each of the beginning service jobs. Although some of the work may be similar, there are specific duties which differ in each job. You may find that your abilities are better suited to one type of work than another. Work experience is one way to help you determine this.

Waiter or Waitress

As a waiter or waitress, you have a chance to work with and meet many interesting people. You are an important member of the employer's sales team because you sell food and service to the public. You are also responsible for the satisfaction and comfort of the customers you serve.

Most of the time, you can have a choice of different beginner's jobs, depending on the type and location of the food service unit. You may work in an informal counter service operation or in the more formal, dignified service of a distinctive atmosphere restaurant. You may start in a simple service job and be promoted to a more complicated one as your skill increases. The knowledge and training you receive will prove useful in any job in food service.

Duties are divided into the three areas of selling and serving food, side work, and closing. You may be assigned any of the following, depending on the size and type of unit and the number of people employed.

Serving Duties

- Seat guests.
- Hand out menu.
- Make menu suggestions to guests. (Know the foods on your menu and their preparation.)
- Take orders and write menu order.
- Serve orders to guests.
- Present guests with check and take money. (Often, guests pay cashier on their way out.)
- Clear tables and reset.

Side Work Duties

- Dust and clean dining room tables, side stands, service station, locker room.
- Set up dining tables.
- Check all the items on the menu to be sure that you have the needed supplies on your stand. Replace as needed during the serving period.

- Always use forks, spoons, or tongs for picking up food from the side stand. Never use fingers.
- Pick up glasses by the base.
- Pick up cups, knives, forks, and spoons by the handles.
- If silverware falls on the floor, place it with the soiled ware and replace with clean silver.
- Be sure tops of condiment bottles are clean before placing on dining table.
- If dishes require wiping, do this at the side stand.
- Use clean side towels to wipe up spills at the side stand or table.
- Plan the arrangement and placement of the supplies on the side stand so they are easy to reach and use.
- During slack periods, organize, check, and perform needed duties such as folding napkins, cleaning and filling condiment containers, cleaning and placing ash trays, and refilling roll warmer and beverage containers.
- Arrange centerpieces and accessories on dining tables.
- Prepare beverages, garnish trays, butter, ice water, breads.
- Cut and serve pastries, cakes, desserts.
- Prepare and serve salads.

Closing Duties

- Put foods away in proper place.
- Empty and wash water pitchers, creamers, sugar bowls, and condiment jars as necessary.
- Wash silver and glassware as directed.
- Reset dining room tables for the next meal.

213

- Check the general appearance of the dining room for any additional cleaning needed.

The tips or gratuities you receive are influenced by the service you give. When you serve guests, what kind of an impression will you make? How can you demonstrate your efficiency as well as your interest in the guest's comfort and welfare? The manner in which you take the customer's order, serve the food, and present the check can help make a favorable impression.

A Day in a Table Service Restaurant

The average work day is eight hours. Eating establishments, of course, have to stay open much longer, from breakfast through the dinner hour and often into the late evening. This means that employees may work split shifts.

A *split shift* means having time off between work hours. An employee may work the breakfast period from 6 a.m. to 10 a.m., leave, and return to work the dinner period from 3 p.m. to 7 p.m. There should be sufficient time between work periods so that workers can use it to their advantage. For example, being off from 11 a.m. to 4 p.m. allows time for personal activity. Only one hour off means that the workers do not have time to leave the premises. This is not desirable and may not be legal. Check the laws in your community.

Some workers must also work on Saturdays, Sundays, and holidays. Since employees can work only five days a week, they must take their two days off during the week.

The hours you work may differ from employer to employer because each table service restaurant must meet the needs of its customers. However, the daily routines tend to follow similar patterns in each shift.

Let us look at a typical day's routine for a waitress working an eight-hour split shift at a resort motel dining room. Two meals are served—breakfast and dinner, with no cocktail service. There is no busboy service.

7:00–7:30 a.m.—Arrives dressed in clean uniform, hose, flat-heeled shoes, and appropriate hair arrangement.

Eats breakfast, washes hands, and freshens up.

Makes coffee.

Assembles juices, cereals, chilled juice glasses, and creamers.

Checks table settings and accessories and turns on lights as needed.

Places menus in convenient location.

Checks with chef or cook on menu items.

7:30–10:30 a.m.—Immediately offers breakfast coffee to guests as they arrive.

Serves breakfast, using the type of service designated by the management.

Gives check to customer, takes money to cashier, returns change.

10:30–11:00 a.m.—Completes serving guests.

Clears tables as each guest finishes. Carries dishes to dishwasher.

Wipes off tables; sets with dinner service as directed.

Cleans pantry or service area. Puts food away.

11:00 a.m.–4:00 p.m.—Off duty.

4:00–4:45 p.m.—Arrives dressed appropriately.

Cleans dining room.

Makes coffee, chills juice glasses, prepares and assembles butter chips, juices, relishes, and ice water.

Checks side stand or service units to be sure all supplies are ready.

Checks table settings and accessories.

Checks menu items with chef.

4:45 p.m.—Eats dinner.

5:00–9:00 p.m.—Hostess or waitress may open dining room, turning on lights.

Serves dinner at assigned tables.

Clears and resets tables as each guest finishes.

9:00–10:00 p.m.—Strips tables and resets for breakfast service.

Cleans up pantry, and/or side stands and work areas. Puts foods away as directed.

Checks breakfast juices in refrigerator and other supplies needed for the breakfast service.

Room Service

Room service is usually performed by a waiter rather than a waitress. Hotels often provide breakfasts, luncheons, dinners, cock-

Jasper Park Lodge, Canada

A waiter on a bicycle delivers a food order to a guest's motel room.

tails, teas, and late snacks in the privacy of the guest's hotel room. Usually, guests will place their orders from a special room service menu. The food is prepared in the kitchen and placed on heated, covered dishes. The food may be carried on a tray to the guest's room or rolled in on a table that is already set. Often the food is placed in insulated carriers designed to maintain the serving temperature of the food.

If you are assigned to room service, your duties will include the following:

- Receive the guest's detailed order slip from the room service clerk or captain.
- Relay the food order to the appropriate food stations in the kitchen.
- Assemble the table or tray for service while the food is being prepared.
- Cover table or tray with clean cloth.
- Assemble and arrange the required number of settings and appointments for convenient service when you arrive at guest's room.
- Collect all cold food items and place on table or tray.
- Collect all hot food items in a heated carrier or place on table or tray.

- Double check the order to be sure everything is there.
- Take table or tray to guest's room.
- Knock, announce "Room service," greet guest, and place table or tray as directed.
- If a table is used, arrange and complete setting of table for the guest.
- Serve ice water, coffee, and hot foods to guests as requested. Guests may prefer to serve themselves.
- Present the check for signature or payment.

Dining Room Helper (Busboy or Busgirl)

Large resort hotels, clubs, and many restaurants generally employ dining room helpers to assist the waiters and waitresses. This is called *bus service,* and so the name busboy or busgirl is used. Bus service speeds up the service of food and allows the waiter or waitress to give more individual attention to each guest. This is a beginning job that can lead to waiter or waitress jobs.

Generally, as a dining room helper, you assist the waiters and waitresses to prepare for the guests' arrival. You keep necessary supplies on hand, and keep the dining area clean and attractive. The qualifications for the job are the same as those for all service work.

As a dining room helper, you would have the following duties:

- Prepare the side stand or station for service.
- Sweep and dry mop the floor.
- Dust the woodwork and furniture.
- Arrange linen and silver in order on the serving table.

- Set up the dining tables.
- Prepare and perhaps serve ice water, butter, bread, and rolls.
- Prepare and/or care for condiments, relishes, salts, peppers, sugars, creamers, ash trays, and accessories.
- Pour water for guests.
- Remove trays of soiled dishes from dining tables and take to dish machine room.
- Reset dining tables.
- Carry loaded trays from kitchen to serving stand.
- Clean dining tables and service station at close of meal period.

Cafeterias usually provide minimum service with low prices. In these self-service units, the customer, after eating, removes his tray to a dish cart or station. Dining room helpers, called floor boys or girls, are often used to supply extra service to customers and to keep the dining room in order.

Commercial cafeterias may use floor boys or girls to create an atmosphere of leisurely dining, with some service similar to restaurants.

In a cafeteria, your duties would be:

- Direct customers to tables. Help with children or disabled persons.
- Carry customer's trays, and possibly transfer food to dining table. Supply napkins and extra silver.
- Remove empty trays and refill water glasses and beverage cups.
- Bring condiments and cooked-to-order foods to guests.
- Order extra foods, at guest's request, correct sales check, and bring to guest.
- Clear and clean tables, chairs, and floor.
- Help clean up when accidents occur.

Counter Worker

The job of counter worker is a responsible one. It requires the sales ability of a waiter or waitress. It often calls for the ability to compute sales and to make change quickly and accurately. Since counter workers deal with the public, they must give careful, efficient, and courteous service.

Counter service saves time and space, and provides rapid service to the customer. This type of service is based on high volume and low prices. Some restaurants use both counter and table service.

Counter service features easy-to-prepare meals, short orders, pre-packaged foods, and fountain items. Frozen, pre-portioned menu items, which can be heated and served quickly, are generally used.

Some counter units operate only as snack bars. They are usually limited to selling sandwiches, beverages, fountain items, and pre-packaged foods such as cookies, cakes, crackers, and candy. Hotels and motels often have snack bars to supplement the regular dining service. In resort areas, snack bars are set up near swimming pools and golf courses. Schools, hospitals, and universities may operate snack bars as an extra service to guests or students.

Snack bars may be open for business 24 hours a day or only during certain hours, depending on the policy of the establishment. For example, some resort hotels do not serve noon meals. Guests use the snack bar at noon as well as late in the evening after the dining room has closed. Hospitals may operate snack bars during visiting hours only.

Counter service is designed to be quick and efficient. All the necessary supplies and some food items are located beneath the counter.

Florida Dept. of Citrus

Food items and combinations are often displayed on counters. This helps increase sales and speed customer selection. As a counter worker, you may be responsible for the arrangement of displays such as this as well as for the service of the food.

The snack bar . . .

Snack Bar

Small snack bars such as this are compact and efficient for quick service. The food is prepared and served in view of the customer.

Orange Julius

Frankfurters are prepared in quantity in this electric cooker on the counter. This tends to attract customers as well as provide fast service.

Snack Bar

The counter worker in this snack bar keeps the cooking unit clean and ready for the preparation of short orders.

Napkins, menus, condiments, and other foods are often arranged on the counter itself.

Food preparation and assembly can be done at a back bar which is behind the counter. This is called a self-sufficient unit, and includes all the equipment needed for food preparation and dishwashing.

In some cases, food is prepared in the kitchen. The back bar is used for serving. A pass-through window from the kitchen to the back bar makes it easy to serve the food.

Even though the counter worker's responsibilities are all basically the same, there will be many variations from one employer to another. The counter worker may prepare some of the foods such as fountain items, salads, sandwiches, and desserts. In smaller operations, as in diners, the counter worker may be responsible for table service as well as counter service.

Generally, if you are employed as a counter worker, you are responsible for serving attractive, good quality food, and providing quick, efficient, sanitary service to customers. As a counter worker, your duties will generally include the following:

- Keep counter top clean and orderly, using clean, damp cloths for wiping counter.
- Group counter accessories such as salt, pepper, sugar, cream, and ash trays within easy reach of customers.
- Arrange the place mat, silver, china, glass, and napkin for one cover in front of guest as directed by management.
- Serve the guests in turn as they come to the counter.

- Place the check face down before the customer as soon as the order is completed.
- Clear, wipe, and rearrange the counter as soon as guests leave.
- Keep area beneath counter and back bar clean and neat.
- Make coffee and other beverages as needed.
- Prepare, portion, and serve menu foods according to the policy of the food service operation.
- Clean and polish the counters, shelves, and equipment.
- Wash glasses, silverware, and dishes used on counter, unless there is a dishwashing arrangement in back kitchen. Snack bars often use paper or plastic containers and utensils.

Counter workers who are employed full time work the usual eight hours a day, five days a week. The days off may be during the week or weekends. Even the daily eight hours may differ. For example, in some operations, employees may start to work at 11 a.m. or noon and work until 9 p.m., or they may work from 3 p.m. to 11 p.m.

There are many different kinds of jobs for counter workers—in restaurants, drive-ins, diners, ice cream shops, or cafeterias. The duties differ a great deal, but the day's routine may be similar.

Here is a typical day's routine for a counter worker who works an eight-hour shift from 4:00 p.m. to midnight in a diner.

4:00–4:30 p.m.—Arrive at work. Put on clean uniform. Freshen up, wash hands.

Check with manager or supervisor for assigned station and work schedule.

Check supplies on counter and back bar. Restock if necessary.

Wash any dishes, glassware, silver, or serving utensils that might be left by counter worker on earlier shift.

4:30–11:30 p.m.—Serve customers as they arrive.

Write sales check, place it in front of guest.

Take money and make change, unless there is a cashier.

Wipe off counter top, and replace accessories in proper place after each guest.

Eat dinner during a slow period. Usually one half hour is designated for meal.

Counter workers may be expected to portion food into the counter serving pans. This is usually done in the kitchen behind the counter. The pans, prepared and portioned in the kitchen, are on the work table, ready to be placed in the counter.

BOCES, Ithaca, N. Y.

The cafeteria counter worker must be familiar with the arrangement of food and supplies on the counter. Study this well-organized cafeteria counter. Note the steam table foods, the cold table setup, the dessert display, and the location of serving tools and extra supplies.

Prepare beverages and other menu items as needed.

11:30–midnight—Carry out closing duties, as directed.

Clean counter and back bar; assemble supplies and utensils for next day.

Clean tables and chairs if there is table service.

Turn off all automatic machines and clean as directed.

Cafeteria Counter Worker

In a cafeteria, the customers serve themselves except for certain foods such as soups, meats, and vegetables. The cafeteria counter worker serves the food the customer requests. Service must be fast so that the line does not slow down. Customers frequently cannot decide on the items they want. As a counter worker, you can help the customer by answering questions and making menu suggestions in a pleasant, friendly manner.

Since food costs in cafeterias are carefully controlled, the prices are usually moderate. Workers therefore must serve exact portions as directed. An extra dip of ice cream or a larger serving of mashed potatoes and gravy may make you seem "a good guy." However, multiplied over and over, it can result in great loss of money to the management. As a result, prices might have to be increased.

The hours worked by a cafeteria counter worker vary with the type of operation. School cafeterias often serve only a noon meal and therefore employ some part-time workers. Industrial and institutional cafeterias may serve two or three meals daily and employ two shifts of full-time workers as well as part-time workers.

The work falls into three parts: The preparation of the counters for service, the service period, and the clearing and cleaning of counters after service. Following are the duties you would be expected to perform during each period:

Preparing the Cafeteria Counter

- Check and polish glass shelves, metal surfaces, and counter tops.
- Supply the necessary number of trays, napkin holders, and silver boxes.
- Arrange the supply tables and shelves neatly.
- Prepare the cold pans or cold table as directed.
- Prepare the steam table and hot counters as directed.
- Assemble an adequate supply of dishes and serving utensils in proper place.
- Assemble supplies of relishes, condiments, crackers, and pre-packaged food items in proper location.
- Make coffee, tea, and/or iced tea according to directions of manager.
- Set up the hot foods, salads, desserts, breads, and beverages attractively and in proper location.
- Prepare foods as assigned.

Service Period

- Take your place at the counter and serve food to customers as directed by manager or supervisor.
- Suggest menu choices to customer if they need help.

- Answer customer's questions about foods courteously.
- Re-stock the counter as needed during slow periods.

After the Service

- Put all foods away in the correct place.
- Empty and clean steam table, hot tables, cold tables, counter tops, glass shelves, and tray and silver holders.
- Clean and refill salts, peppers, condiments, and accessories.
- Clean storage areas and shelves as assigned.
- Empty and clean coffee urn and other beverage containers.

Chef shows student how to hold thumb on the edge of the plate he is serving.

Brookline, Mass., Public Schools

221

Brookline, Mass., Public Schools

Counter workers in a school lunchroom must work quickly and efficiently to serve large numbers of students during lunch periods.

In addition to regular meals, cafeterias may provide snacks for coffee breaks and some made-to-order foods. Slicing meat in view of the customer, as this chef is doing, tends to promote the sale of that particular food.

Canteen Corp.

222

The runner or supply worker keeps the cafeteria counter supplied with food.

Some cafeterias employ *runners* or *supply workers*, who keep the counters supplied. This allows the counter worker to give undivided attention to serving, and thus speeds up the service. Runners keep the cooks informed on the rate of demand for certain foods. They supply the counter with the right amount of food at the right time and notify the dishwashers of the need for dishes, silver, or trays. They also inform the counter worker of the food supply in the kitchen.

Some cafeterias may have an intercommunication system. The counter worker notifies the cooks, through a transmitter, when food supplies are needed. If the kitchen is located below the serving room, the food supplies may be delivered by an electrical conveyer. When the kitchen is on the same floor, a kitchen worker delivers the food to the counter.

Carry-Out Worker

A number of drive-in food operations feature carry-out self-service. The customer drives in, goes to the counter window, orders from a posted menu, receives his order, pays, and then eats in his car or at tables set up outside or inside the drive-in area. There are also drive-ins with carhops who provide service to the customer's automobile. Carhop duties are described in this chapter on pages 226–228.

Drive-ins stress fast and courteous service, cleanliness, and good foods at moderate prices. The drive-in menu varies with the type of operation. It usually offers a wide choice of beverages, hamburgers, hot dogs, fried fish and shrimp, and French fried potatoes.

Carry-outs have counter service, with or without tables for customers to use. The menu in carry-outs tends to feature a specialty, which may be a complete meal, a single item, or meal combinations. The specialties may be such foods as pizza, barbecued chicken, fried chicken, seafood, or local food specials.

A production line type of operation is generally used. For example, the grill cook and/or kitchen helper removes the frozen preportioned food from the freezer to the fry grill or deep fat fryer. When the foods are cooked, they are passed to a helper who wraps or plates them, and pushes them forward onto a heat table to the counter worker. Although systems of food preparation vary, usually twenty to thirty hamburgers are kept prepared ahead on the heat table during rush hours. Frozen or fresh French-cut potatoes are prepared in deep fat fryers, salted, bagged, and kept ready on the heat table. Hot dogs are steamed and kept hot on a steam table, while buns are heated in the bun warmer. Barbecue sauces and chili may be pre-prepared and kept hot in the steamer.

The carry-out . . .

Carry-out workers must be able to adapt to a variety of situations. Here the worker prepares instant mashed potatoes in a mixer.

Some carry-out customers prefer to eat at one of the tables. Note the menu posted on the building where customers can easily read it.

Worker packages orders for customer.

In this carry-out, the customer receives his order of hamburgers and beverages through the counter window.

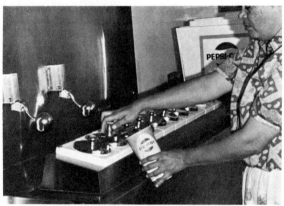

Cape Coral Drive Inn, Fla.

Carry-out worker fills an ice cream cone with soft-serve ice cream.

Counters are designed in a straight line or a U-shape. They are completely equipped with a back bar as a self-sufficient unit. Some drive-in and carry-out counters have a kitchen in the back of the house similar to diners. In such cases, food may be prepared in the kitchen, and the use of pre-prepared frozen foods may be limited.

Drive-ins and carry-outs are usually open for business at 10 or 11 a.m., and close at 10 p.m. on weekdays and 11 or 12 p.m. on weekends. Counter workers are employed full time in two shifts or part time for evening hours.

If you are a counter worker in a drive-in or carry-out, you will have the following duties:

- Check and supply all beverage machines. Prepared and portioned mixes are used. All beverage machines are automatic.
- Check ice cube machine.
- Keep counter top clean and orderly.
- Assemble paper supplies, put cups in racks, check packaged food items, and arrange condiments in proper location on counter.
- Take customer's order. Serve customer, add sales check, and make change.
- Do special periodic cleaning such as polishing stainless steel and washing inside windows, counter light fixtures, supply shelves, storage areas, counters, heat table, and beverage machines.

Automatic beverage machines supply cold drinks such as cola, root beer, orange, and others.

Cape Coral Drive Inn, Fla.

If your job is to pack carry-out orders, be sure to follow management's directions accurately.

National Broiler Council

In addition to taking orders from customers, the fountain worker must know the art of preparing ice cream and soda specialties.

Fountain Worker

Fountain service is often provided in dairy outlets, dairy bars, or ice cream shops. It may also be combined with food service in snack bars, department stores, and counter service restaurants. The fountain worker's job may involve either counter service, table service, or both.

The fountain counter and the area beneath and behind it are carefully planned into a self-sufficient unit. The fountain worker prepares and serves in this limited area, which is in view of the customer. The offerings and the prices may be posted on an easy-to-see wall bulletin board or on a printed menu handed to each customer. Dairy bars and ice cream stores may also handle bulk items such as cartons of eggs, milk, cream, and ice cream. These may be in self-serve refrigerators and freezers so the customer can serve himself.

Fountain workers are the sales force for their employers, so their appearance, manner, and attitude are most important. They are responsible for the prompt, efficient service of attractive, sanitary, quality foods and beverages to customers.

Generally, as a fountain worker, you would have the following duties:

- Clean counter tops, tables, chairs, and fountain equipment.
- Sweep and mop floors.
- Keep counter and display cases supplied.
- Keep counter area clean and sanitary.
- Prepare and serve a variety of milk shakes, sodas, and ice creams.
- Add customer's check, take money, and make correct change.
- Answer phone, and take orders accurately.
- Other duties may be required since ice cream shops and dairy outlets offer ice cream products which are delivered to other operations. Such duties may include dipping and packaging ice cream, storing and issuing fountain supplies, and counting and assembling orders.

Carhop

The carhops' work is similar to that of waiters or waitresses, but they work outdoors instead of indoors. The service is informal, simple, and quick. It involves the sale of a variety of foods served on a tray to customers in cars. Each carhop may be assigned to a certain number of car parking spaces as a station.

With the increase in travel, the popularity of drive-ins with carhop service has grown rapidly. People can enjoy a sandwich or a full-course meal without leaving their cars. They receive fast service and pay moderate prices. The drive-in menu features easy-to-prepare, cooked-to-order foods such as hamburgers, fried fish, fried chicken, and fountain items.

Menus are posted in easy-to-see locations. Some drive-ins have an automatic order system. The customers put in their orders on a

The drive-in menu is placed where it can be easily read from the car window. The customer calls in his order through the microphone placed just below the menu. A carhop delivers the order to the car.

call box, usually installed at the car parking area. The orders are received by the worker stationed at the other end of the call box, who gives it to the appropriate food preparation center. When the food is ready, the order-taker assigns carhops to serve the food to the customers in their cars, collects the money, and makes change.

In some operations, the carhop assigned to the station takes the customer's order, in addition to performing the above duties.

One of the tasks of carhops is to handle money. They are supplied with a change belt and a specific amount of change. They must pay the counter man for each order they receive and then collect from the customer, making change as needed. At the end of the service period, they return the original amount of change to the counter. The money left in the change belt is theirs, as tips for their service to customers. If you are a carhop, you must be accurate in making change or you will lose your tip money. Remember, in this job you are responsible for the sale and service of the correct food orders, conveniently arranged on trays and delivered to the customers in their automobiles.

The carhop arranges the food in an orderly fashion on the tray, delivers the tray to the car, and attaches it to the car window for the convenience of the customer.

As a carhop, you would be expected to perform some or all of the following duties:

- Greet customers promptly in the order of the car arrivals.
- Present menu or call attention to posted menu.
- Record carefully on sales slip, with all the necessary information.
- Deliver order to counter, and prepare tray for service.
- Receive food order, check to see if order is complete, and pay for it.

227

- Assemble food and supplies on tray.
- Deliver order to the car, and adjust tray securely to car door, either inside or outside according to directions.
- Collect the money due, making correct change.
- Return to car later (customers usually honk horn or turn on lights for attention) to check service, take further orders, or remove the tray.
- Empty paper supplies from soiled trays into waste cans. Return tray to dishwashing station.
- Keep customer parking area clean and orderly, picking up papers and trash during slow periods.
- Empty and clean waste receptacles as needed.

SUCCESS IN SERVICE JOBS

It is especially important for all workers involved in serving the public to maintain a good appearance. In aiming to be a top service worker, set your goal at becoming a professional. A professional is cooperative and courteous to all guests and co-workers, and sells the service and food of the eating establishment.

Your personality, mannerisms, and personal habits are also very important, whether you are a waitress, a carhop, or a busboy. Can you answer yes to these questions?

- Do you look well groomed?
- Do you greet guests with a pleasant "Good morning" or "Good evening" and not "Hello" or "Hi"?
- Are you friendly with guests, but not familiar?

- Do you help older persons, disabled persons, and children to feel at ease?
- Do you stand with good posture and not lean on tables and chairs?
- Do you show appreciation for the customer's business by saying, "Thank you. I hope you will come again."?
- Do you handle difficult customers with tact and good judgment?

Your success can also depend on how efficiently you manage your work. How would you answer these questions?

- Do you know and follow your assigned work procedures accurately?
- Do you handle the china, glassware, and silver so that you do not touch the part that touches the food?
- Do you know and practice sanitary procedures in handling all food?
- Do you know your menu, location of supplies, and substitutions so that you can serve customers rapidly, and not waste time and motions?
- Do you avoid jerky movements or work practices that might result in accidents? Wipe up spills immediately? Keep out of the path of servers?
- Do you perform clean-up work willingly without complaining?
- Are you alert to work that needs to be done without having to be told?

The information you have acquired in this chapter on requirements, responsibilities, duties, and ways to succeed in service work is your first step toward success. Much will depend on how well you apply this knowledge, both at school and on the job.

Let's Think It Over

1. There are a number of interesting jobs in the front-of-the-house which require specialized skills and knowledge.

   - List the kinds of jobs found on the service team in large restaurants.
   - What is the general responsibility of a waiter or waitress? What are the advantages of this job? What are the disadvantages?
   - The job of a waiter or waitress in food service includes three different types of duties. For each type of duty, give three different examples of correct procedures.
     Selling and serving.
     Side work.
     Closing.

2. The appearance of waitresses, waiters, and busboys contributes to their success on the job. Listed below are three general aspects of their appearance. Describe two specific practices they should follow for each:

   - Cleanliness.
   - Appearance.
   - Comfort.

3. The responsibilities and duties involved in service jobs depend on the type of food service unit.

   - How do the duties of a room service waiter differ from those of a regular waiter?
   - Why do restaurants sometimes have busboys or girls? What duties do they perform?
   - How does counter service differ from table service? What is the reason counter service is popular?
   - How do the duties of counter workers in cafeterias differ from the duties of counter workers in quick-service restaurant operations?
   - How are the duties of counter workers in various establishments alike?
   - What are the responsibilities of a carhop in taking, giving, and serving an order, presenting the check, and cleaning up?
   - What personal qualities and job skills are employers looking for in hiring counter workers?
   - What is the responsibility of a fountain worker? List the kinds of duties they will perform.

Let's Investigate

1. Interview waitresses, counter workers, and carhops concerning their duties and responsibilities. Write a comparison of the advantages and disadvantages of the work for class discussion.

Chapter 11

Waiting on Customers

Whether you become a waiter, a counter worker, or a dining room helper, an understanding of basic service duties can help you on your job. These duties include taking an order, handling money, setting a table, and providing quality service for guests.

WORDS TO KNOW

American service	Change plate
French service	Banquet service
English service	Family style
Combination service	Cover
Shoulder carry	Silence cloth

TAKING AN ORDER

As a member of the sales and service team, you will need to know how to take food orders

from guests. Whether you work in a table service restaurant or behind the counter in a diner, the procedure is generally the same.

- Greet guests with a pleasant "Good morning (afternoon or evening)."
- Be sure your guests know you have seen them. If you are busy, say, "I'll be with you soon," in a friendly manner.
- Hand the guests opened menus as soon as they are seated. Fill the guests' water glasses.
- Before taking the order, be sure you know the menu choices, preparation times, and substitution policies.
- Serve guests in order of their arrival. Be as quick as possible.
- Take each order on your order pad. If guests are at tables, start at the host's left, if possible. Number each order, the first

#1, next #2, next #3. This will help you to serve the right order to the right person.

- Suggest and help the guests with menu choices in a friendly manner. See Chapter Eight on menus.
- Write or print orders clearly according to the policy of the establishment. It is important that the chef understands your order. Some chefs require you to stay and check as they serve your order.
- Repeat the order to your customer to be sure it is correct.
- Proceed (right to left) around your table, taking the order from each guest.
- If there are a number of guests at the table who are obviously not couples, always ask if they want separate checks.
- Ask the guests when they wish their beverages.
- To save time, abbreviations are often used for menu items when writing orders.

Abbreviation	Menu item
Frank	Grilled hot dog
B.L.T.	Bacon, lettuce, tomato sandwich
A Pie—Van	Apple pie à la mode, vanilla ice cream
F.F.	French fried potatoes
Chef Sal	Chef's salad
O.J.	Orange juice
Hamb	Grilled hamburger
Cof	Coffee

Generally, the form used in taking the order is completed and presented to the guest as the check. The paid check is used by the accounting department or cashier for the records.

231

The waitress writes the menu order on her pad, repeating it to the guest to be sure it is correct. Note that the waitress presents a neat, trim appearance.

People who serve customers should know the menu items and how they are prepared, in case customers inquire. What items has this chef prepared? Broiled stuffed zucchini, tomatoes and cheese, bananas rolled in bacon, and pear halves with cheese.

FOOD CHECK

sun country resorts

Remuda Ranch	Cape Coral	River Ranch	Poinciana	Rio Rico Inn	Cape Eleuthera

DATE	SERVER	TABLE NO.	PERSONS	CHECK NO.
2/10	Peg	4	2	654686

1.95	1	1 ov E Bac Pot	1.95 FD:		
1.75	2	1 up Ham Gr	1.75 FD:		
40	3	1 S oj	0.40 FD:		
40	4	1 S gj	0.40 FD:		
40	5	2 C	0.80 FD:		
			0.22 FD:	05.30:	SV
	6				
	7			05.52:	SV
				05.52:	CP
	8			05.52:	CA
	9				
	10				
	11				
	12				
	13				
	14				
	15				

GUEST RECEIPT

Blue — FA 211   © TAT CHEQUE • Miami, Florida 7/75   **TOTAL AMOUNT OF CHECK**

DATE	SERVER	TABLE NO.	PERSONS	CHECK NO.
				654686

Sheraton Inn

Sales checks must be accurate. Here, the waitress has filled in the date, her name and number of guests, and their orders. The prices, sales tax, and totals are rung through the cash register and then collected from the guests by the waitress. This order reads, ''One egg over easy with bacon and potatoes, one egg up with ham and grits, one small orange juice, one small grapefruit juice, and two coffees.''

232

232

Thank You!

YOUR PATRONAGE IS APPRECIATED

TABLE NO.	NO. PERSONS	CHECK NO.	SERVER NO.
6	2	44052	4

7⁹⁵	Sea & Steer	7	95
7⁹⁵	Prime M	7	95
2⁷⁵	1 Caesar	2	75
4⁰⁰	2 Irish coffee	4	00
		22	45
	TX		90
		23	35
	TAX		
	STYLE DK		

Sheraton Inn

A good waiter or waitress should know where each order goes without asking the guests. How? Write the order in rotation as shown on the dinner check. The first guest gets the sea and steer entrée and the next guest gets the prime ribs of beef, medium. The first receives the Caesar salad and both get Irish coffee.

Thank You!

YOUR PATRONAGE IS APPRECIATED

TABLE NO.	NO. PERSONS	CHECK NO.	SERVER NO.		
5	1	44052	6		
c/soup T					50
H burg spec				1	95
F F					65
ms ch.					95
				4	05
					16
				4	21
TAX					
STYLE DK					

Each check should be made out carefully, as it is filed at the cash register for accurate accounting of the day's sales. What did this customer order? A cup of tomato soup, a hamburger special, French fries, and a chocolate milk shake. Is the total correct?

To complete the check:

- Fill out the top part of the check with your number or initials, the date, and/or the table number according to policy.
- Write the price opposite each menu item or meal, clearly and accurately.
- Write other charges at the bottom of the check. These may include cover charges, sales tax, or special services.
- Total the completed check carefully. Recheck your addition.
- Be prepared to explain any charges to the customer.
- Present the check, face down, to the customer and say, "Thank you."
- Indicate to customer, if necessary, whether you collect the money or whether he pays at the cashier stand.

HANDLING MONEY

You may find that one of your duties involves handling money. Many food service units have a cashier who collects payment for the meal from the customer or the waiter or waitress, and who is responsible for handling all the money. However, in some food service operations, the waiters, waitresses, counter workers, or carhops collect the payment and make change. These operations may include diners, drive-ins, snack bars, fountain services, and some counter and/or table restaurants.

Workers who handle money need to be honest, quick, and accurate in making change. They must also be courteous with the customers.

Mistakes in making change can cause problems for both the customer and the employer.

Thank You!

YOUR PATRONAGE IS APPRECIATED

TABLE NO.	NO. PERSONS	CHECK NO.	SERVER NO.
8	2	44051	Kay

3⁵⁰	St Sand m R	3	50
2⁹⁵	Crepes tuna	2	95
.40	1 ht		40
.40	1 Cof		40
.60	1 ice cr		60
.85	1 cake		85
		8	70
	TX		35
		9	05
	TAX		
	STYLE DK		

Sheraton Inn

This type of check is more likely to be used by a restaurant with an automated accounting system. The food prices are written in the left-hand column. The cashier rings the check through the cash register, which computes and totals the food service and tax. What was ordered by each guest?

Salvation Army Nutrition Program

All sales checks go to the bookkeeping department and must agree with the total meal sales. Notice how carefully the cashier inspects the checks for errors.

When making change, leave the bill in sight on the cash register. Count the amount out loud as you hand the change to the customer.

Ponderoso Restaurant

If you are responsible for the mistake, you may have to make good the loss out of your own wages. On the other hand, customers may make mistakes, too, so you always need to be alert for such situations.

When paying their check, customers rarely have the exact amount. Therefore, if you are responsible for collecting payment, you will have to make change.

How do you make change correctly? First, learn to operate the cash register. Your manager or employer will show you how. Then follow these basic steps in the order given:

- Accept payment from the customer.
- Ring up the sale on the cash register.
- Count the change from the cash drawer to yourself.
- Count the change out loud as you hand it to the customer.
- Thank the customer.

Here is the procedure to use in accepting payment:

Suppose the customer hands you a $10 bill, and the food sale amounted to $6.83.

- Accept the $10 and say, "That is $6.83 out of $10."
- Place the $10 bill on the ledge of the cash register (called *change plate*) in full view of the customer. This prevents later questions concerning the denomination of the bill.
- Ring up $6.83 on the cash register. Place the check showing the amount of the sale—$6.83—on the change plate with the $10 bill so it can also be seen. The amount of the sale—$6.83—will be your starting point for making change.

- Take the change needed from the cash drawer, counting to yourself. Start with the amount of the sale, $6.83, and build up to the amount of the $10 bill. Do not try to subtract in your head.
- Count out loud to the customer as you hand him his change, "That was $6.83 out of $10." Hand out the coins one at a time. Give the customer two pennies and say, "$6.84, $6.85." Give a dime, saying "$6.95." Give a nickel, saying, "$7." Give $1 and say, "$8." Give another $1, saying "$9." Give the final $1, saying, "$10."
- Thank the customer. Now, place the $10 he gave you in the cash drawer.
- Sometimes the customer will hand you a bill and all or part of the change. For example:
  The sale is $3.42. The customer hands you $5.42. You repeat the same steps, saying, "$3.42 out of $5.42" and count out $2 change.

Some cash registers figure the correct change automatically. In such cases, you ring up the amount of the food sale, then ring up the total amount given you by the customer. The cash register immediately shows the correct amount of change you are to return to the customer. Sometimes this exact amount is automatically returned to the customer through a change chute.

SETTING A TABLE OR COUNTER

In some restaurants, waiters and waitresses set and clear off tables. In other restaurants, this is handled by dining room helpers.

Table settings follow a standard pattern,

237

although some variations may be used by individual food service units. Most of the rules apply to both table and counter service. However, some are for formal table service only. The standard rules are important for a good reason—they were designed for the comfort and convenience of the guests.

The clatter of dishes can be irritating to guests, so silence cloths may be used under tablecloths, runners, and place mats. Silence cloths should be spread evenly on the tables and not show below the tablecloth.

Table linen should be smooth and without wrinkles, stains, or holes. Tablecloths should hang evenly over the table edges.

Each individual setting is called a *cover*. The space allowed for each cover is about 60 cm [24 inches] by 40 cm [15 inches]. Dishes, silver, and napkins should be placed about 2.5 cm [1 inch] from the edge of the table, counter, or place mat.

Many restaurants and hotels offer private dining rooms for parties and meetings. Note the napkins, folded in a cone shape, on each cover plate.

Canteen Corp.

Setting a table . . .

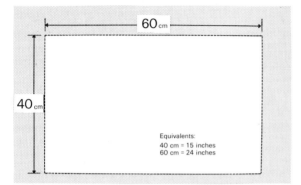

The 40 cm x 60 cm [24-inch by 15-inch] cover in this illustration indicates the space for one cover. This is set up with silver, china, linen, and glassware. Guests do not like to be crowded. This amount of space gives each person room to eat in comfort.

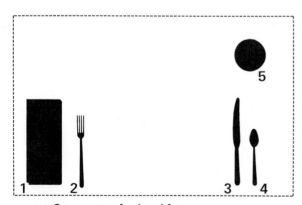

Cover setup for breakfast:
1. Napkin
2. Dinner fork
3. Dinner knife
4. Teaspoon
5. Water glass

If rolls are served in a basket, a bread and butter plate is used in the cover setup.

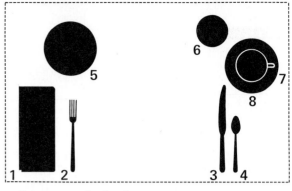

Cover setup for lunch:

1. Napkin	5. Bread and butter plate
2. Dinner fork	6. Water glass
3. Dinner knife	7. Cup
4. Teaspoon	8. Saucer

Cover setup for dinner:

1. Napkin	6. Teaspoon
2. Salad fork	7. Soup spoon
3. Dinner fork	8. Butter spreader
4. Cover plate	9. Bread and butter plate
5. Dinner knife	10. Water goblet
	11. Wine glass

Cover setup for dessert course:

1. Dessert fork	4. Cup
2. Dessert plate	5. Saucer
3. Teaspoon	6. Water glass or goblet

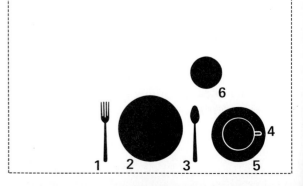

The napkin is folded and generally placed to the left of the fork. Open corners of the napkin should be at the right corner so that the guest can pick it up and unfold it easily. Some restaurants fold napkins in a cone shape and stand them in the center of the covers.

Knives are arranged on the right side of the cover with the cutting edges of the blades toward the center. Spoons are placed to the right of the knives. Forks are placed on the left side of the cover. A space about nine inches wide should be left between knives and forks for the plate. *Silver is arranged in order of use, working from the outside in.* This helps the guest to know which piece to use for each course.

The bread and butter plate is placed on the left side of the cover above the fork. When a salad accompanies the main course, the salad plate or bowl is placed to the left of and slightly below the bread and butter plate.

A service plate is used in formal service. It is on the cover before guests are seated and serves as the underliner for cocktails and the appetizer course.

The water glass is placed on the right side of the cover above the tip of the knife. Wine, liquor, and beer glasses are arranged to the right of the water glass.

The coffee cup is generally placed to the right of the water glass. It may also be put to the right of the knives and spoons. The handle of the cup should be turned to the right.

If a butter spreader is used, it is placed on either the top or right edge of the bread and butter plate, with the cutting edge turned toward the center of the plate. An oyster or cocktail fork is placed to the right of the

Jimbo Restaurant, Cape Coral, Fla.

When waiting on customers in a restaurant with booths, the waitress must serve from the table end.

spoons. It may also be put on the right side of the service plate.

Dessert silver is generally brought in with the dessert. A dessert fork is placed on the left of the cover and a dessert spoon on the right.

HOW TO USE A LARGE TRAY

One of the skills a service worker must learn is handling a large tray properly. Correct stacking, loading, and carrying reduce breakage and make work easier. Good work methods also cut down on fatigue, help prevent accidents, and assure efficient service to the customer.

Large trays may be carried by the shoulder carry or with both hands. The managers may specify which method they prefer you to use.

239

Restaurants often coordinate the colors and styles in tableware, place mats, and menus to give the desired atmosphere. Here, warm colors and informal styles provide a rustic setting for diners.

Corning Glass Works

Simplicity in table settings turns this executive dining room into an informal lunchroom.

Canteen Corp.

In stacking a large tray for shoulder carry, picture the face of a clock on your tray. Load the tray with orders to be served as follows:

- Place the main dish orders at 5, 6, and 7 o'clock, being careful not to disrupt the appearance of the plates.
- Place salads and side dish orders at 3 and 9 o'clock.

Remember, to balance the tray, the greatest weight must come near your shoulder. If you are serving many customers, you may have one tray containing all main dishes. A busboy may follow with salads and side vegetable orders, or salads and bread may have been served first. With balance in mind, stack *soiled dishes* as described below:

- Place the heaviest plates at 5, 6, and 7 o'clock to steady the tray and put the greatest weight on the shoulder.
- Place other dishes at 3 and 9 o'clock with handles pointing toward the center of the tray.
- Place glasses, silver, and cups in the center of the tray so they will not slip off or spill.
- Place other lighter-weight dishes at 12 o'clock.
- Pile saucers and small plates on the large plates when possible. However, do not pile dishes too high. This makes the load too heavy and unbalanced.

What item is missing from this table setting? Judging from the setup, what courses will be served?

Corning Glass Works

241

Dudley–Anderson–Yutzy

Setup for a dessert that can be eaten with a spoon. How would the setup differ if a dessert fork were needed instead of a spoon?

Corning Glass Works

This table for two is completely set up, including filled water glasses.

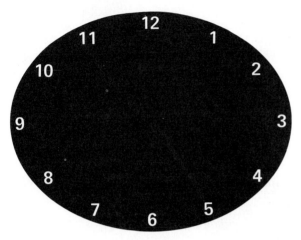

Before you begin to load a waiter's tray with food or soiled dishes, picture the face of a clock on the tray. Place main dish orders or heaviest dishes at 5, 6, and 7 o'clock. Place salads and side dish orders or lighter dishes at 3 and 9 o'clock. Place lighter items at 12 o'clock. Place cups in center of tray so they will not slip off.

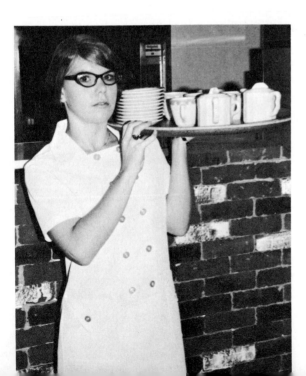

Waitress carries tray on left shoulder, leaving the right hand free to steady the tray. Note that the heaviest load is on her shoulder. Teapot spouts are turned inward toward center of tray so that tea cannot accidentally spill on floor or on guests.

Slyvan Hills, Ithaca, N. Y.

242

- Place coffee pots or pitchers between the center of tray and 3 o'clock with spouts facing inward.
- Place soiled linens on top of the loaded tray.
- Carry the loaded tray to the dishwashing area and unload it according to the procedures outlined by management. Such procedures are known as *policy of the house.*
- On each return trip, bring back a tray of clean dishes, glasses, and silver. Make every trip count!

The tray may be carried on the left or right shoulder, whichever is most comfortable. If the tray is carried on the left shoulder, the right hand is free for opening doors and steadying the tray.

The following directions for left-shoulder carry can be reversed for right-shoulder carry.

- Crouch at the right of the tray stand with the left foot forward. Have the 6 o'clock side of the tray nearest the left shoulder.
- Place the left hand, palm up and fingers spread, underneath the center of the tray.
- Cup the hand slightly so the tray rests on the cushion of the fingers.
- Grasp the edge of the tray nearest your left shoulder with right hand.

- Slide the tray from the stand to the left shoulder until you feel the weight and balance of the tray.
- Stand up straight, using your leg muscles to lift.
- Move the left arm in towards the body until the weight of the tray is balanced by the left shoulder, left palm, and left side.
- To set the loaded tray down, follow the same directions in reverse.

When carrying a tray in front of you with both hands, another method of stacking *soiled dishes* is generally used.

- Place plates and large dishes in the center of the tray for an even balance of weight.
- Place the silver on one side of the tray with handles together.
- Place glasses and cups on opposite sides with handles toward center of tray.
- Pile saucers and small plates on large plates.
- Keep dishes within rim of the tray, and do not overload tray.
- Place soiled linens on top of the loaded tray.

A clean tray cloth is carried over the right arm or in the right hand during service to use in handling hot dishes from the tray. The small trays used in beverage service are usually carried on the palm of the left hand so that the beverage may be served with the right hand to the right of the guest.

BOCES, Ithaca, N. Y.

To place loaded tray on tray stand, waitress bends at hips and knees. She keeps back and shoulders straight to keep tray in balance.

Then she lifts the tray to her shoulder and carries it. The tray may be supported with one or two hands.

Ithaca Country Club

243

Friendly, courteous service encourages customers to return.

Although beverages are usually served from the right side of the guest, this may be difficult to do in booth service. Here, the waitress must reach across the guest to pour the coffee. She must be especially careful not to bump the guest or spill the coffee.

QUALITY SERVICE

Be observant when serving customers. Some may be in a hurry and must be served promptly. In return, they will leave with a good image of the food service operation. Other customers may want a more leisurely service, so you will want to avoid rushing them.

By serving the food neatly, you can make it more attractive and appealing to the customer. You are responsible for upholding the standards of quality set by the manager. Therefore when serving, you should take care to see that:

- Food is not dripped or spilled on customers.
- There are no stains or fingerprints on plates, glasses, and silver service.
- Butter pats and ice cream have not melted.
- Food is served on dishes large enough to hold it easily. Food should not hang over the edge of the plate.
- Fat from fried foods has not collected on the serving dish.
- Cups and glasses are three-fourths full. This helps to prevent spillage.
- Foods have been placed on the serving dishes so they do not run into each other.

STYLES OF SERVICE

Each food service unit determines the style of table service that will best fit its particular kind of operation. It is important to understand efficient, gracious table service and to know the difference between the styles of service used in most restaurants.

In table setting and meal service, you must always follow the pattern established by the restaurant in which you work. However, your knowledge of the many acceptable styles in table service will help you to learn the procedure wherever you work.

The styles described here are currently in use, and all are correct.

American Style

American service is used by many restaurants. It is fast, inexpensive, and easily learned by inexperienced waitresses and waiters. The food order is portioned onto plates in the kitchen, carried on trays to the tray stand, and placed before each guest.

- Ladies, when present, are served first.
- All food is served with the left hand, from the left side of the guests.

- Beverages are served from the right side of the guest with the right hand. When serving beverages, the small trays are carried in the left hand.
- Dishes are removed from the guests' left side, using the left hand.
- Beverages are removed from the guests' right side, using the right hand.
- In some restaurants, dishes are served and removed from the right side of guests, with the right hand, and transferred to a tray held in the left hand.
- The important point to remember is that dishes are served and cleared with *the hand away from the guest*. Why do you think this is a good rule?

French Style

Some of the more elaborate restaurants use French service. It is not as popular, though,

In the French style of service, final food preparation is done on a wagon or trolley in view of the guests.

Dudley–Anderson–Yutzy

This restaurant uses the English style of service. Guests can watch the waiter serve food from service platters placed on a stand near their table.

since it requires professionally trained waiters and is more expensive than American service. Two waiters, each with specific duties, work as a team at one station. All the food is served from a special cart close to the guest's table. Each cart, sometimes called a wagon or trolley, is fitted with gas or electricity. The final cooking such as flaming entrées or desserts is done in view of the guest. All food is served to the guest from his left side. Coffee is served only with the dessert. A choice of desserts may be brought to the table on another cart for the guest to make his selection. This service is

slow, elaborate, and gracious. Of course, more space is required for this style of service.

Russian Style

Russian service, which is simple, fast, and less expensive than the French style, is now being used in many of the more elegant restaurants. The cover can be set and served by one waiter. Food is fully prepared, precut, and arranged on silver serving platters in the kitchen. The waiter serves from the guest's left side, using his right hand, and holding the platter of food in his left hand. Service is always clockwise around the table, starting with the host.

English Style

English service is elegant, requires well-trained waiters or waitresses, and is found in some of the finer eating places. Each guest is served his portion from the service tureens and platters, which are on a trolly or a table in view of the guests. The "host" performing this service is the waiter or waitress assigned to the particular table.

Some restaurants use a waiter and a waitress, who work as a team. The waiter assembles each course on a tray or mobile cart and serves the individual orders in front of the guests. The waitress places the orders before the guests and clears the table after each course.

Combination Style

Restaurants often combine styles to suit their specific type of operation. An example of this is the use of the American style service in which some of the food is served on individual plates in the kitchen. Often vegetables that accompany the entrée are served *family style*. This means that the vegetables, and sometimes salads, are placed on the table in large serving dishes to be passed from one guest to another. This style of table service is popular and is easily handled by the waitress.

Buffet Style

In buffet service, a variety of appetizers, hot and cold entrées, vegetables, and salads are arranged on a long table. The table is usually placed so that guests may walk around it. Beverages and desserts may be on the buffet table, but more often they are served to guests at their tables.

A similar style of service is called smorgasbord. How does it differ? Smorgasbord is a Swedish name taken from "smorgas," meaning sandwich and "bord," meaning table. It could be called a sandwich table. It, too, is a long table. Sometimes it has three tiers, which is usually described as the skyscraper effect. How does smorgasbord differ from buffet? A smorgasbord is more elaborate than a buffet, with a greater variety and number of dishes offered. Scandinavian specialties such as pickled and smoked fish, cheeses, cold meats, salads, and

vegetables are featured. Hot dishes are more often served to guests at their tables.

In buffet or smorgasbord service, the guests help themselves, taking their food to a previously set dining room table. Fewer waitresses are required. However, food preparation requires skill because of the great variety of dishes served and the beautiful decorative effects desired.

Any of the above styles of service may be used in serving the three main meals of the day—breakfast, lunch, and dinner.

SERVING BREAKFAST

A cheerful, friendly manner when you serve breakfast will do a great deal to help put customers in a good mood. Many guests are "low" in the morning until after they have had their coffee. They also appreciate having a cup of coffee while waiting for their breakfast.

In the family style of service, food is placed in serving dishes to be passed around the table by the guests. Here, six servings of broccoli are garnished with grapefruit sections.

Dudley—Anderson—Yutzy

247

Institutions/VFM

Most guests appreciate having a cup of coffee while waiting for their breakfast. Notice the orderly arrangement of this side stand.

Therefore it is customary in most restaurants to serve hot coffee immediately.

Serve the freshly prepared breakfast foods at the proper temperature. Hot foods, especially, should be served piping hot on warmed plates, direct to the guests. Do not let your completed order stand on the counter, waiting for you to pick it up.

Be sure the dining tables are clean, attractive, and appropriately set up. This is generally done before the meal service, but they must be kept neat throughout the serving period.

Order of Service

Knowing the generally approved method of serving breakfast can give you confidence on a job. It can also help you to do your work without having to ask too many questions.

- Fill the water glass, present the menu, and serve the coffee if the guest wishes it.
- Take and write the order.
- Serve the fruit and juice orders in the proper dish or glass on an underliner in the center of the cover.
- Remove the fruit service when the guest is finished.
- If cereal is ordered, place the cereal bowl on an underliner, in the center of the cover. Cut the individual box of cereal partway so the guest may open it easily.
- Check to be sure that cream and sugar are on the table.
- Refill water glasses and coffee cups.
- Remove cereal service.
- Place breakfast plate of hot foods in center of cover, toast plate at the left of the forks.
- Ask guests whether anything else is needed, and refill the coffee cups.
- Remove the used breakfast plates quietly.
- Place the sales check, face down, on right of the cover or present it on a clean change tray.
- Take money and check to cashier, if this is the procedure of the restaurant.
- Clear table and reset as directed.

From what you have learned about the breakfast menu, you can see that good breakfast service is carefully planned. The comfort and pleasure of the customer is always considered. No doubt your own experience in eating out or working on a job has already made you aware of this.

A cheerful setting greets breakfast customers. The cover is set up for a breakfast of cereal, sweet roll, and coffee. How would it be set if the guest had ordered a grapefruit half, scrambled eggs with ham slice, a side order of hash brown potatoes, toast, and coffee?

Corning Glass Works

Place setting for a lunch of chicken on rice, buttered zucchini squash, roll, butter, and coffee.

SERVING LUNCH

Luncheon service can range from a quick meal in a coffee shop to a leisurely one in an elegant restaurant. Be sure to pace yourself according to the type of service needed. If the customers are business people on limited lunch hours, they will want quick service. On the other hand, many shoppers and people who combine business with lunch will generally want a more leisurely meal. Be careful not to hurry them.

Order of Service

The generally accepted order for serving lunch is given below. Special instructions are also given for serving main-course salads.

- Present the menu to the guest (the hostess may do this) and fill the water glasses with ice water.
- Take each guest's order.
- Place chilled butter pats on bread and butter plates or place dish of iced butter pats on the table.

- If appetizer or soup is ordered, place it in the center of the cover on an underliner.
- Remove first service.
- Place the entrée, main dish salad, or sandwich in the center of cover.
- Place individual vegetable dishes above the entrée plate; individual salads, at left of the fork.
- Place the tray or basket of bread and rolls at left of the salad or near the middle of the table.
- Place the hot or cold beverage at the right and below the water glass.
- Remove main course service and extra silver.
- Brush crumbs from table, if necessary.
- Place dessert service in center of cover; place dessert silver in right position—fork on left, spoon on right.
- Refill or serve coffee.
- Remove the dessert dishes and silver.
- Place the check face down on right of cover.
- Clean and reset the table as directed.

Serving food . . .

Photos this page courtesy of BOCES, Ithaca, N. Y.

Waitress serves food from left side of guest with left hand.

From guest's left side and using her left hand, waitress offers a selection of salad dressings.

Coffee is poured from right side of guest with right hand.

Dishes are removed from guest's left side, using left hand.

251

To serve main-course salads:

- Cold salads should be served cold, crisp, and colorful on chilled plates.
- They should be attractively arranged and garnished on individual plates or in bowls, according to the practice of the eating establishment.
- Salads should have pleasing flavor, crisp texture, and be easy to eat.
- If no knife is needed, the fork is placed to the right of the plate and the salad in the center of the cover.
- Rolls, quickbreads, toast, crackers, or sandwiches may be served with salads.
- Often a choice of salad dressings is offered to the customer.

SERVING DINNER

Dinner service is generally more formal and leisurely than breakfast and lunch. Be alert to the needs and requests of guests and serve each course promptly. Before the dinner begins, check with the kitchen and the dining room supervisor for any special information and instructions concerning the service.

Order of Service

- Unless the hostess is responsible for presenting menus, place opened menu before each guest from the left side.
- Fill water glasses.
- Take the guests' orders accurately.
- Serve the appetizer from the left and place in the center of the cover.
- Remove appetizer dishes, usually from the left.

- Serve the soup course from the left and place in the center of the cover.
- Place the salad (if it is the procedure of the restaurant) at the left of the fork. The breads are often placed on the table with the salad service.
- Remove soup service, usually from the left.
- If the entrée is served on a platter, place it directly above the cover with the serving silver at the right of the platter. Place the warmed dinner plate from the left in the center of the cover.
- When plate service is used, place the dinner plate from the left in the center of the cover.
- Place beverage to the right of the teaspoons. Guests may want beverage with the entrée or with the dessert.
- Offer rolls and breads, or place them in the center of the table.
- Remove the main course dishes from the left.
- If the salad is served as a separate course either before or after the entrée, place the salad plate in the center of the cover and the salad fork at the left.
- Remove the salad service from the left.
- Remove crumbs from the table if this is part of the restaurant procedure.
- Place the dessert in the center of the cover from left. Place silver in appropriate positions.
- From the right, serve hot coffee or demitasse, or refill coffee cups, as the guest desires.
- Remove dessert service, usually from the left. Place finger bowls (if this service is used) in center of the cover.

- Refill ice water and coffee cups as needed during the meal.
- Present check face down to right of guest. Take money or indicate where bill is to be paid.
- When guests have gone, clear the table and reset.

SERVING BANQUETS

Your usual duties may be varied somewhat for a special banquet service.

Hotels, motels, and commercial restaurants provide formal banquets, buffets, smorgasbords, informal coffee breaks, wedding receptions, and cocktail and dinner dances for the public. Schools, hospitals, and universities usually serve banquets and provide special party functions as a service to the institutions and the community. These special party services are seldom alike, since they must meet the specific needs of the customer, and the policy of each food service establishment. However, banquets tend to follow a general pattern of service.

Banquets can be served in either the American or Russian style of service.

In *American banquet service,* the banquet tables are completely set, including all cold foods such as water, butter, bread, salads, and appetizers. The hot food is served on heated plates in the kitchen, covered with metal covers, and carried on large trays to tray stands. The covers are removed, and the servings are placed before the guests. All dishes are served and removed from the left, except the beverages.

Russian banquet service is more elaborate and formal. The food is brought in on silver platters and served individually onto the dinner plates on each guest's cover, as in the regular Russian service.

The seating arrangement at banquets is carefully planned so guests will not be overcrowded and can be served quickly and simultaneously. Tables of six, eight, or ten, rather than long banquet-type tables, tend to speed up service. Traffic patterns are more efficient and the worker assignments easier.

Service facilities generally include tray stands for large trays, conveniently placed near dining tables; duplicate service stations for supplies, beverages, breads, and other needs; and equipment for keeping foods at proper temperature during the service.

In all banquet service, waitresses and waiters serve and clear each course at the same time, on signal from the head waiter or hostess. The head table is always served first. Busboys or girls may carry heavy trays from the service room to the serving stand or station. *Floaters* (similar to busboys/girls) may pass rolls and relishes and fill water glasses. The use of busboys or girls and floaters speeds up the service and assures that each course with its accompaniments is on all tables at the same time.

As a waitress or waiter at a banquet, you will need to adapt to the type of service required for each function. Generally, your duties would involve the following:

- Determine the location of your station. You will be assigned a certain number of tables or guests to serve.
- Set up tables. Follow instructions carefully. The kind and amount of china, glassware, linen, and silver will depend on the menu and the style of service.

Bussing or clearing the table . . .

Here is a table of dirty dishes after the customers have left. The busgirl has placed a buspan on the edge of the table and is beginning to remove the tableware.

A *BETTER WAY!* Plates, saucers, cups, and paper are put in one buspan. Plates are stacked, and the paper is put to one side. There are many methods of bussing, and this is only one of them. The important point to remember is that each type of method has to be well organized, or it will not be efficient.

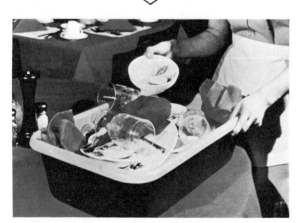

NOT THIS WAY! The busgirl is putting every kind of tableware into the same pan in a haphazard manner. This may seem to be the fastest way for her. However, it creates a mess in the dishroom when this pan has to be unloaded. It also makes extra work for others.

Glassware and silver are put in another pan. The busgirl puts as many similar pieces together as possible. This saves time and work in the dishroom. The buspans can be unloaded easily and quickly, which helps to keep dishroom activities flowing smoothly.

NOT THIS WAY! If the busgirl brought the loaded buspan into the dishroom and the soiled dishtable looked like this, what would she have to do? She would probably have to place the whole pan in any space she could find.

A BETTER WAY! The soiled dishtable is well organized, making it easy to unload the buspan. Silver is placed into the silver pre-soak and detarnishing solution. Note that one plate of each size has been set out so that workers will put the same kind of plates in one stack. Empty cup and glass racks are on the overhead shelf.

Tables seating ten persons each have been set up for this banquet.

Slyvan Hills, Ithaca, N. Y.

Generally, a banquet is served in the same manner as regular table service—food is served from the guest's left, beverages from the right, and dishes are removed from the left. If there are exceptions, these will be explained before the banquet starts.

After guests have left, tables must be cleared.

- Know the location and kinds of supplies and serving utensils you will need such as pitchers for water and beverages and trays for serving.
- Always serve and clear at a signal from the captain or head waiter.
- Use the correct general procedure for serving food and clearing tables, unless instructed otherwise.
- Collect tickets from guests as directed.
- Follow the policy for menu substitutions as determined before the banquet.
- Clear tables at end of banquet except for coffee cups and water glasses.
- Perform closing duties as directed.

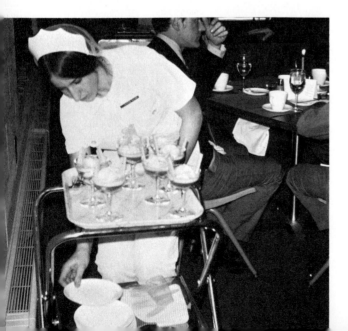

Tray stands, located at each station at a banquet, make serving easier.

256

Let's Think It Over

1. You are waiting on tables in a restaurant. Four businessmen come in for lunch and sit at one of your tables. What procedures would you follow to:

   - Set the table?
   - Take the orders?
   - Serve the orders?
   - Clear the table?

2. Practice counting change for the following restaurant checks and payments:

   - $3.61 check; customer gives a five-dollar bill.
   - $.82 check; customer gives two one-dollar bills and asks for five dimes in change.
   - $8.73 check; customer gives two five-dollar bills and three pennies.
   - $.52 check; customer gives a ten-dollar bill.

   - $15.31 check; customer gives two ten-dollar bills, two quarters, and a penny.

3. You are a counter worker. How would you set up the cover for the following orders?

   - Pie and coffee.
   - Luncheon salad, toast, coffee, and ice cream.
   - Open-faced toasted cheese sandwich, French fries, milk, and cake.
   - Bowl of soup, toast, coffee, and pudding.

Let's Investigate

1. Observe counter workers in the school lunchroom and local eating places. Compile a list of work methods or skills that would make a counter worker efficient. Discuss in class.
2. Report good and poor procedures you have observed waiters and waitresses using at their station and/or side stand.

257

Chapter 12

Managing

Yourself

The success of a food service unit depends upon good management. What does *management* mean? It is the process of planning and organizing to reach a definite goal. When you *plan*, you decide on certain steps that need to be taken to reach the goal. When you *organize*, you arrange the order of these steps so that your plan can work out as well as possible.

Now let us think of management in relation to food service. In Chapter Three, we discussed the management team. This team is responsible for managing time, money, labor, food, and equipment. However, managing does not stop with the management team. Workers must know how to manage their responsibilities and their time. Good management, whether by a hostess, a cook, or a dishwasher, can mean success. Poor management can result

in loss of customers and perhaps even business failure.

For instance, let us look at a drive-in operated by Dave Lincoln. His goal was to make money by selling hamburgers. He achieved his goal by managing himself and his business. First he located his drive-in on River Road, the main route into town. He decided to serve the biggest and best hamburgers in the area. He organized his drive-in operation so that service was fast and good. His workers were efficient, courteous, and friendly. As a result, his customers were well satisfied and returned again and again. The word spread, and soon Dave's drive-in was the most popular in town.

Part of Dave Lincoln's success depended on Bill Evans, the carhop he had hired. Why? Because Bill practiced good management, too.

Good management of time, energy, and equipment helps this worker avoid wasted motion and extra steps in preparing pies.

Bill decided on his goal: "The best carhop on River Road." First, he learned the responsibilities of his job quickly. He learned the menu and planned his work so that he served his customers efficiently. Not only was he courteous, but he was also friendly and interested in those he served. By *managing* his own job well, Bill reached his goal and also helped Dave Lincoln to reach his.

Like Bill, you too can learn to manage successfully on the job, especially when you have the ambition and desire to get ahead. In this chapter, we will discuss good management in food service work.

WORDS TO KNOW

Management	Five steps of
Short-term goal	management
Goal	Human resources
Decide	Long-term goal
Control	Material resources
Plan	Evaluate
Attitudes	Plan sheet
Simplify	Organize
Resources	Work schedule

FOOD SERVICE WORKERS NEED TO MANAGE

Have you ever heard someone say, "He is a born manager."? Some people have a natural ability to plan and organize. Most people are not born with such an ability. However, almost anyone can learn to become a good manager.

Day in and day out, you manage your own activities. Sometimes you do it very well, other times poorly. You manage your schedule to get to school on time and to get your homework done, or you manage your money to get a new outfit for the dance. These are everyday, familiar activities. However, there are many different kinds of management. For instance, what kind of management will your employer expect from you in return for the money he is paying you?

Consider what you will need to manage in food service work:

- *Time*, so that your work is finished on schedule.
- *Energy*, so that you get your work done but do not become over-tired through wasted movements and extra steps.
- *Knowledge*, so that you can do your work correctly.
- *Attitudes*, so that you show interest in the work and a willingness to learn, and that you cooperate with co-workers.

BOCES Vocational School, Ithaca, N. Y.

Students learn correct use of tools and equipment. This will help them to work safely and efficiently on the job.

BOCES Vocational School, Ithaca, N. Y.

Good food handling techniques are an important part of managing self. Here student learns to fill small cream puffs for canapés.

- *Tools of the job,* so that you work efficiently and safely.
- *Techniques of food handling,* so that you can produce and serve food that meets the standards of the unit.

HOW CAN YOU LEARN TO MANAGE?

The management process can be broken down into five essential steps. By understanding and practicing these five steps, you can learn to manage your activities. We will discuss these steps in relation to food service, but you can also use them in your daily personal activities.

What are the five essential steps in learning how to manage?

1. Select your goal.
2. Consider your resources.
3. Develop a plan.
4. Carry out the plan.
5. Evaluate the results.

Let us explore each step.

Step 1. Select Your Goal

A *goal* is an aim—something toward which you direct your effort. There are two types of goals—short term and long term. A *short-term goal* is one that can be reached in a short time. For example, your short-term goal may be to

These students have set a short-term goal for themselves—to learn to prepare large quantities of salad at a fast rate.

Broward Vocational and Technical Education, Florida

260

This student's long-term goal is to become a top-ranking baker. He is preparing a special occasion cake in the shape of a book to fit the theme of a banquet.

earn enough money to buy a stereo. A *long-term goal* is one that takes a long time to reach. If you desire to own a restaurant some day, it may take you years to reach this goal. Therefore this is a long-term goal.

When you are deciding on a goal, it may help you to ask yourself these questions: Why do I want this goal? Would something else be better? Do I have the ability and means to reach this goal? If I do not, can I get them? Will I hurt anyone by reaching for this goal?

Tom Kowalski, a member of the food service training class, has a definite goal. He wants to be a chef. How did Tom set his goal? He not only enjoys cooking but he also has a talent for working with food. He can think of no other type of work he wants to do. Before he made his final decision, however, he talked to several chefs. They encouraged him and showed him many interesting features of their work. They also explained that most chefs earn good salaries. Do you think that Tom has selected the right goal for a successful career? Why?

Have you ever started out with one goal in mind and then found that you had to change it? This often happens, especially as one is growing up. Perhaps your goal was not realistic. Perhaps there was something else you could do and be more successful. Juanita Ramerez wanted to be a waitress. Unfortunately, she spent so much time fussing with table setups that she could not meet the schedule deadlines. Then she tried the job of salad girl. She found it much more satisfying. Her fussiness and interest in detail resulted in beautifully arranged salad plates. With practice, she learned to meet production schedules by working faster. She created salads that be-

came the specialty of the restaurant. Juanita changed her goal and is much happier now.

Step 2. Consider Your Resources

Resources are the means available to you to carry on your daily activities. There are two types of resources—human and material.

Human resources are those within you such as energy, knowledge, attitudes, skills, talents, and personal traits. Think about your own human resources. You may have a special talent such as a sympathetic understanding of people. This can help you to get along well with others, which is important for any job.

By good management of their material and human resources, food service workers can turn out exotic sandwiches such as finger sandwiches with fruit salad, Polynesian pork with water chestnuts, and broiled grapefruit with tuna.

261

Creativity is an important part of food service work. This worker uses her talents to create attractive, flavorful salads.

Dudley–Anderson–Yutzy

Perhaps you have creative ability, or you can always be depended on to get a job done. These, too, are important human resources. What human resources do you think would help a person to qualify for food service work?

Material resources are those found in the world around you. In food service, material resources are the food and equipment you use in your work and the money that is used to operate the unit.

In this step of managing, it is necessary to evaluate your resources. To do this, make a list of the human and material resources that are available to help you meet your goal. Do you have enough resources? How can you best use them to meet your goal?

Mary O'Hara, the dessert maker, had a creative flair. She was bored with her job—she wanted to do something artistic. One day one of the waitresses complimented her on the appearance of the desserts. "You make them look so pretty and appetizing," she said. Mary took a second look at her job. She decided that she could use her creative ability to make the desserts even more attractive. She created appealing garnishes and arranged the desserts so that each was a work of art. She became so interested in her work that she learned how to handle the food and service dishes more efficiently, thereby speeding up production. Instead of being bored with her job, Mary looked upon it as a creative challenge. She combined her human and material resources to meet her goal—using her artistic talent successfully. What were her human resources? Her material resources?

Step 3. Develop a Plan

Planning involves making choices regarding your course of action. These choices are then organized into a workable procedure.

You may have many or few choices, depending on your goal and your resources. Picture in your mind the courses of action that you can take and try to decide what the results of each might be. Ask yourself, "What would happen if I did this?" Try to imagine all the things that might possibly happen. It is not always easy to select just one from all the choices that may face you. When you plan, you need to settle on what you consider the best possible choice you can make.

Next, organize your plan. This means that you develop a step-by-step procedure which will make the best use of your plan and your resources. Plan your actions on the basis of what must be done first, what should be done second, then third. Continue the steps until you have your plan organized. Write out a *plan sheet*, listing the steps in the order they are to be done. Include the resources you will use in each step of your plan.

Keep your plan simple and flexible. Then, if something unexpected happens, it will be easier for you to make changes.

Go over your schedule carefully to be sure it is complete. It can be disappointing if you make a plan and then find it will not work because you forgot something important.

Consider how your plan will fit in with those of others. On a food service job, your plans need to fit in with the policies and procedures set up by the manager.

Althea Washington was assigned to prepare cabbage salad in her food service class. She

Friendly Ice Cream Shops

Planning and organizing are essential in food service work, whether you are a short-order cook . . .

. . . or an assembly line worker.

Canteen Corp.

263

Cape Coral Country Club, Fla.

The chef usually prepares and stores the pies early in his schedule. He is then ready for other food preparation as needed.

Good work habits and efficient methods help food service workers meet their schedules. This student will have her salads prepared and refrigerated, ready on time.

BOCES, Ithaca, N. Y.

planned and organized her assignment by asking herself important questions and providing thoughtful answers.

What is my goal? In twenty minutes, I must prepare enough cabbage salad to serve thirty people. *How can I do this?* I consider the resources I have. This includes the food handling techniques I have learned as well as recipes, supplies, and time. *Will anyone else be involved?* I include others who may be assigned to help me and we decide how we can work together. *How do I complete the assignment?* I plan and organize my resources in a step-by-step procedure. As a result, I can prepare the cabbage salad, including the work that must be done by others, in twenty minutes.

Althea completed her assignment successfully. Can you explain why?

Step 4. Carry Out the Plan

This step in management is exciting. When you put your own plan into action, you are *doing* and having the satisfaction of accomplishment. For example, Althea was successful in putting her own plan into action. First, she assembled and checked her supplies and equipment. Then she set up, cleaned, and cut the vegetables, and mixed them. She checked, and made sure she followed directions. With the help of a co-worker, she arranged the salad in serving dishes and stored them in the refrigerator.

Whether your plan is in your mind or on a slip of paper, use it as a guide. Take one step at a time. Cross off each item as you do it. Refer to your plan often, just as Althea did, so you will not forget any part.

To be successful, stick to your plan so that you reach your goal. This is known as *control*. In food service this means practicing good work habits and using efficient methods. You need to complete your work in the allowed time, in spite of distractions and temptations. You also need to be prepared to adjust to emergencies. However, if you always keep your plan in mind, you can generally do whatever is needed to get the job done.

At the Manor Inn, the entire kitchen staff was working hurriedly. In a few hours, they had to be ready for a banquet for three hundred people, in addition to the regular dinner trade. José Gomez knew just what he had to do. He had studied the cake recipe and the directions that the chief baker had given him, and he had made a plan.

José went to his work table and selected the utensils he needed. When he went to the storeroom to get his supplies, he brought everything in one trip by using a cart. As he followed his recipe, he made every motion count and used both hands efficiently. He used the best methods and shortcuts he had learned in school and on the job. He did not let the noise and the activity in the kitchen distract him from his job.

By carrying out his plan and controlling his actions, José made the job easier for himself. Because he could be counted on to do his job

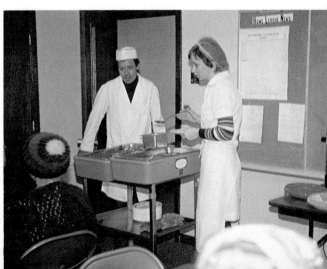

Edison Community College, Ft. Myers, Fla.

The food service worker may be assigned the preparation of salad plates such as these for the cold table. They must be attractively plated and ready on time.

On the job, you may need to take responsibility for part of a food program. These workers developed and carried out a plan for feeding a small group from a portable cart.

Salvation Army Nutrition Program

265

Broward County School Lunch Program, Florida

Food service employees must be dependable and get their jobs done on time. Here, each school lunch worker follows a planned pattern of work to prepare lunch for students.

well, José became important to his boss. What do you think would have happened if José had allowed himself to be distracted by the noise and activity in the kitchen?

Step 5. Evaluate the Results

In this final step, take time to examine the results of your plan. This is called *evaluating*. It is important to do this *before* you select new goals and make new plans. As a result of your evaluation, you may want to change or improve the product or the method used.

In order to evaluate the results you will need to ask yourself and others questions such as, "Was it well done or poorly done?" "Could I improve my plan next time?" "Am I using my resources in the best way possible?" "Am I just doing things as I happen to think of them?" "Do I blame other people for my mistakes?" "Through this plan, have I reached my goal?" "If not, why not?"

To answer these questions, measure your results against acceptable standards. Keep in mind that it takes training and experience to develop high standards of workmanship. For example, you have washed off your work area with a dish cloth and consider it well done. However, the kitchen supervisor is not satisfied. She wants the work area scrubbed with a brush and cleanser, then washed and rinsed off with a cleaning sponge. In other words, the supervisor wants you to meet the standards of cleanliness and sanitation that have been specified by the manager.

When you make your evaluation, ask your co-workers, teachers, or boss to help you. They can assist you in recognizing high standards and in measuring your own work performance.

MANAGING ON THE JOB

In food service work, there are three important areas where management skills can help you to succeed on the job. These are: managing yourself so that you get along with people; managing materials; and managing methods.

Getting Along with People

The food service business is made up of people. You not only work closely with people but you also serve other people. Some of these people are easy to get along with, others are not. Many of the people you work with will be kind, considerate, and helpful. Others, however, may be selfish, moody, or sarcastic. Some may gossip, cheat, or not do their share of the work. In addition, food service employees often have to work under pressure, which may make them tired and irritable.

How will you relate to others in these situations? Can you be understanding of the people you work with, of your boss, of the customers? Can you manage yourself so that you can get along with all kinds of people? There will be times when you may fail, but with each experience you can learn to manage yourself a little better the next time. Here are some ideas for managing yourself so that you can learn to get along with others.

To Get Along with People

Be dependable—Take responsibility for all parts of your job. Get your work done on schedule. Be on time. Be truthful.

Be thoughtful of others—Try to understand other people's needs. Give help to co-workers when needed. Do not gossip. Do not blame other people for your mistakes. Do not expect more of others than they can do. Be friendly, but quiet. Be polite. Ask for help and advice when needed.

Be appreciative—Thank others for help.

Can you put these ideas to work for you so that you can manage yourself and get along with all kinds of people? Janet Danke tried it. Do you think she succeeded?

Janet Danke was a new counter girl at the Home Dairy Cafeteria. Not long after she began her job, she decided that some of the customers seemed unreasonable. Mr. Dobbs bothered her the most. He always seemed to be in a hurry, complaining about the slow service. When pushed too far, Janet had a quick temper and was apt to lose it.

One busy day Janet could take it no longer. Giving Mr. Dobbs a cross look, she said, "Mr. Dobbs, if you don't like our service, go somewhere else. We're busy."

Later, during a break, Janet and Effie Wilson, the food supervisor, were talking about the noon-hour rush.

"Boy, I sure told that complaining Mr. Dobbs off today," said Janet.

"Oh?" answered Effie, questioningly. "Our policy here is that the customer is always right. I don't think the manager would like to have you talk to customers that way."

"Well, I sure don't go along with that policy. I'm going to say what I think," said Janet. "It's a free country."

Later, however, Janet began thinking things over. It was true that on other jobs she had been in trouble because of her quick temper. Maybe she ought to try to do something about it. "I manage my work well," Janet thought to herself, "so why can't I manage my reactions to people?"

Janet selected a goal. (Step 1.) She was determined to control her temper, especially when she was under pressure.

Janet considered her resources. (Step 2.) She liked people, and she usually had a friendly manner. Also, she now knew more about the cafeteria's policies and where to go for help when necessary.

Janet made plans. (Step 3.) She decided she needed to understand people better. In addition, she needed to think before she spoke out. After considering her problem carefully, she

BOCES, Ithaca, N. Y.

Equipment and supplies are efficiently arranged in this work area so that they are readily available to the worker.

decided to look for ways in which she could be more considerate of others. She also decided to observe how others managed to stay calm under the pressure of work.

Janet carried out her plan. (Step 4.) Each day she made a conscious effort to be considerate of the customers and her co-workers. Since the cafeteria was close to his office, Mr. Dobbs soon came in again. Although he complained about the service, Janet smiled pleasantly and said, "I'm sorry, we're pretty busy today, but we'll take care of your order in just a minute. I'm sorry, Mr. Dobbs, that I was so short with you the other day."

Janet evaluated the results. (Step 5.) After working a whole week without losing her tem-

per, she felt she was doing well. On this particularly busy day, Janet realized she had finally succeeded when she controlled her temper with Mr. Dobbs. "How did I do today, Effie?" asked Janet after an especially trying noon hour.

"Good job! And don't you feel better about it?"

What do you think would have happened to Janet if she had not learned to control her temper? How could her temper have affected business? If you had been Mr. Dobbs, would you have returned? Why?

Materials

A well-planned, organized work area can help you to work faster and to become less tired. It can also enable you to produce more in the hours you work.

Generally, the kitchen area in a food service unit has been efficiently organized by a trained person. However, many kitchens may be outdated or even too small. Therefore workers need to know how to manage the work area so they can do their job as well as possible.

Managing materials involves placing equipment and supplies so that they can be used most conveniently. Here are several suggestions for organizing materials in a work area. (See the table on the next page.)

To give you an idea of how this works, let us review a problem which the Monarch Restaurant faced.

The Monarch was having one of its busiest dinner hours. Most people waiting in line were good-natured, but some had become impatient and had left.

Organize Your Work Area

Pre-position tools and materials.	Analyze where each tool and supply will be used first, and/or most frequently. Then place it at or near that spot.
Place items where they are easy to see and reach.	Place the most used tools and supplies in direct line with your sight and reach. Place the less used tools and supplies at full arm's reach. As much as possible, avoid placing supplies where a great deal of bending and reaching is required.
Place items in terms of their weight.	Locate heavy articles close to you on lower shelves. Locate lighter ones at full arm's reach on higher shelves. The very lightest can be located at fingertip reach.
Select and use the right tools for each job.	Read and follow the directions and recipes accurately to find out what tool to use. Observe the tools that experienced workers use for each job.

Bob Chang, the busboy, was clearing off the tables quickly. Why was it taking so long to get the tables reset? Everyone seemed to be working faster, but it did not seem to help.

Ruth Steiman, the head waitress, called impatiently, "Speed it up, can't you, Bob? I've got customers waiting for tables."

"I'm doing all I can," snapped Bob. "I can't get the set-ups fast enough from Jim."

Jim Jackson, the dishwasher, was working at top speed to get clean dinner plates to the chef, salad plates to the salad counter, and set-ups to Bob.

Later on, when the restaurant was not so busy, Jim commented to Ruth, "On busy nights there sure is a bottleneck in this dish machine area."

"Well, let's take a look at the problem," answered Ruth. "Maybe we can figure something out."

"Good idea, let me think about it," said Jim. *Jim set his goal.* (Step 1.) He was determined to find a way to eliminate the bottleneck and to have a large enough supply of clean dishes to meet the demand.

Jim considered his resources. (Step 2.) He had an excellent dish machine, plenty of dishes, and he knew he was a fast and careful worker.

Jim planned and organized. (Step 3.) He carefully looked over his work area. Did it need rearranging? Perhaps if he had shelves for the dishes near the door to the dining room instead of at the dishwasher, he and Bob would not always be bumping into each other.

Jim put his plan into action. (Step 4.) He went to the manager and suggested his idea of adding shelves.

"That sounds like a good idea," said the manager. "We'll have the shelves put up tomorrow."

Jim judged the results. (Step 5.) His plan worked! The whole procedure operated more smoothly the next night. The shelves were within easy reach for Jim, and he could see at a glance when the supply was low. Bob could get his dishes without interfering with Jim's work. Everyone was glad that Jim had been able to find a way to break the dishroom bottleneck so that service was improved.

Can you see how Jim showed good management? Often, there are ways in which you can organize your work materials to improve production. You need to be alert to these opportunities, although you may also need to ask for help from a trained person.

Work Methods

Managing your work methods means organizing your time, energy, and knowledge for the job that has been assigned to you. Remember to observe, learn, and practice the five steps to managing described in this chapter, so that they will become easy for you.

When you are on a food service job, you will be given a work schedule or told what is expected of you. The schedule usually lists the work you are to perform that day. Sometimes a job will be divided into several parts. The time you should normally take to complete each part may also be included. A *work schedule* may be defined as a plan for using your time, energy, and abilities to accomplish a specific task.

Employers expect you to have the ability to manage your own work schedule and responsibilities.

How can you manage your work methods skillfully?

This worker has efficiently organized fruit juice service.

Florida Dept. of Citrus, Denver Schools

Organize Your Work Methods

Simplify your work methods.

List or think of each step in doing a particular job. Eliminate any unnecessary steps in the method you are using. Combine one step with another when possible. Rearrange the order of the steps, the materials, or the equipment if it will give better results. Try other methods or routines to see if they make the work easier or simpler.

Practice and develop efficient work habits.

Use efficient short cuts. Develop and/or follow a planned pattern of work so it becomes habit and requires less effort. Plan your own work schedule to meet deadlines. Be prepared to adjust to changes and emergencies. Do one thing at a time. Proceed logically from one step to another. Observe others to improve your work methods.

Streamline your movements.

Practice speedy, smooth movements. Make every motion count. Use both hands. Lift, carry, and push properly. Stand, walk, and sit with correct posture. Try to gather food and equipment in one trip. Use trays and carts to save energy. If you return anything to the supply area on a cart, do not roll back an empty cart. Instead, bring back equipment that you may need later.

Practice and develop your own managing ability for each job assignment. Use the five steps discussed earlier to help you. Here is how Mrs. Snyder and her vocational food service class used the five steps in organizing a job.

"We've just been asked by the Superintendant of Schools to put on a banquet for 150," announced Mrs. Snyder in food service class one day. "Do you think we can do it?"

"Sure, why not?" said Keith Branski. "We served a luncheon last month. It turned out good."

"I think it sounds exciting," answered Athena Jones, "and we can wear our new uniforms, too!"

The next day the class began planning. As plans were made, Mrs. Snyder wrote them on a large chart so that each class member could check the day-by-day progress they were making. Athena was especially interested in management and made a chart to show the major points of their management process.

Management Chart For Banquet

Our goal. . . . . To prepare and serve an attractive banquet for 150 adults.

Our resources. . . . . A dining area with the necessary number of tables and chairs; a kitchen with the necessary equipment; the ability and experience of class members; knowledge of menu planning, food preparation, and service.

Our plan. . . . . Decide on appropriate menu that can be prepared during class time in the cafeteria and class kitchens. Decide on type of service. Experiment with recipes. Determine costs, and decide what to charge for the dinner. Plan to have cafeteria worker prepare the meat and vegetable; class members to prepare the appetizers, breads, salads, and desserts. Plan work schedules for each class member.

Management Chart for Banquet (Continued)

Carrying out our plan.

Several days before the dinner........ Prepare and freeze breads and desserts.

Before the dinner. .... Arrange worktable. Assemble supplies and equipment. Follow work schedules step by step. Use work methods learned in class. Prepare appetizers and salads. Wash and put away equipment. Set up and arrange tables attractively.

During dinner.................... Assemble and dish up food. Keep supplies replenished. Serve at dining tables.

After dinner. .... Clear dining tables. Put food and supplies away. Clean and arrange tables. Wash and put away dishes.

Our evaluation. .... Judge the appearance, taste, and quality of the food. Judge the attractiveness of the table settings, and consider any improvements needed. List ways to improve timing, organization, and work performance. Consider individual problems, their causes, and ways to improve them.

Economics Laboratory, Inc.

A disorganized soiled dishtable encourages careless work habits and slows down food production. If you were working in this dishroom, how would you use the five steps of management to solve this situation?

To be successful in food service work, think about and practice the five steps of management: (1) Select your goals realistically. (2) Consider your resources carefully. (3) Develop a plan. (4) Carry out your plan efficiently. (5) Evaluate the results and try to improve where possible.

Can you see how the five steps in managing help you to improve your skills in this area? Remember, food service work—preparing and serving food to people on definite time schedules—requires skillful management.

Let's Think It Over

Everyone manages in one way or another—both at home and on the job. If you can learn to manage your resources effectively, you can be productive, happy, and satisfied with your work.

- Define the terms *managing, resource, goal.*
- Give examples of short-term goals and long-term goals.
- Give examples of human resources. Material resources.
- What are the five steps that will help you to manage effectively?
- What should you consider when you make plans as part of managing?
- Explain the meaning of *control* in management.
- Why do you need to evaluate the results of your work?
- What are the three areas that require management skills in food service jobs?
- Why is it important to manage to get along with people? List some ways that this can be done.
- What skills are needed to manage effectively the materials in a work area? Explain how each skill can be developed.
- Describe ways to use the five steps in organizing work methods and simplifying movements.

Let's Investigate

1. Show by diagram, charts, or written explanations how you would apply good managing procedures in the following job assignments.

   - Waitress at 3 tables, seating 6 each, at a banquet for 100 people.
   - Preparing tossed salad for 50 customers.
   - Setting up a buffet table with a supper service for 75 people.

• Clean-up duties in a dining room seating 60 customers.

2. Why do you think these food service workers are having problems? What would you recommend each one do to improve the situation?

  • Penny Drake, a waitress, gave her customer a cross look and said, "I don't know what is in the seafood casserole."

  • A customer complained to Jerry Lee, the carhop, that his hamburger was cold and undercooked. Jerry answered, "That's too bad!"

• Dottie Traymore spent so much time visiting with her friends that she could not get the salad counter ready on time. She was behind schedule for three days in a row.

• Susie Shaw, a tray girl in a hospital, kept dropping dishes and cutlery. She did not place items in correct positions on the patient's tray.

Chapter 13

Be Smart

About Sanitation

If food is to be safe for people to eat, it must be sanitary. *Sanitation* is defined as the science of cleanliness. In food service, this means *sanitary* work habits, or the utmost cleanliness in storage, preparation, and service. It includes *sanitary* or clean and healthy personal habits of workers. Sanitation helps to prevent harmful bacteria from developing.

Another term closely related to sanitation is *asepsis*—keeping free from germs. You probably are familiar with the word *antiseptic,* which means preventing or arresting harmful germs and bacteria. Nursing homes and hospitals must maintain aseptic conditions in patient areas and operating rooms. This means extreme cleanliness of all work areas, tools,

and materials. Areas where food is kept and handled must also be kept immaculately clean.

Wherever there is uncleanliness, certain kinds of disease are likely to spread. High standards of cleanliness guard against diseases.

WORDS TO KNOW	
Sanitation	Food-borne disease
Asepsis	Salmonellosis
Sanitary	Staphylococcus
Bacteria	Trichinosis
Sanitary codes	Sanitizers
Toxin	Contaminated food
Botulism	Detergents

Through carelessness, anyone can bring germs and harmful bacteria into a clean, sanitary area. How can you avoid this?

Wherever food is served, sanitation is the responsibility of not only the management but every employee as well. This chapter discusses the facts that you need to know about sanitation.

LAWS AND REGULATIONS

Standards for sanitation in food service are established and enforced by laws known as *sanitary codes* or regulations. These are the result of a great deal of study and research by national, state, and local agencies. Some of the agencies that make and/or enforce the sanitation and safety standards are U. S. Department of Public Health, National Sanitation Foundation, and National Safety Council. Many other groups such as university research centers, equipment manufacturers, and food service managers cooperate in studying and setting standards that will protect the public and the workers.

Local and state public health departments set up and enforce sanitary codes for the physical facilities and the operation of all food services in their areas. In order to enforce these laws, health departments have sanitation inspectors, who regularly check all types of food services.

Food service operators and workers, therefore, must know, understand, and follow the local sanitary codes. Your local health department can provide this information as well as booklets and posters which can help you to understand the sanitation codes in your community. The personnel of your local health

H. J. Heinz Co.

Sanitary codes for restaurants are the result of extensive research by national, state, and local agencies.

Modern, well-planned snack bars provide different types of deep and shallow sinks for sanitizing utensils and equipment.

Orange Julius

department are often available to give short courses in sanitation. Perhaps your teacher can invite someone from the local health department to speak to the class.

Why is sanitary food handling and personal cleanliness stressed and enforced so strongly? At home or at work, you sometimes may be careless in handling food, with no ill effects. Therefore you may fail to see the importance of sanitation. It is necessary to realize that by being careless or unclean, you may contaminate any food you are handling. *Contaminated food* contains harmful germs and bacteria, which are capable of causing illness if anyone eats the food.

Since good health is treasured by everyone, sanitary food service is vital to all. One of your responsibilities in food service work is to understand the facts about bacteria and food protection, as well as the cause and prevention of illness caused by contaminated food.

BACTERIA

Bacteria are all around you—on the equipment and supplies you handle, on your body, your face, your hands, your hair, and your clothes. *Bacteria* are small plants, so small they can only be seen through a microscope. That is why they are called microscopic plants. Although you cannot see them, you can understand how they function.

Not all bacteria are harmful. In fact, some are essential in making foods such as cheese, vinegar, and sour cream.

This chapter is especially concerned with disease-causing bacteria, called *pathogenic*. They can multiply at a rapid rate and cause infections. These bacteria live on tissue and fluids such as those found in the human body and in food.

Bacteria need the right temperature, moisture, and food to grow and reproduce rapidly. If one of these conditions is missing, the bacteria will not grow and may die. Good sanitation prevents the conditions which cause bacteria to grow.

Most disease-causing bacteria grow rapidly in temperatures ranging from 16°C to 49°C [60°F. to 120°F.]. This is the most dangerous temperature zone in food preparation. High temperatures over 77°C [170°F.] kill most bacteria. Cold temperatures between 0°C and 5°C [32°F. and 40°F.] slow down their growth. Freezing temperatures below 0°C [32°F.] stop growth of bacteria but do not kill them. The average temperature of the human body is 37°C [98.6°F.], which is ideal for the growth of bacteria. Can you see why it is important to wash your hands before working with food?

Bacteria cannot live without moisture. Some bacteria also require oxygen to live, but other bacteria will grow without oxygen.

As was mentioned, bacteria prefer certain foods which are high in protein and moisture.

Areas where food is handled must be kept sparkling clean at all times to help prevent the growth of harmful bacteria.

Atlanta, Ga., Public Schools

278

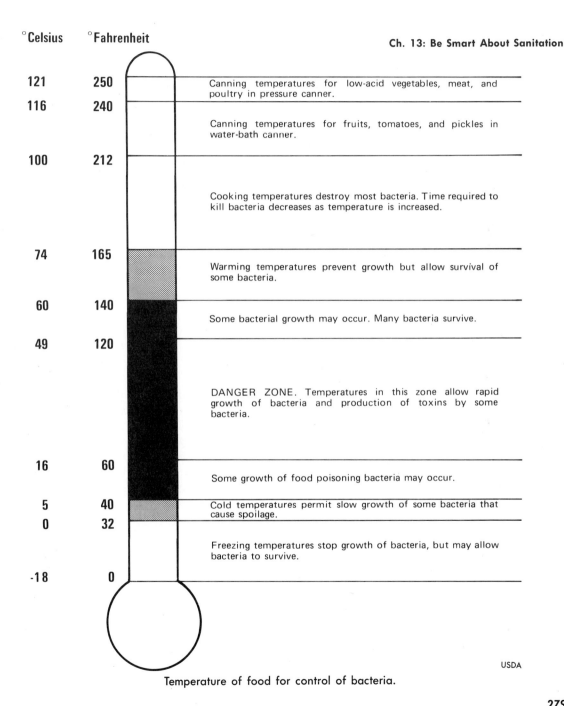

121 250 Canning temperatures for low-acid vegetables, meat, and poultry in pressure canner.

116 240

Canning temperatures for fruits, tomatoes, and pickles in water-bath canner.

100 212

Cooking temperatures destroy most bacteria. Time required to kill bacteria decreases as temperature is increased.

74 165 Warming temperatures prevent growth but allow survival of some bacteria.

60 140 Some bacterial growth may occur. Many bacteria survive.

49 120

DANGER ZONE. Temperatures in this zone allow rapid growth of bacteria and production of toxins by some bacteria.

16 60 Some growth of food poisoning bacteria may occur.

5 40 Cold temperatures permit slow growth of some bacteria that cause spoilage.

0 32

Freezing temperatures stop growth of bacteria, but may allow bacteria to survive.

-18 0

USDA

Temperature of food for control of bacteria.

Cold foods such as poultry, meat, salads, and sauces are served on a bed of ice to keep them cold enough so that harmful bacteria do not form.

They do not grow readily in heavy sugar solutions or in starches. Dried, salted, or acid foods retard the action of bacteria. Fats and protein foods are most commonly contaminated by bacteria.

The most common foods and food products in which bacteria grow are:

Milk and milk products.
Casseroles.
Eggs.
Meat and meat products.
Poultry.
Fish.
Shellfish.
Salad dressings.
Gravies.
Cream pies and fillings.
Pastries.
Custards.
Sauces.
Salads.
Stuffings for meat and poultry.

This does not mean, of course, that bacteria do not grow in other foods. The danger comes from carelessness in selecting, cleaning, preparing, refrigerating, storing, and serving food. The foods themselves are not dangerous, but the way they are handled can make them so. Poor sanitation may result in bacterial growth, which may cause infection and illness.

If harmful bacteria are allowed to grow and multiply in foods, they produce a *toxin* or poison, which can cause serious illness in people who eat the food. These illnesses are called *food-borne illness* or food poisoning.

PESTS

It is important to protect food from pollution by pests. The most common pests are rats, mice, flies, roaches, and ants. As they walk and feed on garbage or other waste matter, they pick up germs on their feet and bodies. The germs are left on food. Pests, therefore, are dangerous carriers of harmful bacteria.

You, as a food service worker, need to be alert for any signs of pests. Report such signs to the supervisor at once.

Careful control measures are a vital part of any sanitation program. These controls eliminate pests from storage and food service areas. Lack of control will result not only in the spread of disease but in costly spoilage as well. Some of these control measures are:

- Rat-proof buildings. Close all small openings. Place ratguards on all wires and pipes coming into the building. Be sure joints at walls and foundations have no cracks.
- Screen windows and doors to keep out flies.
- Dispose of garbage and waste in covered containers, incinerators, or heavy-duty disposal units.
- Close all cracks and crevices in walls around pipes and equipment.
- Keep storerooms and all work areas clean.
- Be alert to insects that may be on cartons or in linens.
- Keep all animals out.

Sprays and poisons, called rodenticides and pesticides, help control rodents and insects. Remember, however, that sprays and poisons are often dangerous to humans and pets and must be used with extreme caution.

- Label and store all poisonous compounds or sprays in a safe place.
- Use compounds for rodent and pest control that are harmless to pets wherever possible.
- Do not use sprays and poisons around food.

- Hire reliable specialists for periodic control of rodents and insects.
- Follow regular work schedules for sanitation.

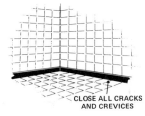

Buildings should be rat proof.

Use sprays and other poisons to control insects and rodents.

FOOD-BORNE ILLNESS

What are the food-borne illnesses caused by poor food handling and how do they affect people? The chart below lists several.

Although these are the most commonly recognized food-borne illnesses, there are others which also relate to food handling. These are:

• *Typhoid fever* from contaminated water,

FOOD-BORNE ILLNESS

Disease	Cause	Effect
Salmonellosis (one of the major food-borne illnesses).	Improperly cooked shell-fish; poultry; eggs; egg products; dairy products; meats; salads with mayonnaise or cream dressings; foods contaminated by unwashed hands and pests.	Results in a serious intestinal illness within 12 to 24 hours. Usually lasts 1 to 3 days.
Staphylococcus (usually called staph food poisoning).	Cream-filled pastries and custards; chopped foods; fish or meat; egg and milk products; food contaminated by cuts, sores, boils, and unclean hands and equipment.	Results in illness within 2 to 4 hours; lasts 3 to 6 hours.
Trichinosis.	Raw or undercooked pork. A tiny worm in the muscles of pork is the direct cause. Recent development in eliminating the worm from pigs will result in better control of this disease.	Results in serious illness.
Botulism.	Canned non-acid foods improperly prepared. Usually home-canned foods, but has also been caused by commercially canned foods.	Results in a serious disease which is often fatal.

milk, shellfish, or food contaminated by flies or unwashed hands.

- *Dysentery* and *diptheria,* caused by germs found in or on defective plumbing; impure water; unwashed hands; flies; dishes or silverware contaminated by a carrier sneezing, coughing, or spitting. A *carrier* is a person who carries the disease-causing germ but who is not affected by it.

Prevention of illness caused by contaminated food is one of the most important responsibilities of the food service industry. Although good sanitation is practiced, it is estimated that two million cases of food-borne illness occur every year. Many of the cases may be mild or may be confused with another illness such as flu or an upset stomach.

Food-borne illness occurs when the people who prepare and serve the food fail to follow sanitary regulations.

Food-borne illness occurs after eating:

- Foods containing disease-producing bacteria.
- Foods containing toxins produced by harmful bacteria.
- Foods containing parasites such as worms in meat which can infect man.
- Food which is contaminated either accidentally or carelessly with harmful chemicals such as the use of cooking containers made with poisonous metals (antimony, zinc, cadmium, and lead); or mislabeling or misuse of chemicals found in food preparation centers.
- Food which is naturally poisonous such as some varieties of mushrooms and greens.

It is most important to protect food so it will not cause food poisoning. *Food protection*

BOCES, Ithaca, N. Y.

To prevent food-borne illness, food must be properly stored, prepared, and served.

means guarding food from harmful bacteria in every way possible. To protect foods, the conditions that promote the growth of bacteria must be removed.

Methods used to protect food from spoilage include:

Trayline worker portions cold food into serving dishes on trays and places trays in a cart. The cart will be rolled into the refrigerator, and the food kept cold until serving time.

Caddy Corp.

283

Frozen turkeys, just received from the supplier, are immediately carted into the walk-in freezer. This prevents partial thawing and growth of harmful bacteria.

A state restaurant inspector checks the condition of the refrigeration unit with the owner to be sure it meets state standards for eating units. All areas of the restaurant are thoroughly checked before a license is issued.

- Drying—removes the moisture, thus killing the bacteria.
- Refrigerating and freezing—removes warmth. Cold temperatures slow down bacterial growth and freezing stops it. However, the bacteria are not killed.
- Heat—kills bacteria. Canning provides high heat (boiling or above), which sterilizes the food and containers. Sealing excludes the air so that bacteria cannot enter. Pasteurizing heats milk to kill harmful bacteria that carry disease. Thus it makes milk safe for people to drink. Cooking provides high heat, which kills the bacteria.
- Pickling, salting, and spicing provide a salty, spicy, or acid solution which helps preserve meats, fish, cucumbers, and other foods. Sometimes chemicals are used. Sugar is used in jams or jellies to preserve the food. In these methods, air must be excluded to stop bacterial growth.

When food is not protected from harmful bacteria in one of the above ways, it may become contaminated. If people eat it, sickness and disease may result.

It is the responsibility of everyone in food service work to cooperate in preventing foodborne illness. There are standard procedures that can help to protect people from foodborne illness:

- *Purchase Safe Food.* Use reliable vendors. Write specifications that follow federal, state, and local laws. Examine food products for signs of spoilage. Check purchases to be sure that only high-quality food is received.

284

- *Store Foods Properly.* Keep unrefrigerated foods in clean, dry, well-ventilated storage at temperatures of 5°C to 21°C [40°F. to 70°F.]. Store foods covered. Use proper refrigeration and freezer temperatures. Refrigerate foods immediately. Do not allow perishable foods to stand for long periods at room temperature. Use the oldest-stored foods first. Maintain good pest control.

- *Prepare Foods Properly.* Discard any questionable foods. Wash raw fruits and vegetables thoroughly. Cook foods till done. Keep all work areas, utensils, and equipment clean.

- *Practice Safe Food Handling.* Food handlers must be healthy and free from disease, have clean personal habits, and be free of cuts or colds. They must wash hands frequently.

- *Follow Sanitary Housekeeping Practices.* Always use clean equipment, utensils, and tools. Keep all areas free from pests.

YOUR PART IN GOOD SANITATION

You have a vital part in the sanitation program.

Keep in mind that bacteria cause:

- Food poisoning.
- Foul odors.
- Food spoilage.

You must do everything possible to prevent bacterial growth. The sanitation practices described in the following pages will help you to be a clean, valuable worker.

285

USDA

Meat inspector looks for characteristics that indicate quality.

Students need to develop and maintain high standards of cleanliness as they work with equipment. This will protect them and the public.

BOCES, Ithaca, N. Y.

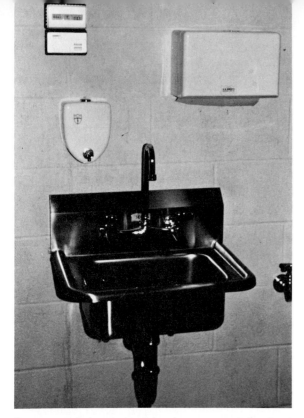

Do not wash hands in sinks that are used for food preparation. Special hand-washing sinks such as this one are usually provided close to the food production areas.

Personal Hygiene

You and the other persons who prepare and serve food to customers must maintain high standards of personal cleanliness. Why? Because this helps get rid of germs. If you are not careful about cleanliness, germs will increase in number.

- Always wear a clean, fresh apron or uniform.
- Wash your hands with soap and hot water often:
    - Before you begin work.
    - Before you handle food.
    - After you visit the rest room.
    - After you handle raw, unwashed food.
    - After you cough, sneeze, blow your nose, or touch your hair or face.

- Do not wear jewelry or fingernail polish.
- Keep your fingernails short and clean.
- Brush your teeth twice a day.
- Take daily baths.
- Wear clean undergarments daily.
- Wear a hair net or cap to cover hair.
- Shampoo hair frequently.
- Use an antiperspirant.
- Work only when free of disease or illness.
- Do not work if you have a cold, sores, cuts, or wounds.
- Have regular physical checkups.
- Do not smoke in the kitchen area.

Sanitary Food Handling

Remember, germs multiply rapidly under unsanitary conditions. Make it a point to develop sanitary habits in handling equipment, supplies, and food. This is a vital responsibility. Good habits can prevent food contamination and the spread of colds to customers and fellow workers.

- Do not touch the "eating" parts of silver—tines of forks, blades of knives, bowls of spoons—or rims of glasses and cups.
- Use disposable plastic gloves, tongs, or scoops when serving ice cubes, butter, rolls, or pastry.
- Use clean spoons for tasting food.
- Never lick your fingers. Do not nibble crumbs.
- Throw away unopened individual containers of sugar, salt, and pepper that are returned from the dining area.
- Scrape leftover food from plates with rubber scraper, not hands.

- Always wash fresh produce, such as fruit and vegetables, before serving raw or cooking.
- Keep food refrigerated at proper temperatures.
- Report any questionable foods.
- Keep hot foods hot and cold foods cold.

Sanitary Clean-up Methods

Good sanitation practices for clean-up are an essential part of the program to protect the public against food-borne illnesses.

- Keep paper and food off the floor at all times.
- Be sure you have enough convenient waste containers.

Atlanta, Ga., Public Schools

Food service worker puts on disposable plastic gloves before mixing a salad with hands.

Kitchen worker prepares to wash pots and pans in a three-compartment sink. The first compartment, on the right, is used for washing, the center one for rinsing, and the last one for sanitizing.

Ithaca, N. Y., City Schools

Food Service Careers

A movable belt takes soiled dishes and trays from the dining room into the dishwashing area.

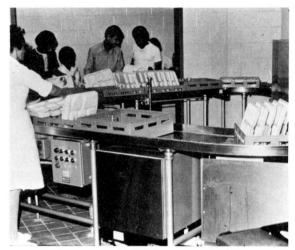

School lunchroom worker arranges soiled compartment trays in dishmachine racks.

School lunchroom worker checks dishmachine racks to be sure cups are properly loaded.

- Wipe up spilled foods and liquids immediately.
- Do not dry sweep while food is being prepared.
- Follow the methods outlined by your employer for cleaning floors, tables, chairs, and work areas.
- Use germicides and sanitizers to wash anything that comes in contact with foods. (*Germicides* and *sanitizers* are chemicals that kill or stop the growth of bacteria on the surfaces of dishes, pots, pans, tables and floors.)
- Use the proper *detergent* (chemical cleansing agent) for any cleaning job you do. Follow the directions on the label. Sometimes a detergent is combined with a sanitizer and is called a detergent-sanitizer.
- After each use, wash mops, sponges, and brushes in fresh, hot detergent water. Rinse in hot water and sanitizers. Allow to air dry.
- Rinse pots and pans immediately after use. Soak in mild detergent.
- Wash pots, pans, and hand tools in hot water (120° to 140°F.), with the recommended soap or detergent. Use a clean scrub brush or wire brush to remove burned food. Rinse in clean, hot water. Use a sanitizing compound (usually done in a third sink) for further sterilization.
- Wash dishes properly by hand as follows: Scrape and stack soiled dishes for washing. Wash dishes thoroughly inside and outside in hot water (43°C) [110°F.], using a recommended detergent-sanitizer. Rinse dishes in hot water (77°C to 82°C) [170°F. to 180°F.], and a recommended sanitizing

agent. Air dry when possible to avoid possible contact with germs on a towel.
- Store clean pots, pans, and tools on the assigned clean shelves or racks. Store upside down or covered.
- Clean equipment such as ranges, steam jacket kettles, steamers, peelers, grinders, slicers, coffee urns, hot food tables, and carts immediately after use. Use the method recommended by your supervisor.

Dishwashing

Clean glasses, silver, and dishes are noticed by customers. People associate cleanliness with a pleasant atmosphere.

Dirty dishes may give a restaurant a reputation as a "greasy spoon." Customers who are served with poorly washed dishes usually do not return.

As a beginner in food service, you may be asked to hand wash dishes or pots and pans. Although you may not think so, this is an important job. The sanitizing of dishes and pots is necessary to prevent food-borne diseases. You are helping when you do the job as directed.

Most food service units use a dish machine. It may be a small model built into a counter or it may be a large, fully automatic machine. Whatever the type, you need to observe certain rules if you work at the dish machine or in the dishroom.

Order is necessary in the dish area to prevent breakage and to get the work done efficiently. Broken dishes raise the overhead cost of operating a restaurant. They can cause accidents such as cuts, too. Work carefully and avoid breakage.

Loading a dish machine . . .

All photos these pages courtesy Economics Laboratory Inc.

Disorder in the dishroom results in costly breakage and cuts down efficiency. Dirty dishes were dumped on the soiled dishtable with little thought given to order.

Cups and glasses should be placed upside down in dish machine racks. This way the wash water can get in and the rinse water can drain out.

This soiled dishtable has been organized with a plate of each size set out as a decoy. Dining room helpers can unload trays or buspans and place all dishes of one type in a separate stack. Silver is placed in a presoak solution.

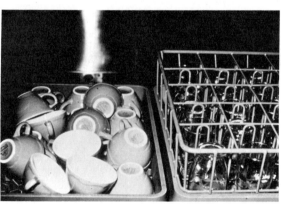

NOT THIS WAY! Do not place cups every which way in the rack. Those that are upright will fill with water and will not get clean. The dish machine cleans by water pressure which scrubs the surface of dishes and utensils. If cups are full of water or nesting on top of each other, the water pressure cannot get to them and clean them. If the cups fill up with water, they must be put through the dishwasher a second time to clean them.

290

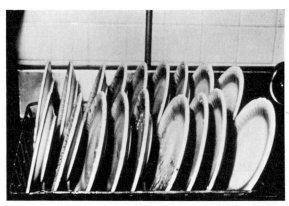

All of one kind of dish should be loaded together in the same rack for best results. Because the dishes were placed in separate piles on the soiled dishtable, it is easier for the dish machine operator to load the racks.

Here is an improperly loaded rack. First, there are too many dishes. Also, they are touching each other which means the wash water cannot hit the entire surface of the dish. If dishes are covering each other when racked, they will not get cleaned. There are also several different sizes of dishes in the same rack. This makes the job of unloading at the clean end more difficult. Remember, wash all of one size and type of dish in one rack.

When loading dishes, scrape off heavy food soil into the scrapping block. Dishes should be pre-rinsed of heavy food soil before they go into the machine. If they are not pre-rinsed, the wash water gets too dirty too fast. The scrap trays and wash arms become clogged, causing poorly washed dishes and repeat washing. The wash solution will have to be changed more often, which means more work and a waste of detergent and hot water.

Silver should be taken out of the pre-soak solution and put into the special silver racks with eating ends up. Knives and forks should be mixed with spoons so that they do not nest. If they nest, the entire surface will not be cleaned. Be sure that the racks are loaded loosely. If silver is jammed tightly and haphazardly with eating ends down, the wash water cannot penetrate well enough into the bottom of the rack. The silver will not be cleaned properly and will have to be washed again.

291

Unloading the dish machine . . .

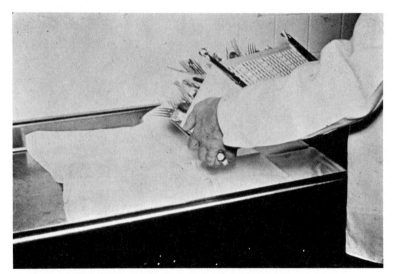

When silver comes out of the machine, it should be allowed to air-dry for a few moments. Then it should be unloaded onto a clean, dry cloth on the silver sorting table. It should be picked up by the handle and placed in clean silver trays. Remember, never touch the eating end of the silver.

Photos this page courtesy Economics Laboratory, Inc.

When the racks of dishes, cups, and glasses come out of the machine, they should be allowed to stand for a short time so that they will dry thoroughly. Racks of cups and glasses should be tilted for a moment to allow the water to run off their bottoms. Cup and glass dollies should be positioned at the end of the machine so the full, clean racks can be placed directly on them.

Allow plenty of room to stack clean plates or put them directly into plate carts. Dishes should be stored in such a way that they will not be resoiled.

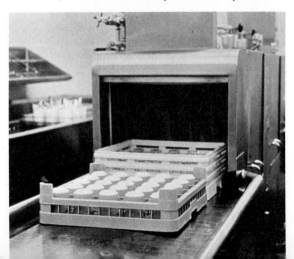

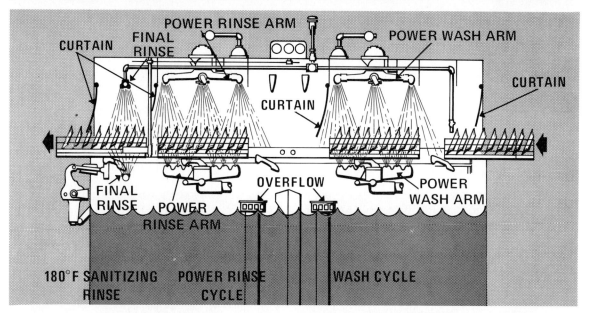

Labels in diagram:

POWER RINSE ARM

CURTAIN • FINAL RINSE

POWER WASH ARM

CURTAIN

CURTAIN

FINAL RINSE • POWER RINSE ARM • OVERFLOW • POWER WASH ARM

180°F SANITIZING RINSE • POWER RINSE CYCLE • WASH CYCLE

This is a diagram of a rack type dishwashing machine. The racks of dishes first pass through the power wash section where the detergent solution is sprayed from both the top and bottom wash arms onto the dishes to clean them. Now you can see why proper racking is important. Next the dishes pass through the power rinse cycle. Here the detergent solution is rinsed off. Then the dishes go through the final rinse section where they are sanitized.

How the busboys stack the dishes makes a difference in the dishroom. Soiled dishes of a kind should be put together. Glasses and silver should be kept separate. Paper should be discarded before the tray or buspan is deposited.

If the soiled-dish table is set up properly, space and utensils will be ready for soiled dishes. Silver may go into a pre-soak. Plates of one size are piled together. Glasses and cups may be placed in dish machine racks. They should be turned upside down so the water can reach all parts and then drain off.

A prerinse section may be built into a dish machine or dishes may be sprayed by hand to remove heavy soil.

Rack dishes as instructed. They should not overlap; if they do, water cannot reach all surfaces. Silver may be placed in special silver racks or washed in a flat dish basket. Be sure not to overcrowd or silver will not be cleaned properly. Silver is usually dipped into a sanitizing solution. When handling clean silver, touch only the handles and not the eating areas so you do not contaminate them.

Allow dishes to stand a few minutes to air dry before loading them in clean-dish areas. Allow room for clean dishes and be sure the area is clean.

Operating the dish machine requires care. Watch the temperature gauge. Wash water should be 60°C to 71°C [140°F. to 160°F.]. The rinse should be 77°C to 88°C [170°F. to 190°F.]. If these temperatures are not maintained, tell your supervisor immediately.

When you operate a dish machine:
- Close the drain valve.
- See that scrap trays are clean and in place.
- Be sure curtains are in place.
- Wash arm should be clean.
- Open the fill valve to fill tank.
- Close valves when water reaches correct level.
- Fill the detergent reservoir.
- Add detergent during washing as instructed.
- Add wetting agent to rinse reservoir.
- Handle clean dishes carefully.

Operating a dish machine . . .

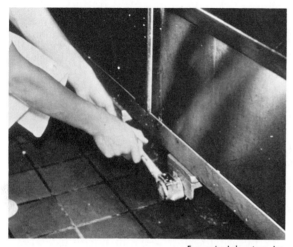

Economics Laboratory, Inc.

Check the machine to be sure that it is clean. Close the drain valve tightly.

Economics Laboratory, Inc.

Check curtains to be sure they are in place.

Check scrap trays to see that they are clean and in place. Be sure there are no bent corners. If they are bent, heavy food soil will drop into the wash tank, clogging the wash arms. Scrap trays should be emptied every few hours.

BOCES, Ithaca, N. Y.

Check the wash arms to see that they are clean. Be sure the spray openings are not clogged with food soil, toothpicks, or other foreign matter. If they are clogged, the washwater cannot spray against all sides of the dishes, and the dishes will not get clean.

Economics Laboratory, Inc.

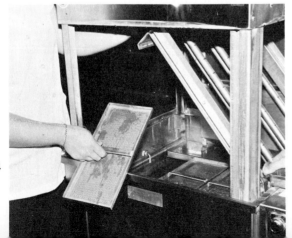

Next, check the wash temperature gauge to be sure that it is between 140° to 160°F. (60° to 71°C). Temperature should be kept at this level for best results.

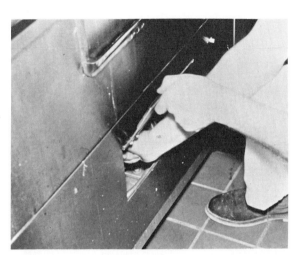

Next, open the fill valves to run the water into the tanks. When the water reaches the top of the overflow, shut the valves tightly. If the fill valve is left open, even slightly, it will waste excess water and detergent down the drain.

Check the power rinse temperature gauge. Be sure it is set at 170°F. (77°C). This temperature insures that the dishes are not only clean but free of harmful bacteria as well.

Then check the final rinse temperature gauge. This should be set between 180° to 190°F. (82° to 88°C) for a proper sanitizing rinse.

Fill the detergent reservoir. If a drying agent is used, be sure that reservoir is filled also.

Cleaning a dish machine . . .

Photos these pages courtesy Economics Laboratory, Inc.

The first step is to turn off the electric, gas, or steam heaters. Then open the drain valves and let all the water drain from the tanks.

Remove the scrap trays and empty them into the garbage can. Never bang them on the edge of the garbage can. That can cause bent corners which will allow foreign matter to drop into the wash tank and clog the wash arms.

Next, wash the scrap trays in a sink with a hot detergent solution. Rinse them thoroughly with the overhead spray and replace them in the dishmachine.

Open the side doors of the machine and remove the wash arms.

If possible, remove the end caps and flush out with a hose at the sink. Make sure that all foreign matter is poked out of the spray jet openings.

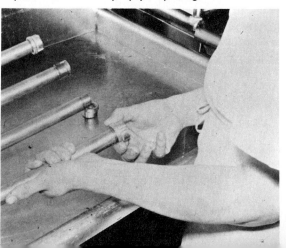

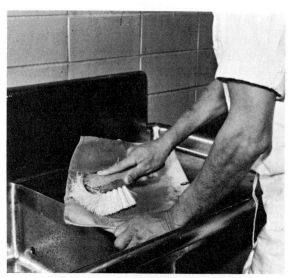

Remove all of the curtains from the machine and scrub them in the sink with a hot detergent solution. Allow to air-dry before placing them back in the machine.

After the machines and work tables have been cleaned and hosed off, they should be wiped with a clean, dry cloth. Boxes, broken dishes, or anything else that is on the top of the machine should be removed. The floors and walls of the dishroom should be scrubbed clean.

Hose out the inside of the machine and clean it thoroughly. Hose off all the work tables and scrub them with a hot detergent solution to remove any greasy buildup that might resoil clean dishes.

The dishmachine and the entire surrounding dishroom should be clean, ready for the next shift.

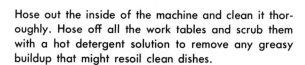

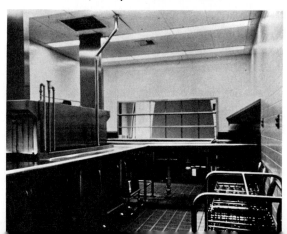

Corning Glass Works

Note the sparkling clean dishes, glasses, and silver. Would this setting be as effective if the tableware had spots and stains?

When you clean a dish machine:

- Turn off gas or electric heater.
- Open drain valves.
- Remove and empty scrap trays.
- Wash scrap trays in sink, using hot water and detergent.
- Remove wash arms and wash, using a brush.
- Remove curtains and wash.
- Hose inside of machine.
- Wipe off machine.
- Clean dish tables thoroughly.
- Hose walls and floors.

The use of sanitary procedures can help make you a valued employee. Remember, food service operations establish sanitary programs according to their needs. It is important for you to know and follow the procedures that your employer sets up.

Let's Think It Over

1. Good sanitation practices in food preparation and service help prevent food-borne illness and the spread of infectious diseases. Every employee must help maintain these standards.

   - Discuss the importance of sanitation in food service establishments.
   - How are people protected by sanitary laws and regulations? Explain how these are enforced in your community.
   - List some poor sanitary practices you may have observed while eating out. Discuss how these may affect business.
   - What types of foods are best for bacterial growth?
   - What can be done to protect food from bacterial growth?
   - List and explain the ways food-borne illness can be prevented in food service.
   - What personal hygiene practices are you responsible for on the job?
   - List the ways you can contribute to sanitary food service in the following areas:
     Food handling.
     Food storage.
     Care of kitchen and dining areas.
     Care of tools, supplies, and equipment.
     Disposal of waste.
     Pest control.

2. Clean dishes and tableware protect the customers. Describe what you would do in each of the steps below if you were using a dish machine:
   - Select temperatures of water.

- Rack dishes.
- Take care of silverware.
- Use detergents.
- Clean machine.

3. Discuss the following cases of food-borne illness as reported by health agencies around the country. In each case, answer the following questions:

   - What was the cause of the food-borne illness?
   - What sanitation procedures would have prevented such an illness?

   a. Seventeen persons aboard a ship became ill within eight hours after eating a noon meal. Nausea, vomiting, cramps, and diarrhea were the symptoms. Macaroni had been cooked prior to the meal, and chopped pimientos, lettuce, boiled eggs, mayonnaise, and mustard were hand-mixed by two cooks. One of the cooks had several minor cuts on two fingers. These finger cuts yielded *staphylococcus aureus*, the same kind of bacteria found in the salad.

   b. About one hundred persons were ill from salmonella food poisoning after a wedding dinner served by a catering company. Investigators discovered that the baked chicken had been stacked in pans on the kitchen shelf and held at room temperature until delivered. It was also found that the catering facilities were dirty and infested with cockroaches.

   c. A number of people were ill from staphylococcus food poisoning after eating custard-filled chocolate éclairs from a restaurant bakery. Upon investigation, it was found that the restaurant had poor sanitary standards. The custard mixture was stored at room temperature for several hours. When filling the éclairs, workers wiped off the excess custard with their fingers into the bowl and re-used it. If éclairs were not sold on the day prepared, they were kept over to sell the next day.

   d. Approximately one hour after the family supper, four persons vomited, became nauseated, dizzy, and had difficulty in swallowing, talking, and seeing. For supper, they had eaten what they thought were collard greens. Actually, these "greens" were the leaves of a wild tobacco plant.

   e. Two persons became ill about 15 minutes after eating mushrooms. Symptoms included nausea, dizziness, numbness, and vomiting. The mushrooms had been picked fresh, refrigerated, peeled, cleaned, boiled, and fried. Examination of similar types of mushrooms showed that these were poisonous.

   f. Sixteen persons experienced acute upset stomachs within five hours after their evening meal. Egg salad was the food suspected. The eggs were boiled and shelled early that afternoon. One of the cooks then added mayonnaise and relish to the chopped eggs. After preparation, the salad was not refrigerated. The cook who prepared the salad had tonsillitis.

   g. At a church dinner, over half of those who had eaten barbecued chicken became ill within six hours. The chickens had been cooked the day before, immediately refrigerated overnight, then reheated the next morning. After reheating, they were cut into quarters with the butcher's meat saw. The chickens were without refrigeration from 10:00 a.m. until 5:00 p.m., at which time they were reheated. Large numbers of *staphylococci* were recovered from the chickens. These bacteria could have come from the meat saw or from the cook's hands which contained numerous small cuts and abrasions.

h. Eleven cases of trichinosis occurred in a small community among seven families who had eaten raw smoked sausage prepared from the same hog. Symptoms were high fever, muscle pain, stomach cramps, chills, and general weakness. This illness was caused by *trichinella spiralis*, a small parasite present in the uncooked pork.

i. Four cases of botulism, including one death, occurred as a result of the consumption of home-canned chili. Symptoms were vomiting, dizziness, difficulty in breathing and speaking, and blurring of vision. There was a paralysis for a time. The chili had been home-canned under insufficient temperature and pressure. This permitted a toxin to be formed in the chili.

Let's Investigate

1. Visit your local health department. Obtain information on inspection practices, number of times inspection occurs, and type of check sheets used. Discuss in class.

2. Obtain information from local food service managers as to the types of detergents, sanitizers, and sprays they use. Experiment with different types on cleaning jobs and analyze the results.

3. Ask your board of health for information about acceptable insect sprays. Why are some types banned?

4. Watch a sanitarian do a "swab test" on the dishes in your school cafeteria or a restaurant. Explain to the class how this is done and why.

5. Visit several restaurants to see different types of dishwashers, or get the information from a catalogue. Report to the class on:

   - Size.
   - Ease of operation.
   - Cost.
   - Efficiency.

6. Ask your board of health if there have been any recent cases of food poisoning. If so, what were the causes? Discuss how the illnesses could have been avoided.

Chapter **14**

Safety Is

Essential

When you eat away from home, do you ever think about or notice the safety practices of the food service unit? Are the exits well marked in case of fire? Are there broken floor tiles or unlighted, unexpected steps that might cause accidents? Perhaps you have had the unfortunate experience of eating in a restaurant that has tables and chairs in need of repair. You may even have been served by a careless waitress who spilled hot soup on you. How do you feel about such places? Would you ever want to go back?

Why is safety so important in the food service business? When accidents occur, there may be serious consequences such as injuries resulting in costly doctor's bills. The safety and

well-being of the employees and customers depends on effective safety programs.

Cities and states establish and enforce minimum standards for safety in all food service establishments. Food service owners should be and usually are deeply concerned about safeguarding their customers and employees. They carefully plan and arrange rooms, entrances and exists, and furnishings and equipment so that no safety hazards exist. They establish and enforce safety precautions and train workers to use safe practices in order to prevent accidents and fire.

The management carries liability insurance, which pays the costs involved in any accidents. Even so, insurance is expensive, especially if

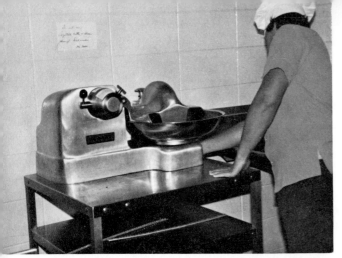

Ft. Myers Tech. School, Fla.

All food service workers are responsible for safe practices, which help prevent accidents. This student carefully checks the vegetable grater before using it.

a restaurant has repeated accidents. Costly law suits have put some restaurants out of business.

The purpose of the Federal Occupational Safety and Health Act of 1970 is to assure safe, healthful working conditions for employees. Under this act, an employer must keep his place free from recognized hazards. He must keep records and report accidents or illness related to the work. Although this law applies to employees, a food service operator would certainly make sure that the premises occupied by customers met all regulations of safety and health.

Can you understand why safety precautions are essential in the operation of a food service unit?

Every food service operator is responsible for establishing safety standards, and every employee must do his share in maintaining them. It is important for you, as a food service worker, to know and understand the safety procedures used in restaurants. These will be discussed in this chapter.

THINK SAFETY

With more than three million people working in food service, accidents are bound to happen. Therefore it is important to develop good safety programs to cut down the number of accidents that occur each year. Recent accident surveys in food service show that *34 percent of the accidents occur during serving operations, 21 percent happen during food preparation, and 16 percent come about while handling materials.*

What causes these accidents? Usually, they happen because workers do not pay attention to what they are doing, they are in too much of a hurry, or they fail to know and follow rules.

Food service managers are aware of the accident problem. They are responsible for developing safety programs to protect both employees and customers. They do this in the following ways:

- They use built-in safety features such as entrances and exits for easy flow of traffic; fireproofing and fire equipment; and proper arrangement and installation of equipment.
- They establish safety rules and procedures and make employees aware of the importance of observing these rules.
- They enforce the safety rules and regulations through constant supervision.

You, as an employee, are responsible for helping to prevent accidents. Organize yourself and your work carefully, and follow the safety rules of the establishment. In helping to reduce accidents, you may prevent injuries to yourself and others. By reducing breakage and equipment repairs, you can also save money for your employer.

Have you heard it said that some people seem to be *accident-prone?* This means that they are apt to have many accidents. Usually, this may be caused by carelessness or lack of physical coordination.

How can you play it safe in the pressure of the many activities carried on in a food service operation? It is not always easy. Pressures build up, causing confusion and nervousness. However, if you try to be conscious of safety at all times, you will find yourself using safe habits, even under pressure. Also, knowing the causes of accidents such as falls, cuts, burns, and strains, can help you avoid those hazards.

There is another important rule to remember. You must report accidents immediately to your superior. The accident report is necessary for insurance purposes to protect the employer and the injured person. Even minor accidents must be reported, in case there are any complications or aftereffects. Often, what seems to be a simple accident may result in permanent injury, especially if ignored.

Be sure you know the location of emergency equipment and how to use it. This would include the fire extinguishers and the first aid kit.

According to recent studies, the following are the most common food service accidents and their causes:

Food Service Accidents	*Causes*
Slips and falls	Spilled food and grease. Tripping over something. Over-reaching.
Cuts	Being struck by objects. Bumping against furniture or equipment. Caught in or between doors or equipment. Broken glass or china. Operating cutting equipment incorrectly.
Burns	Faulty electrical equipment. Scalding liquids and food. Hot ranges, fryers, cooking units.
Strains from lifting	Overloading trays. Lifting heavy objects. Carrying loads incorrectly.

Economics Laboratory, Inc.

Silver and broken glass and china on the floor should be picked up immediately. Otherwise, they can cause serious accidents.

What kind of explanations do food service workers usually give for accidents? What do you think of the excuses given in the cartoons pictured here? Although the workers have "good reasons," the accidents shown can really be traced to human errors. Have you ever used any of the excuses shown in the cartoons?

Remember, it is important to keep your mind on your job at all times. If you do this and also practice the safety guides described on the following pages, you can help cut down on accidents when you work in food service.

Students learn correct procedure for French frying. Basket should be lowered slowly so that fat does not bubble over, causing fire or burns.

Brookline, Mass., Public Schools

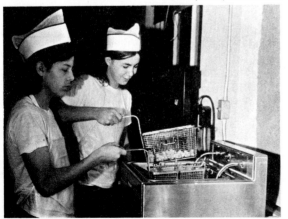

Can you give the *real* reasons for these accidents?

"I was watching George. Boy, was he making a mess of the French fries!"

"Someone told me it was repaired!"

"I was in a hurry!"

"I didn't think it was *that* heavy!"

"I thought I could reach it."

"I didn't *see* him!"

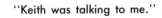

"Keith was talking to me."

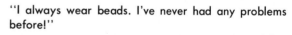

"I always wear beads. I've never had any problems before!"

SAFETY GUIDELINES

To Prevent Slips and Falls

- Avoid storing items on top of lockers or other high units.
- Use a safe ladder and avoid over-reaching.
- Store heavy, bulky material on lower shelves.
- Keep floors clean.
- Clean up wet or greasy spots promptly.
- Walk, do not run.
- Do not leave chairs or carts in passageways.
- Use care in going through doorways or around corners.
- Promptly report any hazards such as broken floor boards, tiles, worn mats, or traffic obstructions.
- Wear safe work shoes with sensible heels.

Be sure knives are sharp, and handle them correctly to prevent cuts.

Harry Hooper, Cape Coral, Fla.

To Prevent Cuts

- Never open cans with a sharp knife.
- Avoid wearing loose sleeves, ties, or jewelry when working with cutting, chopping, and mixing equipment.
- Do not daydream on the job.
- Be sure cutting equipment is sharp because dull knives may cause accidents.
- Pick up knives and other sharp tools by handles.
- Use cutting board when using knife.
- Cut with the sharp edge of knife away from body and away from fellow workers.
- If a knife falls, do not try to catch it in midair.
- Wash knives immediately after use and store in proper place for protection.
- Do not leave knives on work tables or in sink.
- Use safety guards when using cutting or slicing machines.
- Sweep up broken glass and china immediately. Do not pick up broken pieces with hands.
- Put broken glass in separate trash container.
- Discard chipped or cracked glasses and china.

To Prevent Burns

- Use pot holders when handling hot utensils.
- Remove covers by lifting them away from you so steam can escape.
- Keep stoves, ovens, and hoods free from grease.

306

- Get help to handle heavy, hot containers.
- Avoid over-filling containers with hot liquids or food.
- Turn handles of cooking utensils away from edge of stove.
- Wipe hands dry before plugging in electric cords.
- Report any faulty electrical equipment promptly.

To Prevent Fires

- Be sure ovens and hoods are clean and free from grease.
- Be careful when using fats at high temperatures.
- Smoke only in the assigned smoking areas.
- Report any smoke or fire immediately.
- Know where the fire extinguishers are located and how to use them.
- Know the fire exits, and show them to guests if the need arises.
- Keep fire doors, fire exits, and fire escapes and stairs clear of materials and equipment.

To Avoid Strains

- Do not overload trays or bus wagons.
- Place dishes and foods on trays carefully so weight is evenly balanced.
- Carry trays correctly.
- Lift a heavy object by keeping the load close to the body, bending knees, raising it gradually, and straightening the knees slowly.
- Get help to lift and carry heavy objects such as bags of flour.
- Store heavier items on lower shelves.

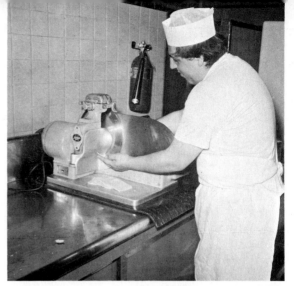

Brookline, Mass., Public Schools

Student concentrates on job assignment—slicing cheese. He knows that if he lets his attention wander, he may have a serious accident with the slicer.

Student made sure that safety guard was in place before using the chopper to make bread crumbs.

Brookline, Mass., Public Schools

307

Brookline, Mass., Public Schools

Student learns to load and lift trays properly to avoid strains.

FATIGUE AFFECTS SAFETY

Have you sometimes felt tired before you even started a job? Have you sometimes worked hard all day and still had enough energy to go to a dance at night? Why was there a difference? You use up a great deal of energy when you work and play. When you have used up more energy than your body can supply, you become fatigued. This makes you feel tired, even though you may not even have started to work.

Accidents are more likely to happen when you are fatigued or tired. *Fatigue* is weariness from labor or exertion. It may come from physical, mental, or emotional causes.

Physical fatigue comes after heavy work or physical activity. For example, carrying heavy pots and pans or standing or walking a great deal can cause fatigue in some people.

Emotional and mental fatigue may come because people dislike certain jobs and try to avoid them. Perhaps they are unhappy or frustrated in some way not even connected with their work. When people are troubled, hurt, or offended, they are likely to feel tired, and their work becomes difficult.

Fatigue is only harmful when you become over-tired and continue to feel tired even after normal rest. Normal fatigue should be overcome by a good night's rest.

How can you prevent fatigue on the job? It is important, of course, that you use your energy efficiently. The following suggestions can help you to make the most of your energy on the job so that you will not become over-tired. This is important because a fatigued person is apt to react more slowly to danger, thus causing an accident.

- Follow good health habits. Get enough sleep and adequate food. Practice good posture.
- Take short rest periods between heavy or hard tasks.
- Prevent emotional fatigue through good human relations with your co-workers and boss.
- Plan and arrange your work and work methods so that you save energy and time.
- Face up to the tasks that have to be done, even if you do not like them. Everybody has to do work at times that they dislike.
- Keep yourself interested in the work you are doing. Develop a good attitude towards work.
- Leave outside problems at home. Do not burden other people with your own personal difficulties.

PRACTICE SAFETY

Think about the kinds of accidents that may happen in food service work and the ways you can help prevent them. Remember safe practices and make them a habit. Know the safe way to use equipment.

Ask yourself these questions:

- Do I wear appropriate and safe clothing?
- Do I avoid wearing run-down heels, plastic aprons, dangling ties or jewelry, loose cuffs?
- Do I follow directions correctly when I use and move equipment?
- Do I use safety guards when operating equipment?
- Do I report safety hazards, accidents, and injuries as directed?

- Do I know how to use fire-fighting equipment and first aid materials?
- Do I use working methods that will help reduce fatigue?

Take time to be careful. Improve your work skills day by day. You can help prevent accidents to yourself and make working conditions safer for co-workers.

EMERGENCY TREATMENT

What can you do if an accident occurs? You should know some first aid rules in case you have to take charge before professional help arrives.

Burns—Immerse burned area in cold water or treat with ice. For instance, have person with a burned hand hold it under cold running water.

Cuts—Wrap severe cuts in a clean towel to absorb bleeding. If the cut is on the hand, elevate the hand and arm.

Falls—A person who is unconscious or badly injured should not be moved. Keep the person

Know the location of emergency equipment and how to use it such as this fire blanket and fire extinguisher.

309

lying down and cover with a blanket to keep warm until help arrives.

Be sure you know whom to call in case of an emergency. Have telephone numbers available.

Let's Think It Over

Food service operators try to prevent accidents through a well-planned safety program. As an employee, you are responsible for the use of safe practices in working with others and in using equipment.

1. What is the meaning of built-in safety features? List as many as you can observe in your food preparation laboratory or school lunchroom.
2. Why is it important to follow safety rules at all times?
3. What accidents occur most frequently in food service? What causes them?
4. List the ways you can prevent each of the following:

   Slips.
   Falls.
   Cuts.
   Burns.
   Strains.

5. How can you safeguard against fire?

6. How would you handle the following emergencies correctly?

   A grease fire on the stove.
   Scalding water spilling on a co-worker.
   The smell of gas escaping from bake ovens.
   A lighted cigarette thrown in a trash can.
   Sparks flying from the electric mixer.

7. How does fatigue on a job affect safety? How can fatigue be prevented or minimized?

Let's Investigate

1. Write to the U. S. Department of Labor, Occupational Safety and Health Administration in Washington or your regional H.E.W. office for a copy of the Williams-Steiger Occupational Safety and Health Act of 1970. Discuss in class:

   • Purpose of this act.
   • Posting of notice of the act.
   • Inspections for safety.
   • Violations and fines.

2. Write to an insurance company for literature on prevention of accidents in food production and serving. Discuss in class:

   • Proper methods for lifting.
   • Care of electrical equipment.
   • Preventing falls and burns.

Chapter 15

Labor Laws

and Regulations

Federal, state, and local governments have laws and regulations which directly concern you as a food service employee. Some of these laws were written to protect your rights and benefits as a worker in the labor market. Others deal with wages, working hours and conditions, social security, and income tax.

This chapter discusses the laws and regulations which directly affect you as a food service worker.

THE FAIR LABOR STANDARDS ACT

The Fair Labor Standards Act is commonly called the wage-hour law. It contains rules for minimum wages and working hours, equal pay, overtime pay, and child labor. This law affects the food service business as well as many other industries. The U. S. Department of Labor is responsible for carrying out this law.

The wage-hour law was established in 1938 to eliminate many conditions that were bad for the health, efficiency, and well-being of workers. In 1966, the Fair Labor Standards Act was amended to broaden its coverage. It is important to understand how this law affects you as a worker, so let us examine those parts related to the food service industry.

The act covers food service employees in hotels, motels, restaurants, and institutions doing an annual gross volume of sales of $250,000 or more. Units involved in interstate commerce are also covered, regardless of gross sales. *Interstate commerce* refers to business

---

WORDS TO KNOW

Social Security Number
Form W-4 Employee's Withholding Allowance Certificate
Form W-4E Exemption from Withholding Tax
Unemployment Insurance
Minimum Wage
Form W-2 Wage and Tax Statement
Form 4070, Employer's Report on Tips
Work permit
Prevailing wage rate
Fringe benefits
Workmen's Compensation
Severance pay
Collective bargaining
Labor unions
Civil service
Job termination

---

carried on in more than one state. An example of a food business engaged in interstate commerce would be a restaurant selling flight meals to airlines or a chain of restaurants located in more than one state.

Any food service establishment which does most of its business from within the state and grosses less than $250,000 annually is exempt from the wage-hour law.

Food service employees working in establishments covered by the wage-hour law must be paid a minimum wage. The amounts increased yearly, from 1974 to 1977.

The reasonable cost of meals and lodging, if furnished by the employer, may be considered as part of an employee's wages. The "rea-sonable cost" does not include a profit to the employer.

Overtime is paid if an employee works more than 40 or 46 hours in a work week, depending on the type of eating facilities. Minimum overtime pay is one and one-half times the employee's regular rate of pay.

The wage-hour law has special provisions for employees who receive tips. A *tipped employee* is defined as an employee who regularly receives more than $20 a month in tips. If all tips are turned over to the employer as part of the gross receipts, the employer must pay the employees the full minimum hourly wage. However, if an employee is permitted to keep his tips, the amount of the tips is deducted from his wage. The amount deducted cannot be more than fifty percent of the required minimum wage. The employer then pays the balance (not less than fifty percent) of the minimum wage rate. This means that the employee must receive at least the minimum wage in the combination of both wages and tips, but with not more than half of the total coming from tips. For example, if you work 40 hours at $2.30, you could earn $92. If you receive tips, your employer could deduct up to $46 or 50 percent. If your tips do not equal this amount, the employer must "make up the difference" so that you do get a total equal to the minimum wage.

If employees are required to wear uniforms, no part of the cost of the uniform and its maintenance may be charged to the employee if to do so would reduce his weekly wage below the required minimum wage provision. This means that your employer cannot deduct the cost of your uniform if in doing so your wage would be below the minimum.

The act also provides for equal pay for employees of either sex who do equal work on jobs which require equal skill, effort, and responsibilities and which are performed under similar working conditions. This applies to all employees who are covered by the wage-hour law.

The child labor provisions of the wage-hour law set a minimum age of 16 years for employment. However, in hazardous occupations such as mining, the minimum age is 18.

Minors 14 and 15 years of age may work during off-school hours in many non-mining and non-manufacturing occupations. However, they cannot work before 7 a.m. or after 7 p.m. Also, they cannot work more than three hours in a school day, 18 hours during a school week, eight hours in a non-school day, and 40 hours in a non-school week.

STATE LAWS

How does this law affect your job locally? It depends on the State Department of Labor and your state and local laws.

The federal wage-hour law allows states to decide what procedures will best meet their specific needs and still satisfy the provisions of the law. Each state, therefore, through its own Department of Labor, sets up procedures to meet the provisions of the Fair Labor Standards Act.

Most states protect their food service employees, as well as many other workers, with laws for minimum wages, employment of minors, working hours, and other labor regulations. However, state labor laws differ greatly. Therefore, contact your local employment office and your state labor department to learn about your own specific state laws and regulations. Be sure to check periodically for recent changes and for interpretations of the regulations.

Although state laws differ, the following general information can help you.

Prevailing Wage Rate

This term, often used in place of minimum wage, indicates the usual wage in the area for a particular job. It means that an employee gets at least the same wage rate generally received by others working in the same occupation in that locality. What is the prevailing wage rate in your community for food service workers? Is this above or below the required federal minimum?

BOCES, Ithaca, N. Y.

Trainee serves canapés at a party. Because she is a minor, she is not permitted to serve any alcoholic beverages.

Since these young men are under 18 years of age, they need a work permit in order to get part-time jobs.

Wage Deductions

The employer must deduct social security and income taxes from employees' wages. Some states permit deductions for union dues, insurance premiums, contributions to charitable organizations, credit unions, U. S. Savings Bonds, and similar payments for employee benefits. The employee authorizes these deductions in writing.

Wage Statement

Many states require that employers provide their employees with a wage statement with every payment of wages. The statement must show at least the gross wage, the deductions, and the net wage.

Liquor Laws

Many states do not allow minors to work where alcoholic beverages are served. The minimum age for working where liquor is served is usually determined by the minimum drinking age for the state. In some states, people under 18 who are in educational training programs can work where liquor is served but are not permitted to serve it themselves. Inquire about this in your state.

Child Labor Laws

States vary in their laws regarding child labor. However, they tend to follow the pattern set by the federal wage-hour law.

Under federal child labor regulations, minors 14 and 15 years old may work at the following food service jobs: office and clerical work, busboys, kitchen helpers (except cooking), waiters and waitresses, and soda fountain and counter workers. Those who are 16 and 17 years old may work in most jobs. No one under 18 years of age may be employed in any of the hazardous occupations as defined by the law.

Federal laws do not apply to minors 18 to 21 years of age. However, some states may have their own laws covering this age level.

State laws usually require that young people under 18 obtain a work permit before they begin a job. The work permit may also be called working papers or a standard employment certificate. A *work permit* shows the employer that the young person is at least the minimum age required for the job and is attending school.

How do you obtain a work permit? The procedure is simple.

- Get the information and application blanks needed for your work permit from the local office, usually the school attendance office.
- Arrange for a physical examination, which is usually provided at the school medical office.
- Complete the application form, which requires parents' signature, your signature, and your birth record.
- Take this form to your employer so he can fill out his part. Then return the completed form to the school office and receive your work permit.

INCOME TAX

When a person's wages go above a certain minimum level that is set by federal law, they are taxed. This is called *income tax*. Most states and many cities also have their own income tax.

After you have been hired for a job, you will be asked to fill out Form W-4, *Employee's Withholding Allowance Certificate*. The form asks for your name, address, social security number, marital status, and the number of dependents you have. In general, a dependent is a person who depends on you for at least fifty percent of his support. You are allowed one exemption for yourself and one for each dependent. Each exemption reduces the amount of income tax that you must pay. If you are single with no dependents, you will have only yourself to claim as an exemption. The information you give on Form W-4 ena-

bles your employer to figure out how much income tax to withhold from every paycheck.

Wages that come below the minimum specified by law are not taxed. Therefore, if your annual wages are below the minimum, you should not have any income tax withheld from your paycheck. To do this, you will need to fill out Form W-4E, *Exemption from Withholding of Federal Income Tax*, which you can get from your employer. By filling out this form and giving it to your employer, you authorize him *not* to withhold any income tax from your wages. However, if you get another job with higher wages, you may find that your total wages at the end of the year may be above the minimum. In that case, you will have to pay the total amount of income tax due when you file your income tax return.

The amount of the tips received must be reported to the employer so that he can withhold social security and income taxes from the employees' wages. If you have a table or counter service job and receive more than $20 in tips each month, you must file Form 4070, *Employer's Report on Tips*, with your employer. This form must be filled out every month. It shows the total amount of tips you received for the previous month. This means that you need to keep an accurate record of the tips you receive. A good way to do this is to count your tips at the end of each day and record the date and amount. You can use a small notebook for this.

In January, your employer will give you Form W-2, *Wage and Tax Statement*, for the preceding year. This shows the total wages you received for the year from this employer. It also shows the amount of federal income tax withheld as well as state and city income tax.

Employee's Withholding Allowance Certificate

Figure Your Total Withholding Allowances Below

(a) Allowance for yourself—enter 1 . . . . |_____

(b) Allowance for your wife (husband)—enter 1 . . . . |_____

(c) Allowance for your age—if 65 or over—enter 1 . . . . |_____

(d) Allowance for your wife's (husband's) age—if 65 or over—enter 1 . . . . . |_____

(e) Allowance for blindness (yourself)—enter 1 . . . . |_____

(f) Allowance for blindness (wife or husband)—enter 1 . . . . |_____

(g) Allowance(s) for dependent(s)—you are entitled to claim an allowance for each dependent you will be able to claim on your Federal income tax return. Do not include yourself or your wife (husband)* . . . . . . |_____

(h) Special withholding allowance—if you have only one job, and do not have a wife or husband who works— enter 1 . . . . |_____

(i) Total—add lines (a) through (h) above . . . . |_____

If you do not plan to itemize deductions on your income tax return, enter the number shown on line (i) on line 1, Form W–4 below. Skip lines (j) and (k).

(j) Allowance(s) for itemized deductions—If you do plan to itemize deductions on your income tax return, enter the number from line 5 of worksheet on back . . . . |_____

(k) Total—add lines (i) and (j) above. Enter here and on line 1, Form W–4 below . . . . |_____

*If you are in doubt as to whom you may claim as a dependent, see the instructions which came with your last Federal income tax return or call your local Internal Revenue Service office.

See Table and Worksheet on Back if You Plan to Itemize Your Deductions

Completing New Form W–4

If you find that you are entitled to one or more allowances in addition to those which you are now claiming, please increase your number of allowances by completing the form below and filing with your employer. If the number of allowances you previously claimed decreases, you must file a new Form W–4 within 10 days. (Should you expect to owe more tax than will be withheld, you may use the same form to increase your withholding by claiming fewer or "0" allowances on line 1 or by asking for additional withholding on line 2 or both.)

▼ Give the bottom part of this form to your employer; keep the upper part for your records and information ▼

Form **W–4**
(Rev. Aug. 1972)
Department of the Treasury
Internal Revenue Service

Employee's Withholding Allowance Certificate

(This certificate is for income tax withholding purposes only; it will remain in effect until you change it.)

Type or print your full name	Your social security number
Home address (Number and street or rural route)	Marital status ☐ Single ☐ Married
City or town, State and ZIP code	(If married but legally separated, or wife (husband) is a nonresident alien, check the single block.)

1 Total number of allowances you are claiming . . . . |_____

2 Additional amount, if any, you want deducted from each pay (if your employer agrees) . . . . | $

I certify that to the best of my knowledge and belief, the number of withholding allowances claimed on this certificate does not exceed the number to which I am entitled.

Signature ▶ _____ Date ▶ _____, 19_____

When you get a job, you will be asked to fill out Form W–4, *Employee's Withholding Allowance Certificate.* It enables your employer to figure out how much income tax to withhold from every paycheck.

Form W-4E

Department of the Treasury
Internal Revenue Service

Exemption From Withholding
(of Federal Income Tax)
For use by employees who incurred no tax liability
for 1976 and anticipate no tax liability for 1977

1977

Type or print full name	Social security number

Home address (Number and street)

City, State, and ZIP code

Employee.—File this certificate with your employer. Otherwise, your employer must withhold Federal income tax from your wages.	**Employee's certification.**—Under penalties of perjury, I certify that I incurred no liability for Federal income tax for 1976 and that I anticipate that I will incur no liability for Federal income tax for 1977.
Employer.—Keep this certificate with your records. This certificate may be used instead of Form W–4 by those employees qualified to claim the exemption.	(Signature)
	(Date)

If your annual wages are below the minimum, you should fill out Form W-4E, *Exemption from withholding of Federal Income Tax.* This authorizes your employer not to withhold any income tax from your paycheck.

For Official Use Only		Wage and Tax Statement **1976**	
	Type or print EMPLOYER'S name, address, ZIP code and Federal identifying number.	**Copy A For Internal Revenue Service Center**	
		Employer's State identifying number	

21 ☐	Employee's social security number	1 Federal income tax withheld	2 Wages, tips, and other compensation	3 FICA employee tax withheld	4 Total FICA wages
Name ▶	Type or print Employee's name, address, and ZIP code below. (Name must aline with arrow)		5 Was employee covered by a qualified pension plan, etc.?	6 *	7 *
			8 State or local tax with-held	9 State or local wages	10 State or locality
			11 State or local tax with-held	12 State or local wages	13 State or locality

* See instructions on back of Copy D

Form **W-2**   See instructions on Form W–3 and back of Copy D   Department of the Treasury—Internal Revenue Service

In January, your employer will give you a copy of Form W-2, *Wage and Tax Statement.* This shows your total wages for the preceding year, and the amount of income tax and social security tax (FICA) withheld. If any state and city income tax was withheld, the amounts will also be shown. This form must be filed with your income tax return.

317

Orange Julius

Part-time workers such as this student generally do not earn enough in a year to pay income tax.

The form also shows the amount of social security tax withheld. This is listed on the form under FICA, which stands for Federal Insurance Contribution Act, the official name for social security. A copy of Form W-2 must be attached to your income tax return.

You must file an income tax return for the preceding year if you had any income taxes withheld. The deadline for filing income tax returns is April 15. Form 1040, *Individual Income Tax Return*, is available at your local post office or Internal Revenue office. If you filed a return the previous year, a form will be sent to you automatically by the Internal Revenue Service. Employers sometimes have the tax forms available for their employees. If you have a state or city income tax, you must file returns for these also. In most areas, your Internal Revenue office can help you fill out your income tax return.

SOCIAL SECURITY

Money is taken out of your wages by your employer for social security. Social security is a federal government program which provides many benefits, most of which will help you when you reach retirement age. There are also benefits for survivors of wage earners.

When you take your first job, you must have a social security number. This enables the employer to deduct the social security tax and credit it to your number.

To get a social security number, ask at your nearest social security office for an application form. After you have filled out and returned the application, you will receive your social security number on a card. Your social security number is the number of your account. You will have only one number for all your working life. Therefore, it is very important to keep your card where you can always find it. A stub, which also shows your number, will be attached to your card. Keep the stub in a separate place. You will need it if you lose your card.

You will need your social security number for employers; banks and others when you receive interest, dividends, or other income; and tax returns.

If you lose your card, take or mail the stub to your nearest social security office. A duplicate card will be sent to you. If you do not have the stub, you can still get a duplicate card. However, it takes longer.

If you change your name for any reason, have your name changed on your card. Get an application blank from your social security office. Fill it out and return it with your social security card. Your record will be changed to your new name, and a new card will be mailed to you. However, you will still keep the account number originally given to you.

UNEMPLOYMENT COMPENSATION

Unemployment compensation is a state or federal insurance system. It gives you some income if you lose your job and are doing everything you can to get a new one.

How can you tell whether you are protected by unemployment compensation? If your state has such a law, every employer covered by it must display an official poster where employees can see it. The employer pays this tax—it is not deducted from your wages.

WORKMEN'S COMPENSATION

Many states have insurance protection for persons injured or killed while on the job. This is called Workmen's Compensation. It provides weekly cash benefits and furnishes necessary medical care to a worker who is disabled. In event of death, it provides weekly cash benefits and funeral expenses to the widow or dependents. This insurance is paid entirely by the employer. If your state has Workmen's Compensation, employers must display a poster where employees can see it.

These laws are constantly changing and benefits are upgraded. Some states require that

Before this student can begin to work, he must get a social security number. His employer will then deduct social security tax from his wages and credit it to his number.

BOCES, Ithaca, N. Y.

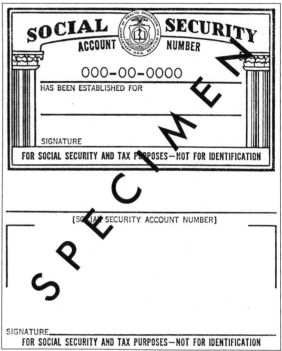

Social security card. The lower part should be detached and kept in a safe place. Carry the upper part with you. If you should lose it, you can use the lower part to get a duplicate.

Food Service Careers

H. J. Heinz Co.

Members of management team discuss employee and food production problems.

where one or more employees, either full or part time, are employed, Workmen's Compensation must be in effect. What are the laws in your state?

LABOR UNIONS

Labor unions are organized for the benefit of employees. They help to promote better working conditions, higher wages, health and welfare services, free education, child labor legislation, and greater job security. They are recognized as the bargaining agent for the members.

The workers in a company vote to decide whether they will have a union. Therefore, some companies are unionized and some are not.

Will you need to join a union? When taking a job, ask if the employees belong to a union. If they do, find out whether membership is required or optional. If it is optional, it means that a union represents the employees but it is up to the individuals to decide whether or not they wish to be members. Since you may have to decide whether or not to join, be sure that you understand the goals and procedures of the union involved. Talk to the union representatives on the job about regulations and dues.

Right-to-Work Law

Some states have a right-to-work law. This provides that the right to work cannot be denied to persons just because they are or are not union members. Does your state have a right-to-work law?

COLLECTIVE BARGAINING

Collective bargaining is a process by which an agent representing the employees meets with management to try to improve wages and working conditions.

The agent may be a union, a municipal or employee group, or any organization that officially represents the employees.

The areas of bargaining are usually covered by a contract between management and the agent. These areas may include wages, working hours and conditions, control of job opportunities, employee security, methods of handling grievances, long-range goals, and fringe benefits.

What are fringe benefits? They are benefits which employees receive. Fringe benefits may include health insurance, paid vacations and holidays, and retirement pension plans. They are paid for by the employer and do not affect the employees' wages.

Some states have laws that regulate negotiations for wages and fringe benefits. Does your state have such laws?

Collective bargaining involves meetings between management and the agent. These discussions usually result in a mutual agreement between both parties. The agreement is drawn up as a written contract, which states the terms agreed upon.

Most employers and employees recognize the values of collective bargaining. When an agreement cannot be reached in a reasonable time, an arbitration agent or conciliator may be assigned to try to bring both parties to an agreement. How does this work in your state? If they cannot agree and the bargaining talks end, labor strikes may result. Generally, a strike is used as a last resort. A labor strike may involve a work stoppage, a slow-down, or a sit-down on the job.

CIVIL SERVICE

If a food service job is in a tax-supported institution such as a school or hospital, it may be a civil service job. Therefore, it is important for you to have some general understanding of civil service.

Civil service protects the status and security of jobs in tax-supported institutions. The law was passed to take government jobs out of politics. This means that when new government officials are elected, the people under civil service continue in their jobs regardless of their political beliefs.

Each civil service job has specifications which give a detailed description of the work and the requirements. Every worker must meet these specifications.

There are three job classifications under civil service—competitive, non-competitive, and labor.

The *competitive* classification covers top management personnel such as managers and directors of food service. They must take and pass a state civil service examination in order to be eligible for the job.

The *non-competitive* classification usually affects chefs and cooks. They may not have to take a civil service examination, but they are required to meet the specifications of the particular job.

Florida Dept. of Citrus

Since the school in which this employee works is a tax-supported institution, she has a civil service job.

The majority of food service workers in tax-supported institutions fall into the *labor* classification. Usually, a civil service examination is not required.

The wage scale is set by the institution and not by civil service. Wages are paid by the institution hiring the workers.

Civil service regulations are enforced through federal and state laws. The state laws are usually patterned after the federal law. However, remember to check the regulations in your own state.

Since the individual institutions are responsible for hiring and firing their own food service personnel, employees may not even be aware that they are part of the civil service system.

Is your local school food service program or hospital under civil service? Are there civil service examinations in your state or community for food service workers?

HANDLING JOB COMPLAINTS

Most unions, associations, and employers have procedures for handling job problems and complaints. Since most of these procedures differ, you will need to go to the person in charge of grievances if you have a problem.

Many state labor departments handle complaints dealing with unequal pay or unpaid wages. If necessary, they can collect unpaid wages for you through their legal department. In this case, you need to file a wage claim at the labor department office nearest you.

Some communities have a Legal Aid Society which may help you in court cases. The society is composed of a group of lawyers who may work without fee or for only a small fee. They help people in trouble by giving legal advice or representing them.

JOB TERMINATION

Leaving a job permanently, whether you quit or are fired, is called *job termination*. Certain procedures are involved.

Employers may ask for one or two weeks' or a month's notice from you if you plan to change jobs. Others may not require any. Be sure to find out what your employer's policy is so that when you decide to leave, you will give the proper amount of notice. By giving notice, you give your employer time to hire and train somebody to take your place on the job. Generally, the amount of notice required depends on how long it will take to find and train a replacement. If you do not give enough notice, your employer may not be able to find a replacement, and his business may suffer.

If an employee is fired, he may receive *severance pay*, but this depends on the employer. *Severance pay* is a specified amount such as a week's or a month's wages, vacation pay, or any fringe benefits due at the time the employee leaves the job. Labor unions often include a statement concerning severance pay in their union contracts with management. Temporary employees are not eligible for these benefits.

On request, employers will usually provide written references concerning your ability and work experience. It is more common, however, to list the previous employer as a reference on a job application. The prospective employer then writes for a letter of reference.

References are important, so try to earn good ones. They will help you in obtaining other jobs. Be fair to your employer. Remember to give notice in plenty of time when leaving a job. If you quit on short notice, it may affect your future references.

Remember, when you accept a job, check with your employer and the other employees as to what is required of you and what your benefits are.

Let's Think It Over

1. It is important to understand the federal, state, and local laws which affect workers in food service.

   - What is the Fair Labor Standards Act? How does it protect workers?
   - What does the law say about tips and uniforms?
   - How would you pay income tax on tips?
   - At what age can you work in your state? Why is this so?
   - Explain the meaning of the following terms: equal pay, severance pay, collective bargaining, prevailing wage rate, Workmen's Compensation, unemployment insurance.

2. Employers are required by law or by written directions from you to deduct certain amounts of money from your wages.

   - Name three legal deductions and explain the purpose of each.
   - Name two other possible deductions, and explain the reason for each.
   - How do you obtain and keep your social security number?

323

Ithaca Country Club

This waitress is trying out for a job. Employers, before hiring you permanently, may ask you to demonstrate your abilities and knowledge during a try-out period.

School bulletin boards often have helpful suggestions such as how to look on a job or where to find a job. If you are job hunting, look through the "Help Wanted" column in the newspapers. Perhaps your school has a job placement bureau. Also, let your friends know that you are job hunting—they may know of someone who is looking for a good employee.

H. J. Heinz Co.

APPLICATION FOR EMPLOYMENT

PERSONAL INFORMATION

DATE _____ SOCIAL SECURITY NUMBER _____

NAME _____ AGE** _____ SEX** _____
       LAST   FIRST   MIDDLE

PRESENT ADDRESS _____
      STREET   CITY   STATE

PERMANENT ADDRESS _____
      STREET   CITY   STATE

PHONE NO. _____ OWN HOME _____ RENT _____

DATE OF BIRTH** _____ HEIGHT _____ WEIGHT _____ COLOR OF HAIR _____ COLOR OF EYES _____

MARRIED _____ SINGLE _____ WIDOWED _____ DIVORCED _____ SEPARATED _____

NUMBER OF CHILDREN _____ DEPENDENTS OTHER THAN WIFE OR CHILDREN _____ *CITIZEN OF U.S.A. YES ○ NO ○

IF RELATED TO ANYONE IN OUR EMPLOY, STATE NAME AND DEPARTMENT _____ REFERRED BY _____

EMPLOYMENT DESIRED

POSITION _____ DATE YOU CAN START _____ SALARY DESIRED _____

ARE YOU EMPLOYED NOW? _____ IF SO MAY WE INQUIRE OF YOUR PRESENT EMPLOYER _____

EVER APPLIED TO THIS COMPANY BEFORE? _____ WHERE _____ WHEN _____

EDUCATION	NAME AND LOCATION OF SCHOOL	YEARS ATTENDED	DATE GRADUATED	SUBJECTS STUDIED
GRAMMAR SCHOOL				
HIGH SCHOOL				
COLLEGE				
TRADE, BUSINESS OR CORRESPONDENCE SCHOOL				

SUBJECTS OF SPECIAL STUDY OR RESEARCH WORK _____

*WHAT FOREIGN LANGUAGES DO YOU SPEAK FLUENTLY? _____ READ _____ WRITE _____

U. S. MILITARY OR NAVAL SERVICE _____ RANK _____ PRESENT MEMBERSHIP IN NATIONAL GUARD OR RESERVES _____

ACTIVITIES OTHER THAN RELIGIOUS (CIVIC. ATHLETIC. FRATERNAL. ETC.) _____
EXCLUDE ORGANIZATIONS, THE NAME OR CHARACTER OF WHICH INDICATES THE RACE, CREED, COLOR OR NATIONAL ORIGIN OF ITS MEMBERS.

*THIS QUESTION MAY NOT BE ASKED IN STATES PROHIBITING SAME. MADE IN U.S.A.
**NOTE: THIS INFORMATION MAY BE ASKED FOR BUT DISCRIMINATION BECAUSE OF SEX PROHIBITED BY FEDERAL LAW. ALSO DISCRIMINATION BY AGE PROHIBITED BY LAW IN STATES WITH FAIR EMPLOYMENT PRACTICES.

(CONTINUED ON OTHER SIDE)

Boorum & Pease W-24

This is a typical application blank that you may have to fill out when you apply for a job. Be sure to

FORMER EMPLOYERS (LIST BELOW LAST FOUR EMPLOYERS, STARTING WITH LAST ONE FIRST.)

DATE MONTH AND YEAR	NAME AND ADDRESS OF EMPLOYER	SALARY	POSITION	REASON FOR LEAVING
FROM				
TO				
FROM				
TO				
FROM				
TO				
FROM				
TO				

REFERENCES: GIVE BELOW THE NAMES OF THREE PERSONS NOT RELATED TO YOU, WHOM YOU HAVE KNOWN AT LEAST ONE YEAR.

	NAME	ADDRESS	BUSINESS	YEARS ACQUAINTED
1				
2				
3				

PHYSICAL RECORD:

LIST ANY PHYSICAL DEFECTS

WERE YOU EVER INJURED?   GIVE DETAILS

HAVE YOU ANY DEFECTS IN HEARING?   IN VISION?   IN SPEECH?

IN CASE OF EMERGENCY NOTIFY

| NAME | ADDRESS | PHONE NO. |

I AUTHORIZE INVESTIGATION OF ALL STATEMENTS CONTAINED IN THIS APPLICATION. I UNDERSTAND THAT MISREPRESENTATION OR OMISSION OF FACTS CALLED FOR IS CAUSE FOR DISMISSAL. FURTHER, I UNDERSTAND AND AGREE THAT MY EMPLOYMENT IS FOR NO DEFINITE PERIOD AND MAY, REGARDLESS OF THE DATE OF PAYMENT OF MY WAGES AND SALARY, BE TERMINATED AT ANY TIME WITHOUT ANY PREVIOUS NOTICE.

DATE   SIGNATURE

DO NOT WRITE BELOW THIS LINE

INTERVIEWED BY   DATE

REMARKS:

NEATNESS		CHARACTER	
PERSONALITY		ABILITY	

| HIRED | FOR DEPT. | POSITION | WILL REPORT | SALARY WAGES |

APPROVED: 1.   2.   3.

EMPLOYMENT MANAGER   DEPT. HEAD   GENERAL MANAGER

Boorum and Pease

give accurate information. Write or print clearly so that the interviewer can read the application easily.

Labor unions have made important contributions in securing job benefits and improved working conditions.

- In what ways might a labor union affect your job?
- What are the major areas of collective bargaining?

Let's Investigate

1. Find out the procedure for obtaining a work permit in your community. Make a step-by-step chart and display on the bulletin board.
2. Survey local food service establishments and find out the following: Are minimum wage standards being met? What is the average amount of tips collected? What fringe benefits are offered? Discuss this in class.
3. Investigate and write a report on the nature and extent of union activities in food service units in your community.
4. Try to get a copy of a food service contract. Discuss in class:

- The wage scale.
- Sick leave.
- Vacations.
- Meal allowance.
- Other conditions of work.

5. If employees in your school food service come under civil service, investigate their duties, responsibilities, and rights. Discuss in class.

Student Resources

Books

Amendola, Joseph. *Practical Cooking and Baking for Schools and Institutions.* New York: Ahrens Publishing Company.

Brown, William C. *Food Service in Industry and Institutions.* Dubuque: William C. Brown Company.

Coffman, CWO James P., USN. *Introduction to Professional Food Service.* Chicago: Institutions Magazine, 1969.

Culinary Institute of America and the Editors of Institutions Magazine. *The Professional Chef.* Chicago: 1971.

Fowler, Sina F. *Food for Fifty.* New York: John Wiley and Sons, Inc., 1971.

Haines, Robert G. *Food Preparation for Hotels, Restaurants, and Cafeterias.* Chicago: American Technical Society, 1968.

Harris, Ellen A. *Professional Restaurant Service.* Toronto: McGraw-Hill Company, 1966.

Kotschevar, Lendal H. *Quantity Food Production.* Berkeley: McCutchan Publishing Company, 1966.

_____. *Quantity Food Purchasing.* New York: John Wiley and Sons, Inc., 1961.

Lateiner, Alfred. *Modern Techniques of Supervision.* West New York: Lateiner Publishing Company, 1968.

Lundberg, Donald and Armatas, James P. *The Management of People in Hotels, Restaurants and Clubs.* Dubuque: William C. Brown Company, 1964.

Lundberg, Donald and Kotschevar, Lendal. *Understanding Cooking.* Amherst: University of Massachusetts, 1970.

McWilliams, Margaret. *Illustrated Guide to Food Preparation.* Fullerton: Plycon Press.

Moosbeig, Frank. *Simplified Manual for Cooks.* Des Moines, Iowa, 50310: 3122 Garden Avenue.

_____. *Quantity Food Management.* Minneapolis: Burgess Publishing Company, 1970.

Terrell, Margaret. *Professional Food Preparation: Techniques and Equipment for Large Quantity.* New York: John Wiley and Sons, Inc., 1970.

Wilkinson, Jule. *The Complete Book of Cooking Equipment.* Chicago: Institutions Magazine, 1971.

Pamphlets

Being a Food Service Worker. 2 manuals, for student and teacher. National Research and Educational Trust, 840 North Shore Drive, Chicago, Ill. 60611.

Choosing Your Career. 1961. J. Anthony Humphreys, Science Research Associates, Inc., 259 East Erie Street, Chicago, Ill. 60619.

How to Find a Job. Francis Roger and Sam Iftikkar. New Readers Press, Syracuse, New York, N.Y. 13200.

How to Get the Job. 1968. Mitchell Dreese, Science Research Associates, Inc., East Erie Street, Chicago, Ill. 61619.

Making the Most of Your Job Interview. New York Life Insurance Company, 51 Madison Avenue, New York, N. Y. 10010.

Modern Sandwich Methods. American Institute of Baking, 400 East Ontario Street, Chicago, Ill. 60611.

Our World of Work. 1961. Seymour Wolfbein and Harold Goldstein, Science Research Associates, Inc., 259 East Erie Street, Chicago, Ill. 60619.

Sanitation of Food Service Establishments. Iowa State Department of Health, Des Moines, Iowa 50300.

Starting and Managing a Small Restaurant. Small Business Administration, U. S. Government Printing Office, Washington, D. C. 20000.

The ABC's of Courtesy for Hotels and Restaurants. Janet Lefler, Ahrens Book Co., 50 Essex Street, Rochelle Park, N. J. 07662.

The Waiter and His Public. Lefton, Sach, and Blanc, Ahrens Book Co., 50 Essex Street, Rochelle Park, N. J. 07662.

What Employers Want. James Worthy, Science Research Associates, Inc., 259 East Erie Street, Chicago, Ill. 60619.

Your Personality and Your Job. Daniel Sinich, Science Research Associates, 259 East Erie Street, Chicago, Ill. 60619.

Brochures may be obtained from:

Food Preparation and Management, Institutions Books, 1801 Prairie Avenue, Chicago, Ill. 60619.

Food Service Industry Training Program and Facilities, U. S. Department of Health, Education and Welfare, Government Printing Office, Washington, D. C. 20000.

Safety, Sanitation and Food Protection, National Restaurant Association, 1530 North Shore Drive, Chicago, Ill. 60610.

Sanitation, Safety, Food and Nutrition, Food and Nutrition Service, Department of Agriculture, U. S. Government Printing Office, Washington, D. C. 20000.

Index

Index

Index

Index